HENDRIK DOEFF

Knight of the Order of the Dutch Lion.
Former chief of the Dutch in Japan
on the island of Deshima

RECOLLECTIONS OF JAPAN

First published in Haarlem by François Bohn in 1833.

Translation and Annotation
Annick M. Doeff

© Copyright 2003 Annick M. Doeff. All rights reserved.

No part of this publication may be reproduced, stored in a retrieval system, or transmitted, in any form or by any means, electronic, mechanical, photocopying, recording, or otherwise, without the written prior permission of the author.

Printed in Victoria, Canada

Cover: The frigates Arinus Marinus and Ida Aleida on the roadstead of the island Deshima in the bay of Nagasaki. Keiga Kawahara, circa 1825. Maritime Museum, Rotterdam, The Netherlands.

National Library of Canada Cataloguing in Publication Data

```
Doeff, Hendrik, 1777-1835
     Recollection of Japan / Hendrik Doeff ; Annick M.
Doeff, translator and annotator.
Translation of: Herinneringen uit Japan.
ISBN 1-55395-849-7
     1. Japan--Description and travel.  2. Doeff, Hendrik,
1777-1835.
3. Japan--Commerce--Netherlands--History.  4. Netherlands--
Commerce--Japan--History.  5. Nederlandsche Oost-Indische
Compagnie. 6. Dutch--Japan.  I. Doeff, Annick M.  II.
Title.
DS809.D64 2003              952'.025              C2003-
900989-0
```

TRAFFORD

This book was published *on-demand* in cooperation with Trafford Publishing.
On-demand publishing is a unique process and service of making a book available for retail sale to the public taking advantage of on-demand manufacturing and Internet marketing. **On-demand publishing** includes promotions, retail sales, manufacturing, order fulfilment, accounting and collecting royalties on behalf of the author.

Suite 6E, 2333 Government St., Victoria, B.C. V8T 4P4, CANADA

Phone	250-383-6864	Toll-free	1-888-232-4444 (Canada & US)
Fax	250-383-6804	E-mail	sales@trafford.com
Web site	www.trafford.com	TRAFFORD PUBLISHING IS A DIVISION OF TRAFFORD HOLDINGS LTD.

Trafford Catalogue #03-0212   www.trafford.com/robots/03-0212.html

10   9   8   7   6

Chief Doeff with his dog and servant Cupido. Shiba Kôkan (1747-1818). National Museum of Ethnology, Leiden, The Netherlands

TABLE OF CONTENTS

Acknowledgements iii

Translator's Introduction v

Haiku by Hendrik Doeff xl

Author's Preface xli

Chapter I 1
General overview of the government, customs, religion, and history of the persecution of the Roman Catholics

Chapter II 33
Adventures of the author when he was an official and chief of the Dutch trading station in Japan from 1799 to 1817 and information of the Dutch trade there

Chapter III 68
The trek to the court in Edo

Chapter IV 91
My further stay in Japan until my departure

Author's Addendum 159

Translator's Epilogue 164

Appendix 167

Bibliography 172

End Notes 175

i

ACKNOWLEDGEMENTS

To my brother-in-law, George E. van Zanen, M.D., Ph.D., retired chief of the hematology/oncology division of the pediatric department Erasmus University Rotterdam, go my heartfelt thanks. Without the research he did for me in Holland, his extensive e-mails clarifying old Dutch terms and phraseology, and his painstaking attention to detail, this work would not be what it is.

To Johan Stellingwerf, Ph.D., retired librarian at the Free University of Amsterdam, multifaceted scholar and author, I want to express my deepest appreciation. In the process of writing a biography of Hendrik Doeff, he generously shared a lot of the information he had gathered over many years on Doeff and his time in Japan.

To Arthur Dudden, Professor Emeritus of History and Fairbank Professor Emeritus in the Humanities, Bryn Mawr College, I also want to express my deepest appreciation for his time, his interest, his input, and his encouragement after he read a first rough draft of the translation.

To Alexis Dudden, Sue and Eugene Marcy, Assistant Professor of History, Connecticut College, my thanks for all the help with Japanese words and terms which were in Dutch transliterated form.

To Ken Vos, Ph.D. candidate and curator of Japan and Korea at the National Museum of Ethnology in Leiden, my thanks for taking over from his father, Professor Emeritus of Languages and Culture at the University of Leiden. Fritz Vos was ill at the time and could not respond to my inquiries. He subsequently died. Ken Vos, despite the trying time of his father's illness, provided me with much valuable information.

To William Vosburgh, Professor Emeritus of Social Research, Bryn Mawr College, and amateur Japanologist, goes my appreciation for his valuable input, his enthusiasm, and his wholehearted support.

To professors Tetsuo Najita, Donald Keene, and Marius Jansen (deceased), eminent Japan scholars, my deep appreciation for their interest and support.

To my son-in-law, Peter Hall, my thanks for preparing the cover and illustrations.

To my husband Jan Willem Doeff, M.D. go my thanks for his support, for his eagle-eyed last review of the draft, and not the least, for having Hendrik's DNA.

I: Translator's Introduction

1, Publishing History.

The book *Recollections of Japan* by Hendrik Doeff, chief of the Dutch East India Company in Deshima, Nagasaki, was first published in 1833 in Haarlem, Holland. Subsequently, it was translated into Japanese and saw several publications in Japan, the latest one in 2003. It was not republished in Holland, but such a move is under consideration given the renewed interest in Doeff's contribution to the understanding of Tokugawa Japan by Dutch scholars.

Although the book was never translated in its entirety into English, an English historian, Mary Margaret Blait Busk (1779-1863), first discussed Doeff's book extensively in *The Quarterly Review* 1836, vol. 54, pages 415-437. She then edited a series titled *Manners and Customs of the Japanese* which was based, in part, on excerpts of Doeff's book in *The Asiatic Journal*, vol. 29, London 1839. This series was then excerpted "for the proprietors" from the *Asiatic Journal* anonymously in *The Chinese Repository*, vol. 9 from May to December 1840. *The Chinese Repository* was a missionary magazine edited by an American, the Reverend Samuel Wells Williams (1812-1884). This man worked for the American mission in Canton, where he was the honorary Dutch consul as well as the American consul in Hong Kong. He was on board the American ship *Morrison* that wasn't allowed to land in Japan, and in 1853 and 1854 he accompanied Perry to Japan as a translator.

Mrs. Busk's series, *Manners and Customs of the Japanese*, was mainly based on the works of Doeff, Overmeer Fischer, Meylan, and von Siebold, the latter a physician and the other former chiefs or employees of the Dutch trading station in

Deshima. Her series was subsequently published in book form in 1841 in London and New York. On page 120, Mrs. Busk wrote "Mister Doeff, to whom we are much indebted in preparing this work." Her book saw reprints in 1845, 1848, 1859.

In 1856, by order of the Congress of the United States, a book written by Francis L. Hawks for Congress was published in Washington. Its title was *Narrative of the Expedition of an American Squadron to the China Seas and Japan, performed in the years 1852, 1853, and 1854 under the command of Commodore M. C. Perry, United States Navy*. Several pages of the book pertain to the period when Doeff, whom Hawks calls "exceedingly shrewd, adding to the craft of the trader the cunning of the diplomatist," was chief in Deshima. Although no source is actually listed other than H. Doeff writer on Japan, it is clear that the material comes from Mrs. Busk's series.

Andrew Steinmetz, in his book *Japan and Its People* (1859), wrote: "*Recollections of Japan* by Hendrick Doeff, formerly president of the Dutch factory at Deshima (Haarlem 1833). This curious Dutch work has not been translated into English, but numerous passages from it have appeared in the *Quarterly Review*, vol. 56, 1836." This review took excerpts from the *Chinese Repository*, and this time the authorship was attributed to Busk.

In 1973 the Charles E. Tuttle Company of Vermont and Tokyo published a pocket book titled *Manners and Customs of the Japanese in the 19th Century from the accounts of Dutch residents in Japan and from the German work of Doctor Philip Franz von Siebold*. Terrence Barrow's introduction to this book does not mention Busk nor does he acknowledge her authorship. He most likely got hold of her (anonymous) work from the *Chinese Repository*.

Donald Keene, in his well-researched book *The Japanese Discovery of Europe* (1720-1830), excerpts three passages from *Recollections of Japan* and quotes Doeff several times. In a private communication, professor Keene mentioned that he had mastered Dutch sufficiently to be able to translate the passage himself.

A Japanese writer, Agu Saito, wrote a book, *Doeff and Japan*, which was published in 1922. Although translated into English, it was not published officially in that language.[1]

2, Hendrik Doeff

The author of these recollections was born in Amsterdam on December 2, 1777 and was baptized in the faith of his mother, the Lutheran church. He died in that same city on October 19, 1835 and was buried in the family grave at the Lutheran cemetery of Muiderberg, then situated near the shore of the Zuiderzee. His father, also named Hendrik, was a ship broker and one-time member of the Municipal Council of the city of Amsterdam. The younger Hendrik Doeff was educated in a French school and after graduation was employed by the company of I. F. Taunay. This company went bankrupt soon thereafter due to the French occupation of Holland and the Napoleonic wars. Now unemployed, Hendrik applied to the VOC, *the Vereenigde Oost-Indie Companie* or the (Dutch) United East India Company, for a job as second buyer in Batavia (now Jakarta), capital of the Dutch East Indies. On June 7, 1798, he was appointed to and sworn in as second buyer by the Committee for East Indian Trade and Possessions at a salary of forty guilders per month. Like all prospective employees of the VOC at that time, he had to swear an oath to the Batavian Republic.[2]

After his appointment, Hendrik was told to leave at the earliest possible opportunity. This posed a problem. Since Holland was now closely allied to powerful France and thus at war with England, it was no longer able to protect its ships against attacks of the British navy. This meant that only neutral ships, mostly Danish and American vessels hired by the Dutch, could maintain Holland's connection to its colonies in the Far East. Doeff was lucky, and barely a month after being hired, he was able to sail, on July 5, 1798, to Denmark. From Elsinore, he subsequently boarded the Danish ship *Fadrelandet* and set sail for Java. A year later, on June 1, 1799, he arrived in Batavia and was immediately appointed to the position of dispenser and scribe in Japan. As June was the month that ships normally set sail for Japan, he was able, after only a couple of days, to board the American ship *Franklin* under Captain Devereux. He arrived in Nagasaki in July, 1799. Little did he realize that he would live on that little artificial island of Deshima, first built on high ground in the bay of Nagasaki for the Portuguese in 1634, as a virtual prisoner for 18 years.

Hendrik's book was part of our legacy but was tucked away in a drawer as a curiosity rather than as something of value beyond the family. Initially undertaken as a family project, since several of Hendrik Doeff's descendants are now American and no longer speak Dutch, this translation soon took on an unanticipated dimension. It became clear that a lot of historical semantic and bibliographical research was needed to do this remarkable book justice.

In rereading it after several decades, the translator was struck by how lively, fresh, and interesting this book, now almost 200 years old, still is. It represented history in a microcosm with all its human dimensions of national pride and national hatreds, as well as of political and international intrigues. Written from the perspective of one who lived some of that history and built on past history to give his experience depth, Doeff was able to transcend his personal predicament and discomfort. He writes with honesty and eloquence what it was like to live as a European in a closed Japan around 1800 and paints a picture of the Japanese, their culture, and their society that indicates both a dispassionate objectivity and a real understanding of that country. In rereading his book, it became clear what an invaluable insight the book provided into a Japan few foreigners really knew at a time when the country had been closed to the outside world for almost 200 years.

Forced through a fluke of history, the Napoleonic wars, to remain in Japan for eighteen years (Dutch chiefs normally had to be replaced every five years at that time if not sooner), only Hendrik Doeff had both the time and the inclination to endeavor to get a real grasp of this truly alien culture. This fortuitous situation combined with an exceptionally bright and versatile personality, earned him a unique position among Deshima chiefs. With a few notable exceptions, they had not been inclined to learn the language nor had they shown much interest in trying to understand their host country where, to be fair, they were virtually held in captivity. Only a few wrote their experiences down which was perhaps also due to the fact that the VOC was not particularly keen to have its employees write about Japan lest its competitors take advantage of this information.

When almost no ships arrived for several years, Hendrik Doeff used his forced idleness to enhance his knowledge of Japan by truly mastering its language. A natural curiosity about the world in general combined with an instinct for fairness in human affairs, made him a keen and astute observer of this land. He used the knowledge he acquired to hone his skills in dealing with the complicated and difficult Japanese, not only on a commercial, but on a diplomatic and political level as well. These skills also served him well in his dealings with Western nations who tried, peacefully or forcefully, to dislodge the Dutch from their monopolistic position. As his knowledge and understanding grew, so did his respect and understanding of the Japanese character in all its positive and negative aspects. In turn, it earned him respect and trust in his judgment among the basically mistrustful Japanese.

Of all the Dutch chiefs or, for that matter, all the other employees of the VOC, it was Doeff alone who truly mastered the Japanese language, thereby giving depth to his understanding of the Japanese and their culture. He became so fluent in the language that he was able, in addition to writing *haiku*[3] of high quality, to fashion a Dutch-Japanese dictionary. This accomplishment cannot be underestimated given that for over two centuries Dutch was the only official Western language Japan used to communicate with the world and through which all Western knowledge entered Japan. The first two American ambassadors to Japan had to avail themselves of Dutch translators until the Japanese learned English and the importance of the Dutch language declined.

Doeff's linguistic skills also permitted him to forge lasting friendships with scholars, translators, and government officials, low and high alike. This helped him immensely in the many predicaments in which he found himself time and again. In short, Doeff's description of his experiences, of Japan, of its people and its customs, seems as objective, fair and balanced as one would expect of a well-trained modern journalist. It also makes his book a source of great value and interest to American scholars of a pre-Commodore Perry closed Japan and worthy of a larger American readership for this and other reasons as well.

One of these is that the book has a connection with the early history of the young American republic and its relationship to the Dutch. For many years, American ships and their captains who were chartered in the service of the Dutch, regularly plied the sea routes from Batavia to Nagasaki. They in turn brought back stories of this mysterious land to the young republic.

The Americans and the Dutch, who had been the first, in 1776, to recognize the flag of the United States of America and the first to give financial aid, were united at that time in their antagonism toward the English. Holland was at war with Britain, and the British had seized not only the Dutch East Indies but other Dutch possessions elsewhere as well.

In 1793, France and England declared war on each other and each ordered the seizure of neutral American ships bound to the ports of the other. British ships not only seized American ships but kidnapped their crews and pressed them into the service of the Royal Navy, especially if they had been born in Britain or in the colonies before the revolution, and thus, in their eyes, were still British. This situation became so bad that in 1807, under the presidency of Jefferson, Congress passed the Embargo Act prohibiting the sailing of merchant ships from any American port. This act, however widely evaded it was, created economic hardships and left American ships idle. Many of these ships were diverted to the Pacific where the Dutch, no longer able to protect their own ships from the

British, hired these neutral vessels, especially for their trade with Japan. That neutrality however did not deter the British, no doubt still bitter about losing their colonies, from frequently attacking or harassing them. This and other abuses eventually led to the war of 1812.

Another rather interesting incident gives evidence perhaps of lingering American antagonism toward the British. In 1807 a squadron of the British fleet under rear admiral Sir Edward Pellew forced its way into the roadstead of Surabaya, Java. Pellew then sent a delegation, among whom was his son Fleetwood, to shore demanding that all Dutch ships be handed over under threat to destroy the city. The commander in Surabaya refused to comply and, declaring that the English were spies, ordered that they be taken prisoner. This of course was against all international conventions. A curious fact is that the man who gave this order was not Dutch but American, a captain by the name of Cowell, who was in the service of the Dutch. One can speculate that he saw an opportunity, if an unlawful one, to get back at the British who had seized so many American ships and taken their crews prisoner.

Another early Dutch-American link is one of competition. A Dutch historian[4] in a book called *The Battle around Deshima* states that several nations jealous of the Dutch trade monopoly in Japan, in particular Britain, Russia, and the United States of America, tried to dislodge the Dutch from their privileged position.

A good case can be made for the first two nations, as Hendrik Doeff describes so vividly in his book. The case in regard to the United States is a more dubious one. It is based on the actions of a shady character, an American by the name of William Robert Stewart. This man first arrived in Nagasaki in the service of the Dutch, but then returned, apparently on his own, to try and get permission to trade with Japan for the Americans "whose king he declared was named Jefferson." The present translator received a letter from the curator of the Essex-Peabody museum in Salem, Massachusetts who, informed of the existence of Hendrik Doeff's recollections, inquired whether by any chance William Robert Stewart was mentioned in his book. The letter stated that Stewart was an enigmatic figure, that a lot of mystery surrounded him, and that it wasn't quite clear whether he was actually an American or not. Doeff, who mentions him extensively in his book, clearly didn't think so.

That leaves one other possible episode in which the United States might have tried establishing trade relations with Japan. It concerns a ship belonging to the Russian-American Company which landed in Japan, supposedly by accident, because it was in need of water. Some sources claim its true aim was to effect a trade agreement. If that assumption is correct, it would have been more a Russian than an American attempt. Only decades later did the United States, impatient with Japan's isolation policy and desiring normal relations, force the issue. To the translator's knowledge, the United States never tried to dislodge the Dutch from their trade monopoly in the same surreptitious, belligerent or underhanded way as the British and Russians tried to do during Doeff's tenure.

3, Problems of Translation

Given the resource Doeff's book provides as well as its serendipitous relation to America and its early maritime history, the translator decided to contact several historians and explain to them the project as well as the content of the book. To the question whether this book, sight unseen, might be of interest, the answer was a unanimous and enthusiastic yes. They also were willing to read a draft and be of help in any way they could. With this, the project became far more than a "for family eyes only" translation. The challenges then proved to be daunting.

First, there was the problem of translating archaic Dutch into modern American-English without totally losing the early 19th century flavor of quaint expressions and turns of phrase. As an example, the Dutch word *scriba* was retained in it archaic English form of scribe rather than being rendered as secretary. In the same way, the Dutch term *dagh register* was rendered as day register rather than daily log or journal. Second, there was the challenge of finding the location or names of places, cities, or islands mentioned in the book. Not only were most names changed with the Meiji restoration in 1868, but in addition, the old ones were often rendered in Dutch transliteration form. The most challenging and taxing task was finding out the meaning of numerous words, mostly related to import or export articles, that no longer meant anything to the reader of modern Dutch nor could be found in dictionaries. Imagine 200 years hence trying to find out what rayon or orlon was, or any other article or ingredient once perhaps commonplace or popular, but long since supplanted by others and thus gone from the lexicon and from memory.

In order to keep some of the flavor of the time, many of these words, most notably those as unknown to Dutch readers of today as they are to Americans, were kept the way they appeared in the original. Explanatory notes from the author, the original publisher and the translator are at the end of the book so as not to interfere with the continuity of the narrative or take attention away from the text. Translator notes pertain to the meaning of the archaic or cryptic words left in their original form and provide additional information, explanation, clarification, or dates on people, places or historical events. Like names or events now shrouded in the mist of time, dates that were perhaps commonly recognizable at the time, are also given a context. Where indicated or deemed germane, other information is also provided in these notes which, with a few exceptions, are kept short. An appendix is also provided with further biographical information.

In order to place Doeff's recollections in an historical perspective, a short journey back in time may be indicated.

II: Historical Background: An Introduction to Recollections of Japan

From the middle ages on, mainly due to Marco Polo's published travel experiences in the Far East, Japan slowly seeped into

European consciousness. However, it would take several more centuries before the Europeans became fascinated by this mysterious "land of gold." In 1492, the same year that Christopher Columbus discovered America, Martin Behaim, a cartographer in the service of King Joao II of Portugal, made the first map of Japan. It would be another 50 years before the Portuguese became the first Europeans to set foot in Japan, ushering in what would later be called the Christian century in Japan.

Various versions relate how the Portuguese first came to land in Japan. One version states that in 1542 a heavy storm blew a Portuguese ship on its way to China off its course. Shipwrecked, it accidentally came ashore off the southern tip of Kyûshû on a small island called Tanegashima. Another version has it that three shipwrecked Portuguese sailors, rescued by a Chinese junk, were dropped off at that same spot.

Regardless of what the true story is, the Portuguese were to come back and stay in Japan for nearly a century until, after the rebellion of Shimabara was quelled, they were expelled in 1639. Their expulsion contrasts sharply with the warm welcome they and their firearms received when they first arrived. At that time, Japan was nearing the end of a century of civil war which had plunged the country into anarchy.

The history of Japan in the century before the arrival of the Portuguese is turbulent and confusing. It was preceded by the slow and gradual usurpation of imperial powers by the *shôguns*, generals. In the country at large, unstable and shifting alliances of power holders either ignored or used an isolated imperial court in their quest for control for themselves.

In 1338, Ashikaga Takauji was appointed *shôgun* and established the Ashikaga *shôgunate* with Kyoto as its capital. The Ashikaga ruled with steadily diminishing effectiveness until the Onin war, which broke out in Kyoto in 1467, developed into a full scale civil war and marked the eventual end of the Ashikaga family in 1573.

At the same time, the old warrior feudal lords, intent on competing on the national scene, were totally indifferent to the welfare of their farmers, levying heavy taxes and imposing other iniquities on them as well. Everywhere in the land were victims of either famine or war. As conditions deteriorated, small landholders, local leaders, farmers, tenants, and servants started to band together to seek ways of getting rid of the marauding feudal armies marching across their fields and seizing "taxes" as they passed. In an attempt to get some relief from their heavy tax burdens, they sent petitions asking for remission of back taxes and a lighter tax burden for the future which were refused. Rebellion broke out and local strife escalated into provincial wars which rapidly spread all over the country. *Daimyô* (domain lords) and local leaders (or superiors against inferiors) started to fight for power in bitter territorial disputes, plunging the country into chaos. This became known as the *sengoku* or country at war period which lasted from 1467 to 1573.

Around the time of the arrival of the Portuguese, Oda Nobunaga, the son of a *daimyô* and a military genius had begun the slow process of pacification and unification in central Japan that would eventually lead to peace and stability under the Tokugawa *shôgunate*. The fire arms, called *Tanegashima teppo* or iron rods by the Japanese, which the Portuguese had brought with them and which were soon manufactured in Japan, greatly aided him in this process. Oda Nobunaga, at war with Buddhist sects on home territory, also welcomed the Jesuits who arrived in the wake of the Portuguese traders. He granted them several audiences and eventually allowed them to establish a church in Kyoto for the many powerful lords and members of the artistic community who had converted to Christianity. Betrayed by one of his own generals, Oda Nobunaga was forced to commit *seppuku* (ritual suicide) in 1582. He was succeeded by his ablest commander, Toyotomi Hideyoshi, a man of apparent humble birth, who was less well disposed toward the Catholic missionaries. He continued the unification process and managed to get the whole country under his rule. He died in 1598, leaving a minor son named Toyotomi Hideyori in the care of a committee of guardians, one of whom was Tokugawa

Ieyasu. Intent on usurping for himself the power that, according to many, belonged to Hideyori, Ieyasu defeated the supporters of Hideyori at the battle of Sekigahara in 1600, and in 1603 he named himself *shôgun*. In 1615 he was able to get rid of Hideyori for good by conquering his palace in Osaka, thereby consolidating his power and establishing the reign of the Tokugawa family which was to give Japan internal peace for 250 years. The Tokugawa Era, also called the Edo Period, as Ieyasu had established his capital in what is now called Tokyo (Edo), lasted until 1868.

The arrival of the Portuguese in Japan in 1542 fell in the middle of a period in time in which Portugal alone controlled the Oriental trade, the chief source of its wealth and power. Ever since Henry the Navigator had given the impetus to maritime exploration heralding Portuguese expansion into the far corners of the world, Portugal expanded its horizons ever further into the 16th century. Over time, Portugal gradually established fortified trading posts all along the west coast of Africa and on the shores of India and Ceylon. In search of spices, settlements that stretched from Bengal to China were set up with the consent of native rulers.

In the beginning of the 16th century, Alfonso de Albuquerque consolidated Portugal's dominance of the Asian trade in 1511 by his conquest of Goa, which became the seat of Portuguese power. Other conquests followed, securing the trade monopoly of the Orient for Portugal for nearly a century, after which they were displaced by the Dutch. Ormuz controlled the Persian Gulf and Malacca the gateway from the Indian Ocean to the South China Sea. The trade in the principal spice islands was in Portugal's hands after Albuquerque sent two expeditions to the Moluccas. Upon being allowed to settle in Ningpo, China, the Portuguese founded Macao in 1557, the oldest European outpost in the trade with China.

The Japanese trade, like trade elsewhere in Asia, was very profitable for the Portuguese and the Spanish with whom the former were now in a union. At first, their ships regularly came to various *Kyûshû* ports but later exclusively to Nagasaki, a city specially built for them. Lying on a remote peninsula, Nagasaki, though a fine natural harbor, was hemmed in by mountains. This made it somewhat inaccessible for domestic trade, but the Portuguese liked it, as it was easy to defend.

Nagasaki, which Pierre Loti in his *Madame Chrysanthème* described as "an enchanted crack through which one enters a forbidden land, a secret garden where time stood still," became a thriving port city which would remain, even after the expulsion of the Portuguese, the only port for foreign trade, except with China, until 1854.

When Japan's relation with Ming China broke down, it fell to the Portuguese to supply Japan with highly coveted Chinese silk, Indian and Persian luxury items, and European fire arms. In addition, the Portuguese ships, usually galleons of 600 to 1,600 tons and arriving annually from Macao, fascinated the Japanese and soon became the subjects of *namban byobu* or southern barbarian screens.

Apart from having perhaps been instrumental, through the introduction of fire arms, in bringing about the unification of Japan, the Portuguese also turned Japan away from an exclusive orientation to the East, mainly China, and to an expanded view toward the West. This came about through the introduction of Christianity.

Traditionally, trading for the Portuguese was intrinsically linked with spreading the Roman Catholic faith as well. *Kirishitan-shu* or Christian teaching was first brought to Japan in 1549 in the person of Francis Xavier and two fellow Jesuits. They arrived in Kagoshima and from there went to Yamaguchi, where the rulers of that thriving city politely listened to the teachings of this "new sect of buddhism." As Xavier had arrived from India, this was an understandable misperception. Xavier left two years later, after having concluded that it was better to convert China to Christ first. However short his stay, he came to develop a high regard for the Japanese whom he called "the delight of his heart." He wrote to his superior: "we shall never find among the heathen another race to equal the Japanese."

Christianity could not have arrived at a better time in Japan. With their society disrupted by 70 years of civil war and anarchy, the Japanese yearned for something new, especially the war lords who hoped that any innovation would give them an advantage over their rivals. The first *daimyô* to convert, in 1563, was a minor one from north west Kyûshû, Omura Sumitada. He was soon followed by five others.

For the next several decades, a steady stream of Roman Catholic missionaries, mostly Jesuits but Dominicans, Franciscans and Augustinians as well, came to Japan where they were warmly received. The Jesuits in particular focused their missionary attention on the *daimyô* and the *samurai*, figuring that if they could get to them, other Japanese were sure to follow, which they did. Substantial communities of *kirishitan*, Christians, developed, but the increasing numbers of Christian *daimyô* became of great concern to Toyotomi Hideyoshi who feared the Jesuits' influence over them. Upon hearing that missionaries were the preliminaries of a military conquest, Hideyoshi turned against them and ordered them expelled. The ban on missionaries did not apply as yet to Portuguese ships and their traders, but the Jesuits continued their work under cover, entering Japan disguised as merchants. That put the fortunes of the Portuguese/Spanish traders who were once welcomed with open arms, as well as their Christian converts, in serious jeopardy.

Although Toyotomi Hideyoshi's edict was at first not strictly enforced, an incident happened that led to the future persecutions of Japanese Christians. The Japanese had impounded the cargo of a Spanish galleon shipwrecked in Shikoku. Its captain tried to get the cargo back by threats, boasting that Spain, with the help of Japanese Christians, could easily invade Japan. Twenty-six people from the galleon, six missionaries and twenty Japanese Christians, were paraded through the streets of Osaka, Sakai, and Kyoto and then were crucified on Nagasaki's Nishizaka hill. By that time, Nagasaki, taken out from the hands of the Jesuits, had become an imperial city.

When Tokugawa Ieyasu came to power, he initially took a fairly tolerant stance toward Christians and the Portuguese and Spanish traders. In part, this was due to the fact that he had his own internal enemies to contend with, in part because he considered the European trade advantageous for his own ambitions. This attitude changed dramatically when Toyotomi Hideyori, son and legitimate heir of Toyotomi Hideyoshi, closely associated himself with the Jesuits and received a great following among Japanese Christians. The Portuguese and Spanish traders became implicated since it was known that they allied themselves with Hideyori. Priests were declared the enemies of Buddha, creating a period of great unrest with which Ieyasu had his hands full. Some time later, the Portuguese were banished to the island of Deshima and shortly thereafter were expelled for good in 1639. Christianity, once flourishing in Japan, went underground and suffered over 200 years of persecution.

The exit of the Portuguese did not mean the end of a European presence in Japan however, as they had been joined by the people who were to terminate their dominance in the Far East, the Dutch. For a short period, the English joined the Dutch but finding trade unprofitable, they left after a stay of barely ten years.

Traditionally, the date of the first Dutch contact with the Japanese is recorded to be April 19, 1600 when a Dutch ship *De Liefde* (Charity) stranded near present day Usuki on the island of Kyûshû. However, this was not the first time a Dutchman set foot in Japan. A man named Dirck Gerritz Pomp, nicknamed "China" because of the many tales he told about his travels to the Far East, twice visited Japan before 1600. He described it as the "isle where there is a lot of silver and where Portuguese ships arrive every year with silk which is sold for silver." The date of his first visit is not known, but on July 31, 1585 he again set foot on Japanese soil where he arrived on the Portuguese ship *Santa Cruz*.

He stayed for eight months and returned to Holland in april 1590 where he proceeded to focus attention on Japan and the desirability of trade with that country. Pomp also was a friend of the Dutch merchant Jan Huygen van Linschoten, 1563-1611. Both men were in the service of the Portuguese and came from the same province. Van Linschoten had returned from Goa in 1592 and in his famous travelogue published in 1598 under the title *Itinerario*, he devoted some pages to Japan, even though he himself was never there. His knowledge of Japan most likely came from Pomp as well as from his association with the Portuguese. The wealth of information his book gave about other countries in Asia and Africa, as well as his description of the routes to these countries, piqued the interest of the wealthy maritime Provinces of Holland and Zeeland which had declared themselves independent from Spain in 1581. As the union of Portugal and Spain (1580-1640) had ended Dutch trade with Portugal, since the port of Lisbon was now closed to them, the Hollanders were ready to challenge the Spanish/Portuguese dominion of the seas and the Far East trade. Near Cuba, they not only captured the Spanish fleet, nicknamed the silver fleet because of the silver it brought from South America, but also broke the Portuguese hold on the Moluccas from where the coveted and thus very profitable spices were brought to Europe. With these and other successes, the Dutch not only ended the Portuguese/Spanish control of the sea trade, but took it over.

A first Dutch attempt to explore the empires of China and Japan failed, but a second one ended up with one ship out of an original four, *De Liefde*, being cast ashore near the city of Usuki in Oita prefecture on April 19, 1600, a year that would mark the beginning of a century of Dutch trade and naval dominance that led to Holland's "Golden Age." One of the four ships, *Blijde Boodschap* (Good Tiding), was captained by Dirk "China" Pomp who would never set foot in Japan again, as he was captured by the Spanish in Chilean waters.

Originally, the fleet that sailed from Holland in 1598 did not have Japan as its destination but the west coast of South America, where the cargo was to be sold for silver. Only if unsuccessful was the fleet to sail to Japan to obtain silver there, which would then be exchanged for spices in the Moluccas. The two biggest ships of this fleet, aptly named *Hoop* (Hope) and *Liefde* (Charity) (formerly the *Erasmus* carrying a wooden statue of this great humanist on its stern which is now in a Tokyo museum), were subsequently directed toward Japan. The Hope perished in the Pacific Ocean, while only the Charity made it to Japan after losing many of its crew to starvation and disease. Of this expedition, only one fifth of the crew members lived to tell its tale. The *Liefde's* twenty-four survivors and its captain, Jakob Queackernaeck, were well treated by the Japanese. Queackernaeck immediately sent three delegates, the English navigator William Adams, Jan Joosten van Lodensteyn and Melchior van Santvoort to Osaka where they met Tokugawa Ieyasu who took a liking to them. Adams and van Lodensteyn later became his advisors. Eventually, Ieyasu granted the first two[5] a house in Edo where they were in his service and allowed the third man to establish himself as a merchant there. All three stayed for the rest of their lives in Japan and facilitated the establishment of a trading station in Hirado both for the Dutch and for the English.

When the Dutch established a trading station in Patani, India, in 1602, a harbor to which Japanese boats also sailed, Adams got permission from Ieyasu to send Queackernaeck and van Santvoort there, but he himself was not allowed to leave. Most of the rest of the crew, with the help of the *daimyô* of Hirado, were able to sail for home in 1605. In the meantime however, the stage was being set for the Dutch trade monopoly in Japan.

Ieyasu, now well informed about the difference between Catholicism and Protestantism and about the antagonism between the two religions which made the Dutch not only competitors but also adversaries of the combined Spanish-Portuguese crown, decided perhaps to use them in a *divide et impera* policy. He officially granted the Dutch the freedom to travel and to settle in Japan by handing a trading pass to Queackernaeck, which informed the authorities that Ieyasu would allow Dutch merchants to come to Japan. In 1608, van

Santvoort was sent back to Japan to inform Adams and Ieyasu that Dutch ships would be sent to open up trade with Japan.

In July 1609, two ships, *Roode Leeuw met Pijlen* (Red Lion with Arrows) and *Griffioen* (Griffin), arrived in Japan, and from this date on the Dutch officially started their trade relation with Japan. After their arrival, delegates, headed by Abraham van der Broek and Nicolaes Puijck, accompanied by van Santpoort as interpreter, were sent to the court of Ieyasu with letters and presents from Prince Maurits of Orange, *Stadholder* of the United Provinces. They were well received by the *shôgun* who handed them four copies of a trading pass, *goshuin*, that would make the Dutch trade relation with Japan unique. These passes stated that "it is ordered that the Dutch ships, without exception, when they come to Japan, can enter every bay. In the future, they have to continuously come and go, keeping this in mind, they must not ever fail to do this. This order is as stated above. Dated August 24, 1609." This copy was given to Jacques Groenewegen and is the only one that has survived. The Dutch were also free to travel all over Japan, marry Japanese women, and take them and their children with them when they left for home.

On September 20, 1609, the VOC opened a trading station in Hirado with Jacques Specx as the first *opperhoofd* or chief. Initially, it was not smooth sailing for this first chief, as there was a shortage of merchandise to trade since Dutch ships had yet to arrive. Specx even went to Patani to urge the authorities there to send ships to Japan and, shortly after his return, he set out to visit Ieyasu to obtain a renewal of the pass to counteract the Portuguese/Spanish campaign to undermine the Dutch trade. These missions were successful. In 1612, ships started to arrive regularly, but profits apparently failed to meet the expectations of the Lords XVII, directors of the VOC, who, in 1616, recommended that the station be abandoned. The Dutch government in Batavia did not agree, and the Dutch stayed in Hirado.

In 1613, the English joined them there and established their own station. The two nations then banded together.

xxii

Their combined fleets under an English admiral and a Dutch vice admiral started to attack Portuguese ships sailing to Japan and Chinese ships headed for Manila in the Philippines. They confiscated their cargo, divided it up, and then sold it to the Japanese. Understandably furious, the Portuguese complained to the *shôgun*, demanding the expulsion of the English and Dutch, who in turn tried to exonerate themselves by pointing out the attempts of the new *shôgun* Hidetada to eradicate the Roman Catholic faith. Indeed, this *shôgun* was more concerned about the spread of Christianity than the profits of trade, and for that reason, one of his first actions in 1616 would be to confine the Portuguese to Nagasaki and the Dutch and English to Hirado. Nevertheless, in 1621 Hidetada forbade the Dutch and English traders to plunder the ships of their competitors and the combined "defense" fleet was dismantled in 1622. The next year the English, unable to compete with the Dutch, abandoned their station, considering it unprofitable.

Yet the Dutch were not without their own problems. In 1629 and 1630, the station was closed and its employees taken prisoner. This resulted from the fact that Japanese traders on Formosa had refused to pay the import duty imposed on them by the VOC. The less than tactful behavior toward them of the Dutch governor of Formosa, Pieter Nuyts, which was subsequently embellished by the anti-Dutch governor of Nagasaki, had infuriated the Japanese government. Only quick action by the Dutch prevented disaster. It entailed sacrificing Nuyts on the altar of the profit motive by promptly delivering him to the Japanese. Permission to trade was granted again and now profits started to soar while the position of the Portuguese continued to deteriorate. The arrival of ships in Hirado during various periods tell the story; fourteen ships from 1621-1623; twenty ships from 1624-1632, but forty-eight ships from 1634-1638.

By this time also, the Dutch, perhaps more flexible than other European nations, had learned how to deal with the Japanese. Antonio van Diemen[6], who greatly aided Dutch expansion in the Far East wrote: "It is totally different with

Japan than it is with China. With great discretion, gentleness, and humility, we have to preserve Japan's friendship toward us. Once we lose it, it cannot be regained by force of arms." The last sentence was prophetic as indeed, no Western nation was ever able to colonize Japan. Contrary to the Portuguese, who showed little tolerance and respect for the natives, van Diemen's compatriots seemed to have taken his counsel to heart and were thereby able to remain in Japan while other Europeans' attempts to get a foothold there failed. For their part, the Japanese, knowing that the Dutch were only interested in trade and not in spreading Christianity, considered them less of a risk.

That said, the attitude toward foreign trade and foreigners of the Tokugawa *shôgunate* remained in general ambivalent, a tug of war perhaps between conservative nationalism and a strong curiosity about the world outside its confines. Though Ieyasu was well disposed toward the Dutch, his successors were of a less sanguine disposition. They did not trust the Dutch. Despite the fact that they had aided the Japanese at Shimabara, informed on the Portuguese, and promptly obeyed orders, suspicion of them lingered. After all, they were known to have pirated ships and, more worrisome perhaps, had established colonies in the Far East. They were also wary of the Dutch in spite of their well known hatred of the Portuguese and the Jesuits (a hatred they had skillfully used to their own benefit by fanning Japan's own antagonism toward them), because they too were Christian, even if they were not interested in spreading their brand of Christianity. Suspicion however was the hallmark of the Tokugawas. After all, they did not even trust their own people, especially the *daimyô*.

Although the *shôgun* may have seen some advantage in the continuance of foreign trade for the consolidation of their own economic power (they had profitably gotten the monopoly of the gold and silver mines), they nevertheless remained concerned lest the powerful *daimyô* whom they feared would also take advantage of foreign trade and might well seek support from foreigners. In addition, they may have seen some usefulness in keeping the Dutch, as they were aware of their technological and scientific superiority and wanted to avail themselves of their knowledge. Whatever the reason for keeping the Dutch, they were put under strict surveillance and the process of isolating Japan from the world, started by Ieyasu to assure the ascendancy of the Tokugawa clan and to try to eliminate all internal and external threats, continued. In 1635, this process was finally completed by his grandson, Iemitsu, also known as the Nero of Japan, who, in an edict, consolidated the *sakoku seikaku* policy that would isolate Japan from the world.

Japanese citizens, on penalty of death, were forbidden to go abroad, while those already abroad were denied reentrance. Given that there were thriving Japanese colonies in the Philippines, Thailand, and Java and that Japanese mercenary troops were used not only by Asiatic rulers but by the new European rulers as well, this edict affected thousands of them and created untold emotional suffering by ripping families apart. The next year, all seaworthy Japanese ships were destroyed and no such ships were allowed to be built again.

In short order, the Portuguese were relegated to Deshima in 1636 while their Japanese wives and children were ordered out of the country. By accusing them of having fueled the Christian rebellion in Shimabara, the Japanese found a handy excuse to expel the Portuguese altogether in 1639, forbidding them to ever again set foot in Japan. They meant just that. A Portuguese ship, perhaps trying to test this ban, sailed into the bay of Nagasaki a year later. It was captured and its crew was executed.

Whatever glee the Dutch may have felt at the fate of their arch enemies and rivals, their fortunes did not fare so well either. Despite Ieyasu's trading pass, promising free trade all over Japan, they were not only to be more and more restricted in place, but in trade as well. The import of silk however remained very profitable, if perhaps not approaching the 100 percent profit as it previously did. More and more restrictions were applied, partially rescinded then reinstituted, especially in regard to the main export of gold, silver, and copper. Yet trade remained profitable.

Soon, their Japanese wives and children had to leave also and only men directly involved with trade were permitted to stay in Japan. To keep a better eye on them, the Dutch, in 1641, were also banished to Deshima, where they managed to remain until the end of Japan's isolation period. This made them the only European presence in Japan for over 200 years. It is not clear whether it was Ieyasu's pass, the fact that the Dutch obeyed the ban on spreading Christianity, or that the Japanese were not yet ready to give up all foreign trade with the West that prevented them from sharing the same fate as the Portuguese. They stayed, as they were the safest bet for the Japanese, but under most difficult and often demeaning circumstances.

If not actual prisoners, the Dutch in the beginning were at best in protective custody on Deshima, an island Kaempfer described as "being 280 by 136 easy strides" in size. Later reports measured the island as being 120 by 70 meters, though its true size was never really established. A letter of Antonio van Diemen to the *shôgun* protesting his countrymen's treatment was ignored. Life on Deshima was not only very difficult but also very boring and monotonous. Movement was very restricted and the Dutch were under constant scrutiny from guards and spies. Only for good reasons, and with the permission of the governor of Nagasaki, were they allowed outside its gate. This monotony was broken only when the ships sailed in or when they celebrated New Year's or Christmas.

Though any outward manifestation of their religion was strictly forbidden, the Dutch, harking back to the ways of their heathen ancestors, joyously celebrated Christmas under the guise of the winter solstice. The nature-loving Japanese, thinking that this was a splendid idea, happily joined in the festivities, unaware of what they were really celebrating. Later on, the King's birthday and Napoleon's defeat at Waterloo were added as occasions to have a big banquet. Meals in Deshima seem to have been of a high culinary standard and much appreciated by the Japanese as well. Cattle and goats, shipped to Deshima from Batavia and bred there, imported wines and home grown vegetables added to the meals' gustatory excellence.

Another distraction for some of Deshima's employees was the trek to Edo. At first once a year, then every fourth year, the Dutch chief, usually accompanied by the scribe and the company physician, had to journey to Edo to present gifts to the *shôgun* and give him the "Dutch" news, a report about the developments in Europe or in the countries with which the Dutch had trade relations. This was also the occasion in which the *shôgun* had the opportunity to ask any questions of importance to him.

From Kaempfer's description of this trek, it is clear that the Dutch in the beginning were subjected to a treatment that, in Western eyes, could be considered humiliating. Once inside the inner sanctum of the palace and in the presence of the *shôgun* and his screened off ladies and children, the Dutch had "... to walk, to stand still, to compliment each other, to dance, to jump, to play the drunkard, to speak broken Japanese, to read Dutch, to paint, to sing, to put cloaks off and on and to kiss one another like man and wife," the latter to the great hilarity of the ladies behind the screen. Further he states "with innumerable such apish tricks, we must suffer ourselves to contribute to the court's diversion." This type of treatment didn't last long and the trek became a true diversion, erotically but also intellectually. Once the ban on the importation of non-religious books was lifted, *daimyô*, mostly interested in military matters, and Japanese scholars, followers of Western culture and studies, visited the Dutch at their officially appointed *honjin* or inns in Edo as well as on the Tokaido highway and engaged in lively exchanges of ideas.

Apart from good food and good wine, another solace, this time sexual, made the otherwise spartan life of the Dutch more bearable. This was the company of Japanese females. One chief, Isaac Titsingh, describes them thus: "Truly, no country has such charming women as Japan. I have not found any like them in any other (Asian) country." The Japanese, who do not have the western guilt and shame complex about sex, saw to it that the Dutch were not deprived of this, to them, basic need. At first, *yûjos* or prostitutes were allowed to stay overnight only, but this soon extended to three days, then to five, and then for as long as their mates wanted them, provided they reported daily to the guards. Given that, outside the trading months, there wasn't much to do, it is no wonder that rumors about the sexual prowess of the Dutch started circulating. At one point, Doeff reluctantly had to curtail the consolation these women brought when funds were low during the period when no ships arrived. This no doubt added to the tension and hardship of that particular time which is so poignantly described by Doeff.

The *yûjos* were often paid in sugar or other company goods and records show not only that the Dutch had indeed a hearty appetite, but also who consorted with whom. For instance, these records reveal the names of some of Hendrik Doeff's consorts, among whom were to be found Iroha, Kotaki, Sono'o, and Uryuno. While distraught over his wife's forced departure, we also know that Doeff's successor, Blomhoff, soon consoled himself again with his former concubine, Itohage, and added yet another one named Tatsu. Coming from the Maruyama district, these women, mostly lower ranked ones in the beginning, were fearful at first of having to go to these "red haired barbarians." That changed quickly however. Soon, only the highest ranked and most expensive *yûjos* came who quickly took up Western habits.

Still a mystery is why the Dutch going *yûjos* were allowed to bear children, while this was strictly forbidden for all the others. Perhaps the answer lies in a *haiku* which states: "The women of Maruyama give birth to corals." This refers to the rounder eyes these mixed race children had, eyes that are highly desirable in Japanese society. Giving birth to these children on Deshima was forbidden and the children themselves could only stay there until the age of seven, after which they had to move to the city, frequently to live with their grandparents. As many of these relationships became longstanding ones, there undoubtedly was a lot of heartbreak when the men had to go home, leaving behind not only women they had come to love, but also their children. A poignant *Haiku* states: "A farewell from Maruyama means a distance of 13,000 miles." By and large, the men provided well for their concubines and children and some, like Doeff, may have stayed in touch with them. Company doctors often took care of them when they were sick long after their fathers had left.

In time, other Japanese visitors came, mostly artists and scholars, who managed to cross the bridge to the island by disguising themselves as workmen. Mutual respect, learning and admiration grew from these encounters which became increasingly productive, not only for Japan but also for Holland, as it introduced a far superior knowledge of Japan than other European nations at that time possessed.

Over time, restrictions for the Dutch in Deshima lessened. For instance, they were allowed to attend the many *matsuri* or Japanese festivals in town or make trips to the countryside. Often including *yûjos* and their children, these excursions did not come cheap. In addition to the usual retinue of translators, banyos (police), and assorted other personnel, often as many as 200, that was required to accompany them wherever they went, the Dutch also had to pay and feed the extra guards needed for these outings.

At the beginning of the 19th century, the Dutch were allowed to go off the island to visit the *yûjos* in the Maruyama district, and Doeff was the first to be so invited. It is likely that he availed himself of that invitation at the Kagetsu, the most elegant of the district's teahouses. A ceiling painted by a Dutchman, perhaps in payment for his debts, can still be seen at the Kagetsu, which is now a fancy restaurant.

Other restrictions were lifted over time also, notably the ban on the Dutch teaching at the *rangaku* (Dutch science) schools which were established in various cities. So voracious was the Japanese appetite for everything Western, that thousands of books on every conceivable subject, all written in Dutch, were imported.

If Deshima was tiny, so was its population which never exceeded twenty and was even as low as a pitiful six during part of Doeff's term there. In general, this population consisted of a chief, a chief buyer, one or two physicians, a scribe, some clerks and carpenters, and some gunners. Not all of these men were Dutch, however, and sometimes only a third were. Others were of other European nationalities.

In the beginning, the VOC's profit was worth the endless complications of dealing with the difficult Japanese, while the considerable profit from the private or *kambang* trade (and smuggling) compensated its employees for the hardships and lack of freedom they had to endure. Stories had it that two years in Deshima would permit a man to live handsomely in his motherland for the rest of his life.

During 1641-1671, a period of relative free trade, an average of seven ships (twelve perished in this period) arrived per year and profits reflected that number. In the beginning silk was the main product the Dutch imported, but sugar replaced it later on. Among other imported articles were deer pelts and shark skins from Asia and woolen cloth and glassware from Europe. The official trade was called the *conpaniya* or company by the Japanese and the imported goods the *oranda watari* or Dutch wares. Subsidiary to it and increasingly more important was the private or *kambang* trade, which, apart from being a tremendous source of extra income for the employees, permitted Japanese scholars to order not only books but all kinds of scientific instruments.

From 1671-1715, an average of five ships per year arrived, and although profits were still substantial, a steady decline in the profitability of the station began. In 1672, the Japanese reinstituted the so called *pancado* system which was first applied in 1604 to the raw silk the Portuguese imported. Now, it was not only applied to raw silk, but to all the goods imported by the Dutch. The *pancado* system entailed that the value of all goods was estimated in secret by ten of the most important merchants of the five imperial cities, Edo, Miyako, Sakai, Osaka, and Nagasaki, after which the governor of Nagasaki made an offer on the whole cargo on the basis of the highest bid. If the Dutch rejected this bid, they were "free" to take the cargo back to Batavia. The ban on the export on silver and gold, plus the fact that the Dutch now had to pay import taxes from which they had previously been exempted thanks to Ieyasu's trading pass, made profits dwindle even more. This had been the intent of the Japanese government all along, as it wanted to curtail the enormous profits in the first place. A quota system on copper and the appearance of the *kambang* or private trade, which benefited the employees but not the VOC which looked askance at it, continued the downward slide of profits in the 18th century. In 1715 only two ships were allowed per year. This was reduced to one in 1790, but upped again to two in 1799.

During the Napoleonic wars, when the Dutch had to resort to hiring neutral ships, there were years when no ships arrived at all, and in 1807 the Japanese government even forbade the hiring of American ships. This was a very dangerous period for the Dutch. In 1813, an imperial commissioner, Matsuyama Sôemon, arrived in Nagasaki with the mandate to expel the Dutch to China if again no ships arrived. Doeff was privately informed of this, but by his very skillful political maneuvering was able to save the day. During the period from 1641-1847 a total of 606 ships arrived in Deshima, an average of about three per year which reflects perhaps not only the ups and downs of trade, but the tenacious holding on to this station as well.

In direct proportion to the declining importance of trade, the diplomatic, political, and cultural importance of Deshima rose. Rather than abandoning a not very profitable station, the VOC, in accordance with its monopolistic policies mixed perhaps with national pride, deemed its presence important enough to stay on this tiny island which was to have such an enormous impact on Japanese culture, art and science. American textbooks invariably declared that Commodore Perry opened Japan to the West, as if Japan had indeed been hermetically closed. This is far from the reality. Though Japan indeed closed its doors, it left open a window, fan-shaped tiny Deshima. However wary of foreign trade and foreigners in general, Japan nevertheless, out of self-interest, did not want to risk being totally left in the dark. It restricted foreign trade but in not eliminating it altogether, managed to be kept abreast of what was going on in the world and more importantly, learn everything there was to learn from the West.

Often described as a lens through which the Japanese observed the world and the world got a glimpse of Japan, Deshima can perhaps better be envisioned as the eye of a needle. The symbolic camel pushed through this eye was the insatiable thirst of the Japanese for knowledge of Europe and Western science as Holland by now had replaced China as the seat of knowledge. Donald Keene states that by the end of the eighteenth century, the Japanese were better acquainted with European civilization than the people of any other non-Western country. The knowledge gathered through Deshima in turn explains the later rapid expansion of Japan.

In the arts, the Dutch exercised a great influence. First, the detailed illustrations found in Dutch botanical and zoological works greatly impressed the Japanese. Then, upon seeing Dutch books on art, notably Gerard de Lairesse's *The Big Painting Book*[7], as well as etchings, prints and paintings on the walls of Deshima for the first time, Japanese artists came under Dutch influence. They studied Dutch painting and drawing techniques, including copper etching techniques and the use of chiaroscuro and perspective, and broadened the range of objects they painted. The Dutch and their wares, especially the exotic animals they imported, became the subject of countless woodblock prints and their images graced numerous porcelain bowls, plates and vases as well. Japanese porcelain also came under Dutch influence and vice versa. Three of the better known Japanese artists of the time were Hiragi Gennai, Shiba Kôkan, and Keiga Kawahara. The latter two made paintings of Doeff whose clearly recognizable image also graced one of the many erotic prints made of the Dutch.

It was through the medium of the Dutch language that

Western science penetrated Japan. Already early on, Japanese scholars realized that they had to learn Dutch in order to translate the books they imported. Dutch schools or *rangaku* were established and the *rangakusha* or Hollandologists started their painstaking work of translating books and manuscripts on all kinds of subjects. Was their first interest geography, it soon turned to other subjects, from astronomy to medicine, warfare and economics. There was literally nothing the Japanese were not interested in or acquainted themselves with thoroughly. This stood in sharp contrast to the Chinese who were rather indifferent to the West and Western knowledge. Over time, *Oranda* or Holland supplanted China as the seat of knowledge for the Japanese.

It was on medicine however that the Dutch had the greatest impact thanks to some remarkable men who were instrumental in spreading Western knowledge in Japan. In turn, they brought their knowledge of Japan back to Europe and provided the first detailed description of this hitherto unknown land and its culture to the European public. Among the more notable ones were Caspar Schambergen who demonstrated Western surgical methods in a school he established in Nagasaki, the *Casparyû*, which continued to exist until the end of the Tokugawa era. He was allowed to stay on in Edo to teach surgery. Engelbert Kaempfer, physician, scholar, and the first scientific discoverer of Japan as well as the author of a monumental work, *The History of Japan*. Carl Peter Thunberg, physician, scientific explorer, and botanist who introduced the science of botany to Japan as well as the use of mercury for the treatment of syphilis. He also provided the West with the first specimens of the tea plant. Willem ten Rhijne who was the first to give detailed descriptions of Chinese and Japanese medical practices and described acupuncture and moxibustion. Franz von Siebold who was the first foreign physician to systematically teach Western medicine in Japan. He is also considered the father of modern obstetrics in Japan. He gathered a mass of information on Japan, including maps which, when they were discovered, caused his expulsion and created havoc for the

Japanese scholars with whom he was in contact. His mania for collecting all things Japanese brought Holland an unrivaled treasure trove which formed the basis of the oldest ethnological museum[8] in the world. Otto Mohnike, a Deshima physician who introduced vaccination against smallpox. Johannes Pompe van Meerdervoort was the last of the Deshima physicians to contribute greatly to the firm establishment of Western medicine in Japan. Against great odds, he founded the first medical school based solely on Western medicine. It has a five-year curriculum patterned after Dutch medical education. He was also instrumental in the establishment of a teaching hospital and presided over the first dissection ever of a human cadaver in Japan. The company doctors were really the ones who inspired the curiosity and whetted the thirst for Western knowledge of the Japanese scholars. It was from these doctors and others as well as from Dutch medical books that Japanese scholars obtained their knowledge of Western medicine. It is certainly a striking development that between 1756 and 1846 twelve private schools were established in Edo, Kyoto, and Osaka that taught Western medicine. The first, *Shirandô*, was opened in Edo in 1786 by Otsuki Gentaku, one of the greatest *rangakusha* or Dutch scholar.

The flourishing of these interchanges owed a lot to another remarkable man who, despite being educated in medicine and law, entered the VOC as a junior merchant. His name was Isaac Titsingh, who was twice chief of the trading station between 1779-1784. He was the first one to make systematic contacts with Japanese scholars, greatly contributed to the scientific interest of the Japanese, and is considered the first Dutch Japanologist. After he left Deshima, he continued to correspond with them and recently, his correspondence with these Japanese scholars was published in two volumes under the title *The Private Correspondence of Isaac Titsingh*. Together with Hendrik Doeff's recollections, Titsingh's correspondence forms another invaluable source for the study of pre-Perry Japan. It was through the eye of the needle called Deshima and thanks to some remarkable men that European culture, scholarship and science deeply penetrated Japan. It is a tragedy that the Japanese built on this learning and used it for an imperialistic expansion after the fall of the *shôgunate*. Without it, they would not have been able to achieve victories over China (1895) and Russia (1905), occupy Korea (1910) and, later on, achieve their initial victories in the Pacific.

On a diplomatic and political front, the Dutch also played a significant role. From 1640 on, the *shôgun* wanted the Dutch to provide them with information about the West which they called *fusetsu-gaki* or "gathering of rumors." Later on, this was formalized into a yearly Dutch newsletter in which a report was given on the economic, political and social developments in Europe, a report no doubt filtered through the eyes of the Dutch who would, naturally, slant the news to protect their own self-interest. In time, the Dutch became more and more valuable to the Japanese. Whenever the Japanese had a need to deal with a foreign nation, they used the Dutch as intermediaries, having them translate letters and send reports abroad or even asked for their advice.

After the Napoleonic wars, the world grew increasingly impatient with Japan's isolationist position. More and more ships started to appear in Japanese waters, making the *shôgun* even more dependent on the Dutch for self-preservation and to keep them abreast of the rapid developments in the larger world around Japan. Books on shore defenses and fortification were requested and the translators had to familiarize themselves with ballistics. In 1825 a *shôgun's* edict allowed coastal *daimyô* to chase away, with guns if needed, all ships approaching its shores. In this way, the American ship *Morrison* which was on its way to deposit shipwrecked Japanese at Uraga, was chased away. The Opium War between China and Great Britain made the *shôgun* realize however, that their shore defenses were not adequate and they revoked this edict in 1842. Soon thereafter, a French war fleet appeared near the bay of Nagasaki. This was followed by a similar attempt of the American fleet under Commodore James Biddle to approach Edo. Increasingly, Japan's isolation came under heavy pressure.

xxxv

In 1844, King William II of Holland sent a special emissary to Edo to give the *shôgun* a letter in which he urged him to open up Japan by pointing out the dangers of continuing the isolationist policy. This emissary was politely received, but the warning was ignored. In 1852, Jan Donker Curtius, then chief on Deshima, notified the *shôgun* in the yearly newsletter than Perry's warships would soon sail into Edo. The next year they did just that, forcing the Japanese to change their traditional policy of isolation and achieving with might what Dutch diplomacy had failed to achieve. The treaty of Kanagawa opened up two harbors to the Americans and promised them better treatment for their shipwrecked sailors, though no specific mention as yet was made of trade. The Dutch at the same time also received two additional harbors. This in effect ended the unique position of that tiny island called Deshima through which so much knowledge penetrated Japan despite its policy of isolation.

In summary. Hendrik Doeff's role in the history of Deshima and Japan is an important one for various reasons:

1. As a lexicographer, he was able to master the Japanese language to such an extent that he was able to compile an extensive dictionary of this notoriously difficult language. Before Doeff, several Japanese scholars had already attempted to fashion a Dutch-Japanese dictionary. In 1796, a dictionary by Inamura Sanpaku appeared under the title *Haruma Wage*, but the work was too voluminous to be published. Doeff's dictionary, based on Halma's lexicon, the *Dôfu Haruma*, was published and supplanted *Haruma Wage*. Widely disseminated and used, it became a main vehicle through which Japanese scholars in the last decades of the Tokugawa Shôgunate mastered the Dutch language and thereby Western science and culture. In 1838, Ogata Koan had established the Dutch language school Tekijuku where students,

among them such luminaries as Fukuzawa Yukichi, Hashimoto Sanai, and Ômura Masujirô paved the way for Japan's transition to a modern state. As an indication of the importance of Doeff's dictionary in this period, Fukazawa Yukichi once wrote: "This (dictionary) was the work of master Doeff who once lived in the Dutch quarters of Nagasaki. It is revered as the great treasure of all students of the Dutch language." Scholars and students alike hand-copied pages of Doeff's dictionary and sold them to *daimyô* and others. It was said that in doing this, students could earn enough to pay their tuition. In the still existing Tekijuku, the language study room is called *Zûfu-beya* or "Doeff's room."[9]

2. As a Cultural Participant Observer, he was an active participant in various phases of Japanese culture in Nagasaki. The trek to Edo, partially on the famous Tokaido highway along which he traveled in the style of a *daimyô*, and his appearance at the court in Edo were unique events for a foreigner to be able to observe.

3. As a diplomat, he often functioned successfully as an intermediary, advisor, and translator in Japanese relations with the Western world. His role was especially important during the arrival of a Russian Embassy and in the Phaëton incident, when an English ship penetrated the harbor of Nagasaki and threatened to destroy Japanese ships and commit other hostilities. Indeed, Hendrik Doeff may well have prevented a war between Japan and England which might have changed the course of Japan's and the world's history.

4. As a patriot, he upheld the sovereignty of the Netherlands when, under Napoleon, the country had technically ceased to exist as a nation in Europe and when its empire in the Far East had

xxxvii

been lost to the English. He successfully rebuffed British and Russian intrusions and, more importantly, twice thwarted Raffles'[10] attempt to take over Deshima, the last place on earth where the Dutch flag still continued to wave. Doeff's refusal to strike the flag meant that Deshima was symbolically the Netherlands for a short period in history.

In short, Hendrik Doeff was a highly unusual man in a highly unusual situation. He stood up for his principles and steadfastly did his duty for an incredible length of time in spite of all the adversity he had to endure. His triumph was all the greater for it.

"Schip Franklin" is the first image of an American ship. Doeff took
the Franklin from and to Batavia.
Peabody Essex Museum, Salem, MA.

Harukaze ya
Amakoma hashiru
Hokakebune

A spring breeze
to and fro they bustle
the sail boats

haiku by Hendrik Doeff

Original translation into Dutch of this *haiku*, Professor Fritz Vos

PREFACE

This small book about Japan, seeing the light for the first time, will strike many as not being quite comprehensive enough in regard to that empire. One could indeed expect more from someone who spent 19 years in Japan, 15 of which as chief of the Dutch . In the story about my return voyage, the reader will learn how a shipwreck unfortunately robbed me of all my papers and collections. I was not able to salvage anything of what I researched about Japan during all those years. Therefore, nothing remains but these recollections from my stay in Japan, which I wrote down in book form shortly after my return to Holland. These recollections, regarding Japanese manners, customs, and religious beliefs, which I culled from the old papers in Deshima and certain other sources, were then still fresh in my memory. While still in Japan, already several of my friends wanted me to publish these recollections, but since a lot of the memories concern my own person, I was always reluctant to do this during my lifetime. Sometime ago, however, I changed my mind for the following reasons.

First, I wanted our nation to know how our flag of olden fame continued to wave in Japan, even during the French domination in Europe, and that of the English in the East Indies. Twice, and by the most wicked means, the English tried to make that flag disappear from Deshima. From the years 1813 and 1814, you will glean the kind of intrigues of which they availed themselves. You will then be in a position to judge whether such an excruciating ordeal deserved as superficial a treatment as is shown in a recently published book about the Dutch flag. But this was not the only reason that led to this small book. Following the return from Japan of Mr.

xli

Von Siebold[1], the rumors that he would publish a dictionary he wrote of both Dutch and Japanese also contributed to my decision. In a report to the governor general of the Netherlands Indies written by this Mr. von Siebold and submitted in 1825, he did not mention my name, and neither did Mr. Overmeer Fischer, former warehouse master[2] in Japan, do so when he submitted a Dutch-Japanese dictionary to the government. As both men had simply availed themselves of the work I had done, I have been forced to claim authorship of that dictionary, and I take the liberty to refer the reader to an explanatory addendum to this book. I regret my shipwreck doubly now. It deprived me of personally presenting this dictionary, of which I am the author, to His Majesty[3], as had been my intention. By doing this, I also wanted to prove that my 19-year stay in Japan had neither been unfruitful for the sciences nor useless in regard to the honor of the Dutch flag and her rescue from the hands of the English. If this present small work will at least partially achieve those last two aims, I would feel doubly rewarded.

CHAPTER I

I. General overview of the government, customs, religion, and history of the persecution of the Roman Catholics.

The empire of Japan, which lies at the extreme eastern end of the old hemisphere, has been frequently described by the Portuguese, French, Germans, and Dutch, yet it is not really well known in Europe. The reasons for the many mistakes other writers make is, on the one hand, the difficulty of getting to know the interior of the country because of old laws which by now have been in existence for two centuries; and on the other hand, the real difficulty of learning the language. How can you really describe a country well without being able to understand the language? You could perhaps assume that the translators, whom the Japanese appointed to trade with us on Deshima, and who were supposed to be versed in the Dutch language, were able to enlighten us about the history and customs of their country and give us its peculiarities. You would be quite mistaken in this however. During my 19-year stay in that country, from 1799[1] to 1817, it was my experience that the translators, who only learn Dutch[2] through association with the *Dutch* in *Japan*, had the greatest difficulty understanding newly arrived employees whose use of language was as yet alien to them. At the same time, the new arrivals had a most difficult time understanding the translators' pronunciation and their use of the language, which was geared to Japanese speech patterns. My lengthy stay gave me the opportunity to eliminate this difficulty. After having assiduously tackled the Japanese language, I started to draft a Japanese dictionary for Dutchmen in 1812 on the model of Halma's Dutch and French dictionary, with the help of the ablest translators[3] whom I chose myself. The Japanese government considered this endeavor so useful that I was asked to complete it, which I did before my departure in 1817. This work as well as all my other papers were, to my deepest regret, lost on my way home in the ship wreck of the *Admiraal Evertsen*.

It is necessary here to go a bit deeper into the development of this dictionary, now lost to me. Despite the fact that the original one, written in my own hand and the fruit of five years of labor, has been swallowed up by the sea, there is a neatly written copy remaining in Japan.[4, 5]

Only after 12 years in Japan, and with diligent efforts to truly master this language, did I feel able to profitably undertake this work. If, to my great regret, this work had not been lost as mentioned before, I would have been flattered to present it to His Majesty, our venerated King. As the neatly written and aforementioned copy is now at the Municipal Translators College in Nagasaki, it is very easy to make a transcript or abstract with the help of a few translators. Someone else could thus conceivably get the honor and the pleasure of which the shipwreck deprived me. It would be rare indeed that someone again would stay in Japan for as long as circumstances forced me to stay. No stay of four to five years will give the required knowledge, even to the most gifted person, that is necessary to produce a dictionary of that most difficult language.

The obstacles that stand in the way of thoroughly mastering that language are as follows:

1. The existing law that no foreigner may ever learn the Japanese language.[6]

2. The lack of contact with the Japanese, as even a translator can only come to the home of a Dutchman under the surveillance of a district warden (in reality a spy) of Deshima.

3. The lack of free access to the homes of Japanese families in Nagasaki, even during the trek to the Court in Edo once every four years during which one is always surrounded by guards or spies.

Taking all this into account, everyone must agree that a short stay, filled with other obligations one must see to, will give little opportunity to fruitfully undertake such an important work.

It took an exceptional permission and a Court order to the town governor of Nagasaki to allow the translators who helped me in writing this dictionary[7] to come to my house. The many services I provided to the Court during the first 12 years of my stay were instrumental in getting me that exceptional permission.[8] Although my long stay in Japan allowed me of course to make many observations about its government, religion and customs, I will not describe this most remarkable country in any great detail. For this, I refer the reader to the work of Engelbert Kaempfer[9] published at the beginning of the last Century. It is still the best. Yet it should be noted that this work is less his than it is that of the Governor General, Mr. Camphuys[10], a very literary and able man who wrote the history of the founding[11] of Batavia which Valentijn[12] included in his great work. The famous Onno Zwier van Haren[13] found Camphuys worthy of a separate biography. Kaempfer was only in Japan for two years, spoke no Japanese, and availed himself of a Japanese servant whom he had to teach Dutch in order to be able to gather his most important information.

It was Camphuys, a former chief on Deshima, who provided Kaempfer with the detailed observations that he had gathered during his stay. With this treasure, the German physician presents Camphuys' observations as his own. In this case as well, foreigners once more do not adequately credit the Dutch.

My aim in this book is only to correct the many misperceptions about Japan that exist in Europe, and to offer the necessary clarifications. We will start with the history of their form of government.

The origin of the Japanese nation which Kaempfer, according to his Japanese sources, describes as being extremely old, millions of years even, is very uncertain. According to the Japanese themselves, *Tensio Daisin* (descendant of the heavenly Gods) is considered the first man on earth, but there is obviously no record of this. The beginning of their actual and certain history dates from the first lord, or *dairi*[14], of Japan, Sen Mou Ten Oo, 660 years B.C. From this date, some 25 centuries ago, the Japanese can trace their history and the unbroken chain of their real and lawful hereditary emperors in a reasonably orderly way. In this respect Kaempfer deserves full credibility. It is strange however that he and all the other writers constantly speak of a *spiritual* and a *worldly* monarch in Japan, namely the *dairi* and the *shôgun*[15], the first residing in Miyako, the second in Edo.[16]

In my opinion, it is a mistake to call the *dairi* a *spiritual* monarch. Rather, the *dairi* is the old absolute monarch of Japan whose ancestors had the sole authority in religious as well as civil matters. This unlimited and exclusive power diminished through the appointment of a *shôgun*, or chief general, of the people's army (85 or 86 years B.C.), a title the then reigning *dairi* gave to one of his sons. It was almost 13 centuries before the chief generals extended their power, or somewhat infringed the *dairi's* power. Only around 1160 or 1170 A.D. did the *shôgun* Yoritomo[17] avail himself of the opportunity to weaken the power of the *dairi* under the guise of protecting him but only to elevate himself to the status of hereditary chief. He was all the more successful in this, as several of the ruling princes of the 63 domains into which Japan is divided and who vied for the favor of the *dairi,* waged war against each other and claimed second sovereignty for their own princely domains which sovereignty they did not have before. Against this backdrop, Yoritomo acquired a power from the *dairi* which he never again gave up, but instead bequeathed to his heirs.[18]

The disturbances and wars[19] nevertheless continued with greater or smaller intervals until the year 1590 when Taiko[20], a man renowned in Japanese history, came to power. From a very lowly background[21] as servant to a medicinal herbalist, he achieved the highest office of *shôgun* through his courage and ability. Through sheer statesmanship, he used the authority of the rulers of several provinces who constantly strove for greater power to enhance his own authority, at the expense of the remaining power of the *dairi*.

He eventually realized that this maneuver to restore the peace would be dangerous to himself. He therefore decided to keep these subordinate princely rulers busy elsewhere. It is not clear whether Taiko's ambition would have extended as far as the conquest of China, though he waged war on the island to the west of Japan that is on the way to China, the Korean peninsula. For this war, he preferred to engage the troops of those princely rulers from whom he had the most to fear in the pursuit of his ambitious projects. By doing this, he achieved a dual aim: if the princely rulers were killed in that war, his ambition had free reign; if they won, it gave him the opportunity to bestow land on them in conquered Korea. He would thereby tie *them* to his own interests while in the meantime, his followers were kept in Japan. This was bound to assure him supremacy at home. He was only partially successful in this. Korea was not totally conquered but only made subject to paying tribute to Japan. This situation still exists insofar as the ruler of Tsushima occupies a territory on the shore of Korea in the name of the *shôgun* up to this day.

I do not know if Korea still pays tribute money to Japan, but it is a fact that the Koreans are forced, at every new ascension to the throne, to come and greet the reigning *shôgun*.

At the elevation of the present *shôgun*, this caused many an unpleasant situation. The Japanese government now desired that the Koreans bring their homage *not* to the *shôgun* at Edo as they had in the past, but to the subordinate ruler of the island Tsushima. The Koreans considered this an insult and refused to comply. After this dispute had lasted several years, the Japanese government formed a commission in 1811. It consisted of the ruler of Kokura, the chief treasurer, and the chief accountant of the realm. They went to Tsushima as representatives of the *shôgun* and received the homage of the Korean delegation there. On their way back home, this commission, minus the ruler of Kokura, but accompanied by the governor of Nagasaki, visited me on Deshima.

Taiko (to get back to this conqueror) did not fully achieve his goal, as many of the princely rulers whom he had sent to battle in hopes of getting rid of them returned. In addition to these problems, there was the one of a nephew whom he had named as his successor, as he had expected to remain without male issue. When a son was born to him, he wanted him to relinquish his territory which he, Fidetsuge, showed absolutely no inclination of doing. Both sides disguised their true intentions. The nephew secretly armed himself, but Taiko's expressions of friendship lulled him to complacency. While in this lethal peace of mind frame, Fidetsuge was summoned by his uncle, who was now well enough armed to demand obedience. His nephew didn't *dare* decline to come. Without even seeing his uncle, Fidetsuge was ordered to go to the mountain Koyasan, the usual place where grandees condemned to exile were sent.[22] There is a monastery on this remote and lonely place. Here, the ambitious nephew who found it unbearable to be thus in disgrace far from the Court, committed suicide by cutting open his belly,[23] the way the Japanese grandees are in the habit of doing.

Taiko died in 1598. He would have liked to have seen his son, Hideyori (1593-1615), established as his successor, but, given his son's tender years, he had to seek a trusted guardian for him. He thought to have found him in his best friend and counselor, Iyeyas[24]. He had showered this friend with favors, adding to the territory he already ruled seven other ones. Could he have trusted anyone more? This friend did now have the power to protect the young prince, and certainly the will to do so should not have been lacking in someone who owed so much to the house of Taiko. The more so, as a marriage had been arranged between the young prince and the daughter of his guardian. After Taiko's death, Iyeyas ruled the country under the name Daifusama and was supposed to hand over the reign to the young prince on his fifteenth birthday. It soon became clear that Daifusama had no intention of doing this. The first five state counselors got wind of this and added four more counselors to their ranks, in an attempt to rein in the ambition of the country's ruler. Dissension paralyzed all of their attempts, however. Violent civil wars broke out, and in 1616 Daifusama was able to conquer the palace of Osaka[25]. Some rumors had it that the young emperor burned in his palace; other claimed that he had fled to Satsuma. Soon after this event, Daifusama died in solid possession of supreme power, which he bequeathed to his heirs up to this day. After his death, the Japanese gave him the title *Gongen*. He left five sons, and designated his second son, Hidetada, as his heir. He did not choose his eldest son, whom he had appointed ruler of Suruga during his life time. At the same time, he made his three youngest sons rulers over the estates of Mito, Kyûshû, and Owari. The oldest brother could not swallow this humiliating displacement, as he was now a mere subject. While his father was away at the Owari estate, he tried to conquer the castle Nagoya through trickery and force. The wet nurse of the crown prince got wind of the attack and, under the guise of having to take the baths for health reasons, left for Owari to inform Gongen. He immediately returned to Edo. This oldest son came to meet him in Kawasacki but, upon learning that his father knew everything, returned to his estate in Suruga. There he was ordered to stay for the rest of his life in the castle Futsiyu. To prevent all further attacks against his second son, Gongen introduced him publicly as his heir under the name of Taitokfumi. Gongen died the same year, 1616. After the father's death several grandees, yes *even* several envoys of the *dairi*[26], the truly legitimate emperor, tried to have the exiled oldest son make peace with his brother, but the latter referred to the immutability of his father's sentence.

Not satisfied yet with his answer, and afraid of further attacks from his oldest brother, Taitokfumi sent some of his boldest nobles to kill him. The oldest brother's vigilance thwarted this attempt, and all the secret murderers met with their death in Futsiyu. The ruler of Suruga did realize however that his life was now irrevocably forfeited. To avoid a shameful death sentence, he committed *seppuku*[27] as is the Japanese custom. Only then did Hidetada, or Taitokfumi, rest safely on his throne, as his younger brothers had no reason to dispute his legitimacy. Since that time, their heirs always carry the title "princes of the blood," and are consulted in all important matters. The *shôgun's* wet nurse, married to the counselor Mino-Sama and instrumental in having brought the attack of the oldest brother to light, was so revered during her lifetime that one had to give presents to her as well as to the *shôgun*. For a long time afterwards, the descendants of the Mino-Sama clan continued to be highly esteemed.

Since that time, Japan has remained free of all civil unrest and foreign wars. But Gongen had restricted the power of the *dairi*, once the supreme ruler in Japan, to such an extent that he now stands completely under the guardianship of the *shôgun* in Edo, who provides him and his court with a fixed annual allowance.[28] The *dairi* did however retain the right to bestow certain dignities or ranks, which consists solely of titles that provide him with many important gifts of money from the beneficiaries to whom the titles are given. Yet he cannot even bestow these ranks without the recommendation of the *shôgun*, who puts his seal on them.

In two instances I witnessed how the Court of the *shôgun* deemed it useful to consider the feelings of the *dairi*. The first occurred during the arrival of the Russian ambassador de Rezanov (1804 and 1805), whose proposals, I'm told, led to a consultation with the Court of Miyako, the *dairi's* Court. The other occurred when the astronomers at the Court of Edo proposed to count, from now on, the years by the sun instead of by the moon, as had been the Japanese custom and to arrange the almanacs accordingly. The Court of the *dairi* opposed this, however.

From this, one cannot come to the conclusion that the *dairi* had any authority in important matters. In the first instance, it seems to me that, in the event the *shôgun* had had to call the princes or lords to arms if a war between Russia and Japan had resulted from the rejection of the Russian proposals, he would have made them more willing to do so if the *dairi* had proven the necessity for this in a declaration. But I'm equally convinced that, had the *dairi* disagreed with the *shôgun*, no one would have paid any attention to him. As I will show later, the *dairi* was feared even less because all the rulers suspected to be particularly loyal to the *dairi* were kept under strict surveillance.

As concerns the second instance, one has to seek the reason for this in the fact that the Almanacs, traditionally calculated in moon years, were manufactured in Miyako under the supervision of the *dairi*. As Gongen himself had instituted this, the Court did not dare change this in order not to jeopardize the whole form of government.

One can therefore see that the *dairi* is not a *spiritual* and the *shôgun*[29] not a *worldly* emperor as many writers claim, but only that the *dairi* was once an absolute ruler until his generals, taking advantage of the civil unrests and their influence over the army, usurped for themselves the highest power, leaving the *dairi* but the splendor of his noble lineage. As for the rest, they made him as powerless in spiritual as they did in worldly affairs.

As to the former, the *shôgun* himself regulates or supervises everything. He appoints four religious commissioners whom we call temple lords, and the Japanese call *tera bugyo,* or temple magistrates. All temple disputes and all trespasses of the priests come under their jurisdiction.

The *dairi* lives in Miyako (Kyoto), Japan's second city, where an official of the *shôgun*, known as chief judge, keeps an extremely close eye on him. This judge lives right across from the *dairi's* palace. Through his spies, he makes sure no one enters the gate without his knowledge. It is thus impossible that the *dairi* could conspire with whatever princely ruler would be so inclined.

One can regard Gongen as the founder of the present day form of Japanese government. But regardless of how much the Japanese venerate him because of his excellent qualities, and as the progenitor of their present day imperial house, in their eyes the stain of his disloyalty to the son of his benefactor Taiko clings to his memory. In spite of this, they gratefully recognize that the form of government he instituted provided them with an internal and external peace for 200 years.

The wars he waged to obtain unlimited power helped him recognize which rulers or princes would be troublesome to him and his descendants, and, to this day, their descendants are never appointed as ordinary or extraordinary government advisors. That rank is only given to the descendants of his allies *if* they are not lords of too extensive lands. By this statecraft, the *shôgun* prevents his subjects from pulling the same trick on him as was pulled on the *dairi*.

There are five ordinary and five extraordinary advisors. The *shôgun* appoints them, and they act in his name. All orders are signed and executed by them, and are to be obeyed immediately. Yet their authority, as well as that of their *shôgun*, is subject to Gongen's institutions, and to old customs no one in Japan dares to deviate from for fear of causing a revolution. The following example, which occurred during my stay in Japan, may serve as proof of this. The inheritance of office, high as well as low office, is an ancient custom in Japan. However, the choice of the son who will succeed him is left up to the father. If he has no sons, he may choose one from another family. This adopted son then loses his own name and receives the name of his new father.[30] Only in ordinary daily life, but not during solemn occasions, may this adopted son call his real parents "father" or "mother." The predecessor of the present *shôgun* had the misfortune of losing his only son and heir to a fall from a wild Persian horse.[31] Therefore, the *shôgun* had to adopt a child from another lineage, that of the present *shôgun*, whose father was still alive. This *shôgun*, already on the throne, once publicly addressed him as father which created a tremendous uproar. The oldest of the government advisors, Matsudairi Zusho No Kami Sama, came out against this as being contrary to old customs. Since these same customs dictated that no inferior may ever contradict his superior, the advisor recognized his own guilt. He left the council and immediately went home where he imprisoned himself. He then asked his colleagues to inform the *shôgun* in writing of this event. The *shôgun* was thus forced not to address his real father by that name any longer, as he realized how strictly Isu No Kami had upheld the old customs in regard to himself, and had punished himself for this breach. After some time Isu No Kami was set free and was reinstated as government advisor.

In matters of great importance, the highest authority belongs to an assembly consisting of the *shôgun* and three royal princes who are the rulers of Kyûshû, Mito, and Owari, and the descendants of Gongen's youngest sons. They always make decisions based on his institutions. The administration of the treasury is in the hands of a treasurer, or "grand thesaurier," who has an audit office under him. The lands or towns of the imperial domains are ruled by governors who, with the help of several officials, exercise power in judicial, civil, or military matters. In addition, the Court in Edo has two officials called *Metsuke*[32] by the Japanese, and chief spies by us. Their position is equivalent to chief of police. They have a few lower ranked people under them whom we call *dwarskijkers*.[33] Their task is to see to it that no one infringes on the established institutions or customs. They would even have to report the *shôgun* if he himself did so. This profession is necessary in a country where so many small princely rulers, each sovereign in his own territory, reign. These rulers are always on the lookout for an opportunity to declare themselves totally independent.

This explains the need to have people closely watch their comings and goings. This espionage system is so accurate that any attempt to escape from the yoke of old customs and that of the *shôgun* would be known instantly.

Often a *secret* snoop, or *okobito metsuke*,[34] who belongs to the lower classes is sent to one or another landed estate to listen in on the conversations of the common man and write everything down. He continues doing this until he hears something worth returning to the Court for. This may be a rumor of some unusual event that his successor spreads around.

As soon as the first dispatched snoop hears of it, he quickly returns to report his findings. His successor then stays on and continues spying. These jobs are extremely dangerous; if the spy is found out, he will no doubt be murdered. There are no examples of someone coming back alive from Satsuma. All the secret snoops there were discovered and killed, and the one who is sent to this province considers himself as being sentenced to death. From all this, one sees the great power of the princely rulers, especially the one of Satsuma, as the *shôgun* has to let so many murders go unpunished.

Japan is divided into 68 large landed estates, each with its own princely ruler. As Gongen considered some of these rulers too powerful and mistrusted them, he would confiscate some of their lands under the pretext of easing the difficulties of governing them. He would then give these lands to his favorite allies. They did not, however, receive the title *daimyô*,[35] the original rulers' title, but that of *siyomiyô*. Their task is to keep an eye on the original ruler. For this reason, there are more princely rulers than in the 68 provinces which also contain the landed estates of the Crown, Yamashiro, Yamato, Kôchi, Izumi, and Settsu. These princes are subject to a very difficult obligation. They have to reside one year in their own territory, the other at the Court in Edo, where they have to leave their wives and children as hostages when returning home for the following year[36]. This order is so strict and immutable that possible bastard children born in the landed estates of these princes have to be brought, together with their mothers, to Edo as soon as they reach the age of five. During my stay for example, I saw the small daughter of the prince of Omura being brought to Edo.

To escape from Edo is impossible. It is hopeless to even try to pass the guards in the Fujisan mountains and in Arai[37]. When these princes return to the Court from their provinces they, as feudal tenants, have to bring gifts to the *shôgun*, and deliver a certain number of troops in times of war. No two princes who live in adjacent lands are allowed to be there at the same time. When one is home, the other has to be in Edo and vice versa. The day of departure from Edo as well as from the province is so firmly established for these princes that not one of them would dare not leave on the assigned day. They do meet each other en route, but even in that event, the necessary precautions are taken. Those from the south territories, either coming to or leaving Edo, are not allowed to stay more than one night in Osaka, and then only out of view of the castle. They are not allowed to stay overnight in Miyako, home of the *dairi,* whose ties to the princely rulers the *shôgun* naturally fears the most. Only the *siyomiyôs* or descendants of Gongen's servants and favorites who more or less check on the princes, are allowed to stay overnight there. All others have to continue their journey immediately. If the *shôgun* discovers that one or another prince, either through industry or economy, has amassed more assets than he deems desirable, he will get the *dairi* to give this prince a higher title, an honor he doesn't dare refuse, even though the gifts this title oblige him to will relieve him of all his excess monies. Would he refuse, a princely neighbor would quickly offer *his* services to the *shôgun* in order to bring the other to his senses. It is precisely this mutual fear among the princes that keeps them in balance. In addition, the worry about wives and children who are in the *shôgun's* power has also prevented these otherwise sovereign princes to rebel against his authority, which has given Japan peace for two hundred years[38].

The uncertainty as to whether Fideiri, Taiko's son, who according to some died in the castle of Osaka, but might have fled to Satsuma and perhaps left heirs there, still keeps the Court of the *shôgun* wary of the ruler of that province. The more so as he is very powerful and as his soldiers are considered the bravest in all Japan. In his own domain, he absolutely does not submit to orders which the other princes may perhaps obey. For this reason, attempts were made to unite him to the Court through family ties. His daughter is married to the present *shôgun.*

The chief justice in Miyako, as well as the governors of the cities Osaka and Sakai, may take their wives and children when leaving Edo. But both governors of Nagasaki,[39] the only place where associations with foreigners is permitted, as well as all lesser officials[40] of that city have to leave their wives and children in Edo, to be used as hostages in case of suspicious dealings with those two foreign countries, Holland and China. The governors of Nagasaki are replaced yearly in the ninth month (*Sefuguats*[41]). Frequently, the same governor will occupy this office three times. I myself saw one occupy this office four times, but their continuous occupation never last longer than a year. The other officials mentioned are also replaced yearly, in the sixth and ninth month, and then have to go to Edo. They, but foremost the chief banyos,[42] frequently return to their posts in Nagasaki. At my departure from Nagasaki in 1817, I left behind three officials whom I had already met upon my arrival in 1799, and who had, off and on, occupied those same posts.

The governor of Nagasaki is in charge of military, civil, and judiciary matters, but for anything of importance he consults the auditors and chief banyos. The latter are also charged with examining all judicial matters; the governor metes out sentences on the basis of their report, though he may not sentence someone to death without the assent of the Court in Edo. The only exception is engaging in smuggling with foreigners, in which case the execution may follow the sentence immediately.

Outside of the city's jurisdiction, there is also in Nagasaki an estate steward of the imperial domains who is directly responsible to the Court. The city itself has eight mayors, of which the two oldest are commissioners of the imperial treasury and are in charge of the trade with the Dutch and the Chinese. Sometimes they're also called the commissioners of the foreigners. Each of the other remaining mayors is chairman for a year on a rotating basis. Everything has to be submitted to him, after which he consults with his colleagues, and then presents it to the governor. He in turn has the chairman announce all the orders from the court, and he also arbitrates small disputes that may arise between officials.

At first, the office of mayor was not hereditary, but was

chosen from the oldest and most affluent citizens. For quite some time now, this office has been hereditary.

In every street in Nagasaki there lives an *otona*, or district warden, who keeps a list of all the inhabitants of that street. As warden of the street, he has to settle small disputes that may arise and arrest those engaging in fights or other mischief, but has to report more important matters to the judge. Should someone from his street accused of criminal behavior come before the judge, the *otona* is often responsible for seeing to it that the accused is locked up. These wardens are also fire fighters, and in front of their door one can always find fire buckets and a big tub of water. They also keep all other fire fighting equipment in their homes. Two policemen, who are called *geheimmeesters*,[43] are directly under the wardens. They keep track of whatever happens, arrest people on the slightest suspicion, investigate their crimes, and report to the chief banyo. When a *geheimmeester* calls you in, you are required to obey immediately.

Lastly, there is a cadre of lower banyos who fall directly under the chief banyos. They have to see to it that all orders coming from the Court are executed immediately, keep an eye on everything, and perform guard duty wherever they have been stationed. These lower banyos also have two *geheimmeesters* under them, but they are slightly different from those under the just-mentioned district wardens. Whenever something happens that commands the vigilance of the police, factions from both sides do the work, each hoping to be first to uncover the matter. For this reason, it is rare that something happens that the police does not get wind of immediately, and it is rare that a criminal act remains hidden for more than 24 hours, or that the culprit remains free from justice.

After the mayors, the highest ranked are the officials of the imperial treasury. The college of Dutch translators[44] consists of four chief, four under, and several lesser translators, altogether some 60 or 70 people. Chinese translators are more numerous. At the head of all those who work for the treasury, at the head of every translators college and of all other subordinate institutions in Nagasaki, is a so called *dwarskijker*, a snoop, or spy. I can only compare him to the *contrôleurs*[45] *or Arrondissements' inspectors* of our country. He has to make sure that the employees of his college adequately fulfill their office, do not transgress in any way, and do not dishonor their office by their comportment. Once a month at a fixed date, the snoop has to give a report of everything to the governor in person and under four eyes. Woe unto him if the governor has been informed of something beyond what the snoop reported. It is for this reason that he has the right to always demand access to the governor, if need be even at night. He really has to know everything, and such a post is an excellent way to have the officials do their duty. I will not mention several officials of lesser rank.

In short, these people are the urban officials of Nagasaki, and I'm convinced that other cities in the country are organized in the same way, except for the Dutch and Chinese translators, who are only found in Nagasaki.

Concerning the character, mores, and customs of the Japanese, I will briefly sketch what I could observe of them during my nineteen-year stay in Japan. Generally speaking, these people are courageous and not afraid of any danger in all the world. With an absolute blind obedience, they execute whatever command is given to them by the higher authorities, or in the name of the *shôgun*. Japanese subjects do not have any freedom at all to question or judge orders given to them. On the contrary, they consider it the greatest honor to execute those orders to the letter. The country's internal troubles, well described by others, attest the most to this. It is known that they have the habit of cutting open their bellies[46] for matters we would call minor.

One could ask whether this could not be construed as proof of their courage and disdain of death. I myself believe that it is similar to suicide in Europe, and the reader may decide whether this is more or less contemptible in Japan than in Europe. The reason Japanese commit suicide by belly cutting (or tearing the belly apart with a short sword) is foremost the loss of office and dignity, be it through one's own fault or that of others. This would make him live in disgrace, and he would rather die. Remember, for example, the story of Fidetsugi, who was named Taiko's heir but was disappointed in this. Banned to the Koyasan mountain, he chose to commit suicide this way.

Not infrequently will a Japanese resort to this ultimate measure when, as an official, he did not execute or only partially executed an order from the Court. Since he would then be put to death by torture or at least be banned, which means his whole clan would have to share his disgrace and be deprived of any office for the rest of their lives, he prefers to punish himself by cutting his belly. This act means that his family will always be honored.[47] During all my years in Japan, I never heard that the Court *would have ordered* someone to mete out this punishment to himself.

When an English ship penetrated the poorly guarded bay of Nagasaki in 1808, committed acts of outrage which the governor should have prevented, and then escaped the actions taken to stop it, the governor, Matsudaira Zusho No Kami Sama, fell under the just mentioned category of not executing the *shôgun's* orders. He was so sure of the fate awaiting him that he cut his belly barely half an hour after we had talked with him. (I will go into what happened here more fully later on.)

The commanders of the Imperial guards, not really government officials but subjects of the ruler of Hizen, who were not at their post at that time, did likewise, thereby sparing their relatives an otherwise certain disgrace. It is clear that the Court would indeed have punished them severely, as the prince of Hizen himself, though away at that time from his land, in Edo as a matter of fact, was imprisoned[48] for 100 days because he had not seen to it that his underlings executed the *shôgun's* orders properly. Yet the young son of the governor of Nagasaki, who was totally innocent in this matter, immediately came into great favor at the Court, where he got a very lucrative post.

The religion of the Japanese was, up till about 600 B.C., solely that of Shinto, i.e. the Godhead according to ancestral customs. This religion is very simple, and to a certain extent is pure deism.[49] The Shintoists[50] conceive of a simple creature who lives in heaven and desires of man purity of soul and conscience. Among other virtues, it also demands total submission to the laws of the land. They venerate this deity in their temples, which still reflect the simplicity of yore, as they cannot even have roofs of copper or tiles but only of thatch. In size and beauty, they are very different from the temples of Buddha. Shinto temples are small, clean, and devoid of images or statues, but they do contain a large mirror. This mirror symbolizes the clarity with which the deity sees into the depths of the human heart including its evil, just as man discovers the blemishes on his face in the mirror. Shinto priests are indistinguishable from their fellow men, as they do not shave their head or wear special clothing. However, they carry two swords and, at solemn occasions, long tabards[51] and caps that differ according to their rank. They can also marry. The oldest and most important Shinto temple is in the province of Ise.[52] Supposedly, the first inhabitants of the country settled there. Given the antiquity of this temple, it is much revered and protected from falling into ruin. It is the country's holiest sanctuary, to which all inhabitants make a pilgrimage at least once in their lifetime. The major holy days of this place of worship are:

1) New Year's day which usually falls in our month of February. The exact date cannot be established as the Japanese count by lunar years, and alternately have 29 or 30 days in a month. After 33 months, there is a leap month and then the year has 13 months.

2) The festival of girls, or dolls, falling on the third day of the third month. This festival is celebrated in every home that has girls under the age of ten. All kinds of toys are displayed and neighbor children are invited in and given treats.

On the fifth day of the fifth month a similar festival takes place for boys which is called the flag festival. The boys amuse themselves with more male oriented toys like flags, armor, or weaponry. Both festivals are celebrated in communal gaiety.

On the nineth day of the nineth month there is a festival (*Matsuri*) for the Shinto temple Suwa in Nagasaki.[53] The aforementioned mirror is then carried with great solemnity through the streets to a certain straw cabin on the square. The Japanese call this cabin an *ohatta*. The mirror is kept there by the priests of the temple until the eleventh day when, with the same pomp, it is carried back to the temple. Kaempfer describes this ritual extensively in his book.

When the Japanese travel, they first go to the Shinto temple to beseech a happy journey. When the Dutch ships are likely to set sail from Batavia[54], the Japanese translators for the Dutch, for instance, go to the Shinto temple to pray for a happy journey for them. When a new born baby has to receive a name (30 days after the birth for a boy, 29 for a girl), the ceremony must also take place in a Shinto temple. The parents take the child there and give three names to the priest, who chooses one of them. The child frequently does not carry this name forever. It can change, sometimes three times, in childhood, adolescence, or adulthood.

The first, the fifteenth, and the twenty-nineth of every month are designated for ceremonial duties. On these days every Japanese goes to the temple to pay tribute to his deity. This Shinto religion, the oldest and original religion of Japan, does not forbid the eating of meat as some people think. Rather, the reason people do not eat meat lies in the fact that cattle are uncommonly rare in this country. The Japanese do not use cattle for food, but only as beasts of burden, and they forbid their slaughter lest there be a shortage. There is simple proof that no religious reasons exist for their not eating their cattle; for example, every year when the Dutch slaughter one of the cows brought from Batavia, the governor and regents of Nagasaki are happy to receive some of the beef. When the Dutch chief gives his yearly banquet on New Year's Day, the Japanese translators relish the proffered oxen beef.[55] According to the time of year, the Japanese eat deer, wild boar, and all kinds of fowl without any religious scruples. The inhabitants of Nagasaki also eat pork, only found in the environs of that city, on a daily basis. They do not slaughter the pigs themselves however, but leave that to the curriers, who also serve as executioners and are considered by the natives to be of an inferior race.

There are many Buddhist[56] sects in Japan. Their temples are full of all kinds of idols to which many miracles are ascribed. Kaempfer and several others have written extensively about this. One can find Japanese who solely adhere to the Shinto religion and do not practice Buddhism. Yet there is no Buddhist who would neglect the ancient and honorable religious rites of his country. The Buddhist priests have to remain unmarried, except those of the *Ikkôshô* sect.[57]

It has been said that the Japanese have no concept of the deity, that they don't even know the word God. This is only true insofar as they use the word *Kami*, or Lord, for God. The Japanese also use this word for a lord of a domain, but other letters preceding this word indicate the difference. For example, the ruler or prince of Satsuma is called Satsuma No Kami. That same title is also given to high officials of the realm, adding to it the name of their land which, in reality, they do not own. The governors of Nagasaki carry that title as well.[58] With the Chinese characters, which, with the exception of the Court of the *dairi*, have been in use for a long time already in Japan, one can express the name of God or Lord of Heaven with just one character. Should one like to use the old Japanese characters still in use at the Court of the *dairi*, one has to use three characters or letters. Just like we do, Lord of Heaven. They also have a name for the word creator, or *Kaibiakshen*, whom they recognize as the keeper of the universe, which they call *Sekai*. Thus, it is far from true that the Japanese do not acknowledge the existence of a God. The idols of the Buddhist religion are not called *Kami* or Lords, but *Hotoke*.[59]

The eradication[60] of the Roman Catholic religion, after rapid and very substantial gains,[61] has been extensively, but perhaps not completely impartially, described by many writers. Several of them intimated that it was the result of *religious hatred*, but I beg to differ with them. The Christian religion was first introduced to Japan in 1542 by Franciscus Xaverius, and continued to spread, without any opposition, until 1586, a time span of some 44 years. In 1586 however the famous *shôgun* Taiko ordered the destruction of all Christian churches, forbade any of his subjects to follow that religion any longer, and banned the foreign missionaries. Taiko said that this was *not* because there was something wrong with that religion, but because it didn't fit in with the ancient rites and customs of the land, and he feared that it would cause disturbances in the country. Two main events seem to have contributed to the decision of the *shôgun*. The first was the behavior of a Portuguese priest who, upon meeting one of Taiko's[62] government counselors, refused out of sheer arrogance to show him the respect *all* Japanese show him. The government counselor took this as a great slight (the dignataries of this country are easily offended), and reported it in the worst possible light to the Court of Taiko by aggravating the circumstances. The second was perhaps even more significant. A Spaniard arrived in Japan to trade at the time when trade and shipping were still totally free. He found himself in the company of several Japanese dignataries, and when the conversation fell on the great power of the King of Spain, he took a world atlas and pointed out all the wide-spread possessions of his master. Truly amazed, the Japanese asked him what means his master used to get dominion over such vast territories. The Spaniard replied: *oh, nothing is easier. We start out by sending priests to the lands we want to conquer; these priests convert the people to their religion,[63] and as soon as they have largely succeeded in this, the army is sent in and allies itself with the newly converted, and then conquers the rest without much difficulty.*

These two events, through which the Europeans expressed their intentions *and* showed themselves as feeling superior to the natives, certainly caused the eradication of the Roman faith in Japan *as a way to subjugate that country*, but *not* because of its religious tenets. In 1597, for the first time some foreign missionaries were executed also for the political reason that, once banned, they had returned to Japan, a crime punishable by death. Although from 1586 on the Portuguese[64] were not allowed to spread their religion, they could practice it themselves. They were allowed to trade freely, but were not allowed to talk about religious subjects with the natives, or send missionaries to Japan. It seems that this only served as a precaution against the dangers to which the Spaniard's talk had alerted this cautious and distrustful nation.[65] After the first execution in 1597,[66] the persecutions of Roman Catholics escalated dramatically. It was only three years later, in 1600, that the first Dutch ship[67], tossed by a storm, landed in Japan. It had an Englishman by the name of John Adams[68] as first mate.[69] The time of this first arrival shows already just how wrong those writers are who ascribe the main reason for the banishment of the Spaniards and Portuguese from Japan to the Dutch. It is true that the Dutch, at that time at war[70] with Spain, were depicted by the Spaniards in the darkest colors, as is common in times of war. For their part, the Portuguese did likewise. Therefore, when the Dutch arrived for the first time in 1609 with two ships[71] to trade with Japan (just like the English, who started their trade around the same time), they would naturally and for their own advantage have confirmed the story of the aforementioned Spaniard; but the basis for the persecution had already been established long before. It is interesting to see what the famous Onno Zwier van Haren has to say about all this in his all too little known book, which contains a defense of our nation against the calumnies of Tavernier and others. The title of his book is *Japan With Regard To The Dutch Nation and the Christian Religion*. On page eleven he writes:

"The Jesuit priest Charlevoix, at the end of his 12th book on the general history of Japan, relates a conversation the *shôgun* Ongoshio[72] had with the English first mate Adams in 1603. In this conversation, Adams confirms what the aforementioned Castillian had said in Hirado[73] and also adds that the Catholic missionaries had been banished from England, Sweden, Denmark, and Holland for the same reasons. It is Charlevoix's opinion that this conversation served primarily to embitter the *shôgun* against the Roman Catholic priests and their religion. But assuming the veracity of this conversation, assuming that this *shôgun*, one of the savviest politicians history can point to, consulted a foreigner, a gardener to whom he, the *shôgun* of the richest nation on earth, gave 70 ducats for his keep, about the safety of his country and his house; assuming that Ongoshio, to banish the Roman Catholics from his realm, needed to look for an example to the north of Europe, an example Tay-Ko-Sama had already given in Japan, and assuming as well that all of this gave birth to the opportunity to murder thousands of Christian Japanese, it would have been an *Englishman* who caused the persecution and not *the Dutch.*"

After the banishment of the Spaniards in 1624, the Portuguese still remained in Japan for quite some time. Would they have remained quietly on the island of Deshima that had been built for them,[74] and continued to trade there as traders only, without breaking the law by proselytizing the Roman Catholic faith among the Japanese, I do believe indeed that they would still be here, just as they are in Macao. The behavior of their chief in Japan, known as *Capitam Mor* (major), a Japanese by birth and a zealot for the Roman faith, had given rise to their total banishment in 1639. This character had plotted a conspiracy with some of the rulers in Japan who secretly adhered to the Roman faith. A letter of this chief to the King of Portugal, in which all the names of the co-conspirators were listed, was intercepted when the Portuguese ship was captured at the Cape of Good Hope. The Dutch subsequently delivered this letter to the Japanese authorities who, for the first time, paid attention. The co-conspirators could possibly have saved their skins, as they were strongly supported by the governor of Nagasaki; already, the authenticity of this letter was found to be suspect, until another letter of a similar nature also written by *Capitam Mor*, and addressed to the governor of Macao, was found by the Japanese themselves. This convinced them of the truth, and many of the Japanese rulers who were members of the conspiracy were banished from the realm, together with the Portuguese, and sailed on Portuguese ships to Macao. In a nutshell, this is the evil we Dutch perpetrated, something that is completely justifiable according to the rules of war, as we were openly declared enemies of Spain and Portugal, which at that time belonged to Spain.[75] We Dutch alerted our friends and allies, the Japanese, to the deceitful ways of the Portuguese.[76] Can we reproach them for this? It is clear however that this discovery prejudiced the Japanese mightily against the Roman faith, which they came to see as a cover for foreign domination. A law was thus enacted that all inhabitants of Nagasaki and its environs, starting on the fourth day after New Year, had to kick a statue of Christ or some saints with their feet. This law did not apply to the Dutch, who have never done this. Though the Japanese know very well that we are Christians, they do not consider us *like the Portuguese Christians*. (These are the exact words of a Japanese with whom I discussed this matter.)

Another accusation leveled at us in regard to the eradication of the Roman faith in Japan concerns the event that happened in Arima, in the bay of Shimabara at the end of 1637 and the beginning of 1638, a place where the then chief of the Dutch in Japan, Mr. Koekebakker, had arrived on a ship. Ignorant foreigners usually put this matter in the most despicable light.[77] I hereby present the results of my research culled from the old daily diaries of that time, as well as from the mouths of the Japanese themselves. It is clear from this that Mr. Koekebakker was not called upon to suppress the Catholics, but to punish the insurgents who had instigated a rebellion against their ruler in the province of Arima. The former prince, or lord, of Arima had left behind his nobles and warriors when he left his province (for which he received a large landed estate). The prince had believed that the new ruler would keep those people in his service, just like he himself fully intended to take into his service those he would find in his new domain. However, the new ruler of Shimabara only appointed his own cronies as officials and soldiers. The former officials were thus left without a livelihood, and had to resort to agriculture in order not to die of starvation. This in itself would not have led to anything, but the new ruler now also imposed higher taxes than they had been used to or could pay. The ruler then ordered that a cape made of straw be placed on the shoulders of those who couldn't or wouldn't pay and that this cape then be set on fire. This hideous cruelty is still remembered by the Japanese under the name of *mino odori*, or straw cape dance, which was based on the way those wretched creatures jumped in their agony. These and other cruelties led the people of this domain who, as mentioned above, mainly consisted of nobles and soldiers and thus were not unskilled in the art of war making, to a rebellion[78]. This new ruler of Arima, at that time residing in Edo, was summoned by the *shôgun*, who spoke to him, according to Japanese history, in the following way:

"Go, Lord of Arima, and restore peace in your land; if you're unable to do so, you do not deserve to live since you are incapable of governing a people who, through your actions, have become miserable."

The ruler was unable, either through mercy or violence, to achieve this. That was just what the Court had intended. While not wanting in any way to support a rebellion, it nevertheless wanted to punish the unjust prince for his tyranny. Hereupon the neighboring rulers received the order to keep their armies in readiness in case the army of Arima failed to quash the rebellion, but not before. The Court, in order to expedite[79] matters, also invited Mr. Koekebakker, then chief of the Dutch in Japan, to go as a friend of Japan to the bay of Shimabara with the Dutch ships that were anchored in Hirado to expedite the matter. He complied, but only with the sole Dutch ship[80] then at anchor there. The insurgents had declared that they were willing to die for the *shôgun* if he wanted their ruination, but not for their ruler; they had decided that, against him, they would fight to the last man. In the meantime, several Christian Japanese of Amaxa had joined the insurgents, and were rightly accepted as a strengthening of power. Once arrived, Mr.

Koekebakker put several batteries of guns on shore, about twenty in all, and manned by a hundred men. These guns, as well as those from the ship, fired about 425 rounds in fifteen days.[81] Shortly after the arrival of Dutch help, the insurgents shot a letter attached to an arrow into the Japanese army. It contained the following:

"Are there no longer any courageous soldiers in the realm to do combat with us, and weren't they ashamed to have called in the assistance of foreigners against our small contingent?"

This seems to have resulted in the withdrawal of the Dutch soon thereafter, at least before the main attack on Arima. In any event, Koekebakker and his men were *not* present at the attack which took place on April the sixteenth and seventeenth, and in which the insurgents were conquered and killed. Held responsible for the insurgence, the ruler of Arima anticipated to be sentenced into exile together with his two brothers, and to escape that disgrace, he cut open his belly. This is what truly and really happened, regardless of what Kaempfer, Charlevoix, Tavenier and others may have written earlier; and regardless of how often, in later years, people who have never been in Japan brought this matter up again and embellished it even more; it was *not* to fight against Roman Catholic Christians that Mr. Koekebakker was called upon, but to fight against insurgents with whom only *later* those Roman Catholic Japanese allied themselves.[82] Koekebakker assisted the *shôgun* of Japan as an ally, just as around that same time the Dutch assisted several native rulers against the Portuguese with whom they fought in Asia as well as in Europe, as the Portuguese were then still Spanish subjects.

Another point is that there was no time for deliberation. Orders from the Japanese Court had to be obeyed immediately and without delay on penalty of death. As the Dutch on Hirado were in the power of the Japanese, this penalty would undoubtedly have applied to them as well. Proof of this is the order Mr. Caron[83] , a man whose knowledge of Japanese matters cannot be praised enough, received from the Court in Edo to demolish a very big stone house he had built in Hirado. Mr. Caron's reply had been: *"the order of the authorities shall immediately be executed."* This was his good fortune as, according to orders already given, the least bit of resistance would have cost him his life.[84] As erroneously as this matter is viewed in Europe, so is the behavior of the Dutch in Japan portrayed as if they had to show that they renounced the Christian faith by trampling on a statue of Christ. It is possible that the envy of other nations invented this slander because we are the *only* favored *European* nation in Japan according to the law enacted by the founder of the present royal family, Gongen.

This law, as well as all other regulations enacted by this *shôgun*, is considered holy and inviolable; a law according to which we may no more be driven out of that country than any other nation be allowed in. It is this Gongen who, in 1609 and *not* in 1619 as some claim, granted us that everlasting passport without which the Japanese would have expelled us as they did all other nations. Truly, our present relations with Japan are *not* about renouncing our faith for the sake of profit, as both trade and profit are very meager.

A 19-year stay in Japan has given me the opportunity to jot down a lot about the Japanese religion but, alas, those notes as well as all my other papers were lost in the shipwreck of the *Admiraal Evertsen*. Whatever I remember, I will add to several excerpts from the lesser known work on Japan of the famous Onno Zwier van Haren. I found this work to be very accurate, and it reminded me of the many excerpts I made from the old daily registers. In 1629, when the governor of Nagasaki demanded from all its citizens a written statement that neither they, nor anyone in their families, embraced the Christian religion, only two of the first Dutchmen, Melchior Santvoort[85] and Vincent Romeyn, who had been shipwrecked in Japan in 1599 or 1600,[86] were still alive and, no longer in the service of the VOC[87], lived privately in Nagasaki. They did not have to give a statement other than that they were *Dutch*. No statement was demanded from Reijer Gijsbrechtsz[88] either, who was then still in the service of the VOC. The question that needs to be asked is this: would the Japanese have known that we were Christian? They did know this soon enough.[89] Who can really imagine that the Portuguese wouldn't have told them simply to have the Dutch share their fate? Also, if the Japanese truly did not know this, why were the Dutch exempted from the general rule? Although the Japanese did not tolerate the exercise of the Christian religion in their own country, they tolerated it from the foreigners who were admitted to their country. For this reason, the Portuguese were never asked to trample on the cross even though they were banished for the first time in 1639. *Not* because they were *Christians,* but because they did not cease having their missionaries proselytize the Roman faith in Japan. I clearly remember reading in the daily registers that Mr. Caron, long before he became chief (in 1639), was asked by the Regent Fesodonne of Nagasaki whether the Dutch were Christian. The answer of Caron was: yes, whereupon Fesodonne[90] replied: *"That stinks."* Caron then explained to him the difference between Protestants and Roman Catholics, and pointed out to him that there was a protracted war between the Dutch and Spain,[91] precisely to throw off the coercive yoke of the latter. In 1643, the ship *Breskens*, which was to sail to east Tartary,[92] was forced ashore in Nambu, on the east coast of Japan, due to a lack of provisions. The Japanese imprisoned the captain, the second buyer, and eight sailors and brought them all to Edo. The ship then sailed away. It was of little use that these men stated that they were Dutch, as just before this four Jesuits had secretly entered Japan. The Japanese now saw the Dutch as members of that order, until a renegade Jesuit priest by the name of Ferreira, who later assumed the Japanese name of Shovan and who served as a translator in the interrogation of the four missionaries, solemnly declared that they were indeed Dutch. Yet the Japanese still didn't quite believe that they belonged to the VOC. They interrogated them alone several times in Edo, and then in the presence of the four Jesuit prisoners. When asked whether they were Christian, they answered in the affirmative, but stated that they differed from the Portuguese and didn't have as many festive days as they had, but that they went every seventh day to the temple to celebrate their religion. Only after Mr. Elserak, the then Dutch chief in Japan, arrived in Edo and recognized them as being Dutch and belonging to the VOC were the men released. I found in the day registers that many a time the Japanese said to the chief, "We *do* know that you are Christians but you differ in dogma from the Portuguese." It is clear from this that the Dutch never disguised their religion to the Japanese who knew very well that the Dutch were Christians whose faith differed from the faith of the Portuguese, which surely is in accordance with the truth. As regards the trampling of statues,[93] the reality is as follows. Since the eradication of the Roman faith in Japan, all the inhabitants of Nagasaki and its environs, as well as those from the Omura and Bungo provinces, were in the past and are today obliged to trample on a crucifix. No natives are exempted, and the Japanese servants of the Dutch, both Protestant and Catholic, also have to participate. This "trampling of the crucifix" starts on the fourth day after the Japanese New Year and lasts for five or six days. The Chinese[94] are also required to participate in these ceremonies, as they allowed themselves to be used to smuggle in crucifixes, rosaries, books, and even Jesuit missionaries when all Jesuits were banished. As soon as a Chinese junk arrives, several specially designated officials board the ship with a crucifix, upon which the Chinese who have come to Japan for the first time are forced to trample. Yet as far as the Dutch are concerned, the Japanese are so considerate that they do not even talk about this matter. Here is an example: in November of 1801, when Mr. Wardenaar was chief and I warehouse master, a small brig perished on the Gotto[95] islands, and the crew was transferred to Nagasaki to be examined. The city's governor asked our chief as well as the scribes, M. Mak and D. H. Letske, to witness this examination in the government house. The crew of the brig consisted of two Malaysians, a man and a woman; a small boy and two maid servants of that same nation, a black Papuan, a Chinese, and a man from Cochin-China (now Vietnam). The brig was clearly a Portuguese ship, and to a man the crew declared that they came from Portuguese Timor, and that they were on their way to Amboina[96]. The captain and all the officers had died en route, so that they had to let the brig, which they couldn't steer, just drift by the grace of God. Eventually they landed on the Gotto islands.

During the examination, the governor had all the Dutch present leave for a moment. The Dutch thought that this was strange, but they soon learned from the chief translator that the governor had ordered these people, whom he didn't know, to trample on a crucifix. In order not to offend the Dutch, he had not wanted this to take place in their presence. When the trampling ceremony was over, the Dutch were invited in again. From this, one can see that the Japanese know and honor our religious sensibilities. The fact that the Japanese have also softened their previous extreme severity against other faiths is clear from the following event. Although the Japanese took for granted that the crew of the brig was Roman Catholic, the governor of Nagasaki, out of pity for the poor shipwrecked people, put the Malaysians and the Papuan with us on Deshima, in an old house fenced in by bamboo and watched by a Japanese guard. The Chinese and Cochin-Chinese were put on the Chinese[97] island. They stayed there till 1802 when, on orders of the Court, the latter were to go on junks to China, and the former to Batavia on our ship *Mathilda Maria*. In Batavia it became quite clear that the brig had been slated to go from Timor to Macao, but that the aforementioned crew had murdered the captain and officers and captured the ship. They were then sent to Macao, where they were duly punished. Although the oft mentioned demeaning ceremony of trampling a crucifix did not apply to the Dutch, the Japanese, convinced that the Dutch were Christians, nevertheless thought of ways to prevent the Dutch from importing this new, strictly forbidden faith to Japan, something they had accomplished through the banishment of the Spaniards and Portuguese.

The Dutch were forbidden to spread the Christian faith, be it through books or pictures, and were not allowed to practice their faith in the open, so as not to give offense. As a preventive measure, the captains of the yearly arriving ships have to put all books dealing with religion and all external signs of religion such as rosaries, crucifixes, or images of saints, and so on in a barrel, which is then closed on board with the seal of the chief banyos, brought on shore, and kept on the island of Deshima by the *Otona* until the ships depart again, at which time the barrel is returned in the same state as it was received, sealed. Bibles and hymnals were exempted, however, and I myself had several of them, which the Japanese knew about. They never objected. Furthermore, a muster-roll of all those on board is taken when ships arrive, and during loading and unloading as well as the comings and goings of the crew, the chief banyos carefully inspect them. Basically, the sealing of books and other religious articles, and the counting of the men, are the *only things* the Dutch are subjected to in Japan. Is this any worse than what they are subjected to in Roman Catholic countries where their religion is equally not tolerated? My sojourn in Japan, from July 1799 to December 1817, gave me ample opportunity to learn in detail what really had been going on. I can hereby attest that the stories of renouncements of faith, and the trampling of crucifixes by the Dutch, are pure fiction. If these accusations had any veracity, then the Russians who were here for six months in 1804 and 1805 would have learned about them. Yet, neither Krusenstern[98] nor Langsdorff[99] mentions anything about these accusations. Kaempfer,[100] a German who has spent two years in Japan, and Thunberg,[101] a Swede who has spent some time here when he was in the service of the VOC, would also have mentioned something, but the former is silent in this matter and the latter writes in the third chapter of his book, *"Voyages au Japon"* (*Travels in Japan*), pp. 57 and 58:

> *"On February 22, which corresponds to the fourth day of the Shoguats[102] or first month of the Japanese year and the following days, this famous ceremony which is so demeaning to good Christian souls, took place in Nagazacke and its environments.*

The Japanese trampled on crucifixes and images of Christ and Mary. Despite my desire to understand the circumstances of this ceremony, I only found one Dutch officer who once witnessed it, as he was on his way to the governor of the city to confer with him about the preparations of our journey to Edo. This formally exposes as a lie the assertion, which is as ridiculous as it is false, of some writers who claim that the Dutch are only admitted into Japan after having trampled on the most revered images among Christians. I will add that these writers were not even required to offer any ironclad confirmation of these accusations. This confirmation is only required of those writing about all the places where, in the past, Christianity took some root."[103]

These are the words of Thunberg who, if I'm not mistaken, is still alive. In general, his words bolster my argument.

CHAPTER II

Adventures of the author when he was an official and chief of the Dutch trading station in Japan, from 1799 to 1817, and information about the Dutch trade there.

Part I - 1799 to 1806

Since 1639, the European trade in Japan has been exclusively in the hands of the Dutch, even though they traded there thirty years before then. The notion that the Dutch were first allowed to trade in 1611 is wrong. In 1609, in the seventh month of the Japanese calendar (corresponding to our month of September), the *shôgun* Gongen, father of the present reigning dynasty, granted the Dutch a pass[1] or the special freedom to trade. I carefully researched these Japanese periods or *nengos* to this effect. I have already stated before that the laws, customs, and ordinances instituted by this venerated founder of the dynasty are strictly adhered to because their usefulness has been thoroughly tested for two centuries. For this reason, it seems to me that the Japanese government, no matter how it may have hampered our trade from time to time, will never deny us this trade out of respect for the pass Gongen granted us, and provided we show respect for Japan's customs, something that is reasonable to expect from any foreigner. The decrease in our trade with Japan in various periods up until 1752 has been truthfully and extensively reported by many. I myself ascribe this decrease for the most part to the fact that the Japanese, when they first realized how much silver, then gold, and finally copper[2] we and the Chinese exported from their country started to get worried about a possible shortage of these metals for themselves. From 1690 to 1700, we shipped out 25,000 *pikols*[3] at about a $120^7/_8$ pounds per *pikol* of copper, which comes to over three million old Dutch pounds. If we assume that the Chinese took a similar amount of copper, though their trade always exceeded ours, the export of copper would have been six million pounds yearly, and what would have been the consequences! The Japanese realized in time the need for some regulation. The yearly copper tax[4] was periodically lowered to about 9.700 *pikols*. This number was not written in stone. If for example, through a shipwreck or some other accident, the full quota was not taken, the Japanese allowed it to be added to the next year's quota. This rule remained in effect until 1790, when the last quota was instituted, lowering the trade to 6,000 *pikols*. This harmful regulation came about when a Dutch chief who had not been in Japan as a lower ranking official before and thus did not understand the Japanese character and how to handle it, wanted to have the then existing quota augmented. In vain, those officials who had lived in Japan for years tried to point out that this was impossible, but the chief refused to listen to them. Not only did he *not* receive his desired goal of a bigger quota, but his indelicate and imprudent behavior resulted in a much smaller quota. When I left Holland in 1798 as second buyer in the service of the VOC[5] and arrived, via Batavia, in Japan in 1799, I found both the trade and the trading station affairs in shambles. The then chief, Mr. Gijsbert Hemmy,[6] had died the year before during the trek to the Court in Edo. At that same time, a raging fire had destroyed all the buildings on Deshima except the freestanding house of the chief as well as two or three old warehouses. The Dutch staff consisted of a second buyer, Mr. Leopold Ras, in reality a scribe but serving at that moment as chief, two assistants, a doctor, and two sailors. The High Government in Batavia was unaware of what had happened, as its ship, sent to Japan in 1798, ran afoul of a reef and never returned to Batavia.

As the affairs of the trading station were thus in disarray when I arrived, I tried to stay clear of everything lest I be swept away by the confusion. However, when I was appointed scribe to replace Mr. Ras, who became chief, I persuaded him that it was necessary to inform Batavia of all that had happened. To this end I left with the same ship I had arrived with and once again landed in the capital of the Dutch East Indies. At first the authorities were dismayed that I hadn't stayed until order in the chaotic situation had been restored. Soon though, they understood the predicament that had confronted me in Deshima. Restoring order would have entailed that I, only twenty-one years old and totally ignorant of Japanese matters, would have had to take away the authority of a superior who had been in Japan for fourteen years. This I could not properly have done. Mr. Willem Wardenaar was then appointed chief. In 1800, I returned with him to Japan in the capacity of scribe, and in the company of three more assistants. We arrived in the month of July.[7]

Before I continue the story of my activities in Japan, it will be necessary to report briefly on the ships we used for the trade with Japan from the start of the English wars in 1795[8] to the time we peacefully retook our possessions in 1817.[9] In 1795 the company ship, *de Erfprins*[10] under Captain Ditmar Smit, arrived in Nagasaki, but in 1796 no ship was sent. In 1797, because of a shortage of Dutch ships as well as for reasons of war, the VOC hired a neutral American ship, the *Eliza of New York*, under Captain Will Stewart. Within view of Japan and on the roadstead, this ship always had to fly the Dutch flag and, in addition, had two company officers on board. On the assurance of the then chief Hemmy that this ship was truly hired by the VOC and had only Dutch property on board, the Japanese allowed the ship to anchor. This ship made the trip again under the same conditions in 1798. In 1799 the North American ship *Franklin* under Captain J. Devereux arrived. I made my trip from and to Batavia on this ship. On our return trip, we did not go through the strait of Formosa (Taiwan), which is rare, but sailed to the east of that island. I made the voyage to Japan with Mr. Wardenaar and the other officials on the American ship *Massachusetts* under Captain W. V. Hutchings. The Dutch government also put Captain Ditmar Smit on board this ship. Since that time, the following ships arrived in Japan: in 1801, the American ship *Margaretha* under Captain Samuel Derby; in 1802, the Dutch company ship *Mathilda Maria* under Captain G. Belmer and the hired American ship *Samuel Smith* under Captain G. Stiles; in 1803, the American ship *Rebecca* under Captain J. Deal; and in 1804, the hired Dutch ships *Maria Susanna* under Captain G. Belmer and *Gesina Antoinetta* under Captain A. Musquetier; in 1805, the hired Dutch ship *Resolutie* commanded by the colonial officer H. Voorman; in 1806, the American ship *America* under Captain Lelar, and the Bremer (German) ship *Visurgis* under Captain G. Herklots; in 1807, the American ship *Mount Vernon*[11] under Captain J. Davidson[12] with also on board the above-mentioned Voorman, and the Danish ship *Susanna* under Captain Ditmar Smit. No ships came from Batavia in 1808. In 1809 the American ship *Rebecca* was sent with Mr. Hendrik Tilenius Kruithoff on board. He was slated to replace me as chief. However, Mr. Kruithoff's ship was captured by the English, but the Dutch colonial ship *Goede Trouw*, under Captain H. Voorman, arrived safely in Deshima that year. After 1809, the Dutch colonial government did not send any ships until 1817, when the voyage was resumed by two ships, *Vrouw Agatha* under Captain R. Witsen, and the *Canton* under Captain J. Schinderhutte.

When Mr. Wardenaar arrived in Deshima in 1800, he found the same disarray I had found the previous year, as well as a considerable financial deficit. As chief, he could make any arrangements he wanted, and Mr. Ras, who, upon the death of Mr. Hemmy had neglected to do any accounting, was held responsible for the financial shortage. When he arrived in Batavia he had to pay it out of his own pocket. In my opinion, one can ascribe to Mr. Ras more a lack of discernment than dishonesty. In the meantime, Mr. Wardenaar, whose honest conduct at that time deserves all esteem (if only he hadn't tarnished it later!), found himself in a real dilemma. There were still former chiefs in high government positions in Batavia whose conduct during their administration in Japan could only appear in an unfavorable light in his report. These men were his superiors, but if he wanted to honor the truth, Wardenaar had to go through with it. For many years the prices of company goods, such as tin, elephants' teeth, *hamans*[13] and *ducatons*[14] had been put in the books at lower than the prices the Japanese had paid for them, according to the contracts which were renewed for a further fifteen years in 1784. The calculation of the costs of trading, as well as the prices of the exported copper and camphor, was also incorrect.

Mr. Wardenaar, whom I trusted completely at that time, just as he also consulted me in everything, immediately put a stop to these abuses by giving an accurate accounting of everything and by sending proof of sold merchandise, of costs of copper and other merchandise, in sealed envelopes to Batavia. This is still done to this day and it thus presents Batavia with an accurate picture of the state of Japanese trade. Settling the chaotic affairs in Japan which Mr. Wardenaar entrusted to me, and in which the accountant Age Igis was of great service to me, gave me insights that served me well later on, as I had to examine all relevant papers, since the books had not been kept since 1795.

According to the opinion of many, the Dutch trade is no longer as profitable as it was in the past. I readily acknowledge this *if* one considers this past as the time when our trading station was still in Hirado; but if this past only goes back to the time we ceased to export the gold coins called *kobans*, I don't believe that the difference is that significant. As some may disagree with this view, I will show shortly to what this seeming loss of profit is due.

Trade in Japan takes place in a silver denomination called *tael*[15], which is merely imaginary and serves only as a standard for prices. In the olden days of the VOC, the *tael* was calculated to be worth 70 *stuivers*[16]. The ostensible profits on goods sold then were substantial and showed extremely well on the company books in Japan and on the report that was sent yearly to Batavia. When, in the middle of the last century, the order was given to calculate the *tael* at forty and three years later, at thirty-three stuivers, profits on imports fell considerably, and could no longer cover the costs in Japan. The exported copper, which cost twelve *tael,* three *maas*[17] and five *conderin* per *pikol* was then put in the loss-profit column as costing eighteen *tael,* making the Japanese trade cover their own costs but by a strange method. What does it mean whether one already wants to look for profit in Japan rather than in Batavia? Strictly speaking, the latter conveys the real and true profit, and this is the way we prefer to calculate it since I arrived in Japan and until this day. Profits of the Japanese trade are calculated *only* after selling and minting the copper. Camphor, which in earlier years was sent to Coromandel,[18] Bengal, and Europe, now also goes to Batavia for sale. Camphor and copper are presently the only two articles exported for the account of our government which, as I firmly believe, makes considerable profits from the Japanese trade. Our government's trade with Japan entails that we bring in merchandise yearly, merchandise desired by the Japanese treasury at established prices, and that our government in return receives copper and camphor, also at established prices. The Japanese treasury, or the management of the country's finances, buys this merchandise from us at fixed prices, but lets us deliver it from the warehouses to those merchants to whom the treasury has sold it, except for a small portion which it keeps for itself.

Merchandise imported by the Japanese government consists of tin, lead, mercury, powdered sugar, sapan wood[19], cotton threads, pepper, cloves, *putjuk,*[20] *catju,*[21] some *numia,*[22] cloth, twilled wool, superior quality twilled wool, and *perpetuanen.*[23] All wool cloth has to be Dutch made. The Japanese know the quality of Dutch wool cloth, and always pay the fixed price of eight *tael* per *ikje.*[24] for the more common colors, but they pay less for foreign material which they consider inferior in quality. We found that out when we were unable to deliver the Leiden cloth and had to deliver foreign cloth during the war. We only got ten *tael* for fine red English cloth in 1813, while the Leiden cloth always brought in eleven *tael.* Black English cloth went for nine, but the Dutch for ten *tael* and only one piece of purple English cloth fetched the same price as the Leiden one, eight *tael*, but the rest went for no more than six or seven *tael*. The Japanese truly fancy the real Dutch cloth at the exclusion of all others. Other merchandise the Japanese import includes *grijn*[25], though in small quantities, mock velvet, gold and silver cloth, *chitzen*,[26] *Patnachen*,[27] coverlets, coast *taffachelassen*,[28] among other things. Only 3,500 *ducatonnen* can be imported yearly.

Our expenses in Japan consist of:

(1) Court presents payable yearly to the *Shôgun* in Edo. These are mostly comprised of wool cloth, *chitzen*, and *coast taffachelassen*, if they are available. Since the export quota for copper was lowered to 6,000 *pikols* in 1790, the cost of these Court presents comes to about 6,000 *tael*. Before that, when the copper quota was 9,700 *pikols*, the cost was calculated at 12,000 *tael*. The trek to the Court itself costs about the same. Since this trip no longer takes place every year but every four years, the same cost for these journeys is incurred only after every third year. However, the translators still have to send the presents to Edo yearly, and since the total cost for this comes to 2,750 *tael*, the total expenditure for four years comes to 5,060 *tael* per annum. If no ships arrive, we do not have to send gifts.

(2) The *Hassak*,[29] or yearly payment, in Nagasaki. The *Hassak* is paid each time a ship arrives and consists of 1,921 *tael* cash, four pieces of superior twilled wool, 4,000 pounds (more or less depending on the quality) of sapan wood, 87,424 pounds of sugar and, for miscellaneous expenses, 74 *tael* and eight *maas*. This brings the total to about 5,200 or 5,300 *tael*. The *hassak* is not due when no ships arrive.

As mentioned before, we are not *required* to export the yearly allotted copper quota, but we can add the unused portion to the next year's quota. When more than 6,000 *pikols* copper are exported with no ships having arrived the previous year, the payment has to be augmented accordingly. But if there were ships that did not export the total allotted quota, we are not obligated to pay the full amount. The former scenario took place in 1803, the latter in 1808.

(3) Moreover, presents are also needed for the Japanese nobles. Although we receive gifts in return, they are usually of little value. The cost of these compulsory presents, minus the value of the return gifts, comes in my estimate to about 2,500 *ropyen*.[30] The rent of Deshima island plus the rent of the *Inasse*[31] cemetery comes to 5,517 *tael*. If we add to this the salaries for day and night guards in the years ships do arrive, the total cost comes to 7,900 *tael*. If ships do arrive, the fixed expenditures are as follows:

Gifts to the Court	6,000. *tael*
Cost of the trip to the Court in Edo prorated, as it takes place once every four years	5,060. *tael*
Yearly benefits and their related costs	5,300. *tael*
Rent of Deshima island, etc.	7,900. *tael*
Total	24,268. *tael*

Without ships arriving, the yearly rent of Deshima comes to	5,500. *tael*
Cemetery Inasse	17.2 *tael*
Total	5,517.2 *tael*

(4) The Dutch government has to maintain its own employees consisting of:
the chief
a warehouse master
a scribe
a physician
4 clerks
2 sailors

Previously, they were paid a monthly salary by the VOC, which was a pittance. However, the chief, the warehouse master, the scribe, and the clerks received 5% of the import and export, which they divided among themselves. In addition, the chief received the proceeds of 700 *pikols* of copper once it arrived in Batavia. As this was a very uncertain source of income for all these employees who, when no ships arrived, as was the case in 1808, 1810, 1812, 1815, and 1816, had to eke out a living from their monthly stipend, I was able to change this system. On the basis of a proposal I submitted, everyone who shared my unhappy fate during all those years received not only a compensation, but in addition a fixed income which was determined on a yearly basis. This was not only for the chief but for all lower employees as well.

(5) The cost of living allowance of the employees. They get their maintenance from the government according to a fixed rate. Before 1790, this allowance was very high but was reduced in 1792. As is frequently the case, the government went to the other extreme and set the allowance too low. With the arrival of Mr. Wardenaar in 1800, this allowance improved somewhat, but it was unfortunately fixed in the year of peace, 1802, when the cost of living was so low in Batavia that a bottle of wine only cost sixteen *stuivers*, beer cost next to nothing, and the price of butter was astonishingly low. Eventually, those prices rose to such an extent that I — granted that it was during war time in 1807 — had to pay in Japan three Spanish *matten*[32] or eight and a half *guilders*[33] for a bottle of wine. When I returned to Batavia, those allowances were also raised at my instigation.

Apart from the High Government[34] trade, still called the Company[35] trade, employees and ships' officers could also trade for their own profit in Deshima. This was called the *kambang*[36] trade, which is not, as some claim, after the Malay word *kembang*, flower, which makes no sense here, but instead a Dutch bastardization of the Japanese word *kamawanu*, which means *indifferent*. This was truly the way the Japanese regarded this trade, which they also called *waka nin mono*, "things of the inferior ones." The *kambang* merchandise consists of several articles. The main ones are saffron, licorice, Berlin blue porcelain, ratan, sandal wood, banana (or *areek*[37]) nuts, sweet oil, coconut oil, crab eyes, sal-ammonia, balsam copaiba,[38] gold leather, Persian leather, glassware, articles from Nürnberg, scissors, cutting knives, watches, and other knick-knacks. These articles were first bought by the treasury[39] of Nagasaki, which made three bids, but at the third bid the Dutch either had to accept or take the goods back to Batavia. In this manner, two articles, a *caret*, a tortoise shell escutcheon, and buffalo horns were sold at the third bid when I left. All the other above-mentioned articles were sold in the treasury room to the highest bidders by means of sealed envelopes. Two Dutchmen are always present and everything is well organized. In the past, the treasury received 40% of the highest bid price, but between 1792 and 1798 that percentage was lowered to 35%. This meant that the seller only receives 65% of the highest bid, while our government, since 1800, still takes another one percent to cover the warehouse rental cost. This kambang trade may not be engaged in for goods which our government sends to Japan. Both the Dutch and the Japanese government forbid this, and the Japanese government also forbids the *kambang* trade of *eenhorens*[40] and Cantonese *sum*.[41]

In years past, a lot of smuggling[42] in these forbidden articles took place. They were surreptitiously brought on shore or secretly sold at night by the sailors who were in the best position to do so, and who sometimes earned a lot a lot of money doing it. Today, profits on these articles have dwindled, but I don't doubt that smuggling is still going on, despite the strictest vigilance. During my residence in Japan, only one case of smuggling came to my attention; it concerned the warehouse master Maarten Mak who, in 1807, sold 300 illegal scissors to a certain dealer. Had he sold them openly, he would only have made ten *tael* less. Every one who makes money off the *kambang* trade has his accounts written down in the *kambang* book, kept by several translators who are called *kambang* commissioners. Whenever someone buys something, be it from the compradores (our regular suppliers) or from other merchants, he puts a note in the *kambang* till and, when the ship leaves, everyone receives a bill signed by the *kambang* commissioners. It's easy and painless.

Goods not allowed in the *kambang* trade are copper bars and camphor, which are solely traded by the government; and also any kind of weapons, big or small, which are forbidden by the Japanese; drawings or maps[43] of cities or regions of Japan, hard currency, hammered or plain gold or silver with the exception of gold or silver works for which we supplied the raw material. The exports of the Japanese officials consist of lacquer works, most often inlaid with mother of pearl, which is a Japanese specialty, as the lacquer from China is not nearly as pretty; silk and cotton cloth, silk thread, silk *kabaaijen*[44], *sake*, *soya*, all kinds of fruit preserved in *sakemoer*[45], iron pans, coarse porcelain, *martevanen*[46], medicinal rice, and fans - some of those marvelous transparent ones which some think are made out of rice paper but are really made out of a kind of seaweed. The rest consists of all kinds of knick-knacks.

I'll explain what *sake* and *soya* are. The former is a strong beer brewed from rice but not distilled. *Soya* is neither buffalo blood — there are no buffalos in Japan — nor oxen meat, as beef is extremely scarce, and there were years in which I never tasted any; nor is soya rotten fish. It is nothing but a mixture of wheat, salt, and some kind of white beans, called *mieo-mams*[47]. This mixture is put in a pot and buried in the earth, where it is kept to ferment for a certain length of time. After that, it is cooked so it can be preserved longer.

Aside from the *kambang*[48] trade in which he shares with the other employees, the chief also has the privilege to export yearly 100 *pikols* of processed copper products which consists of copper plates (no bigger than a regular small sheet of paper), copper thread, plaited copper frames, copper shovels, kettles, pans, etc. In earlier days, the treasury charged the chief forty or thirty-two *tael* for that merchandise, but since 1790, fifty to fifty-two *tael*. This is why I never took advantage of this privilege, which I sometimes gave to other employees or ship's officers. The relationship between *kambang* money and Company money, often called *light money*, consists of the fact that twelve Company *tael* are worth not more than ten *kambang tael*. There is an even greater discrepancy in the accounts of the Compradores,[49] or regular providers. Say they deliver 100 Company or "light" *tael* worth of merchandise; they will only receive 75 *kambang tael* for it.

This was the way trade took place in Japan when I arrived for the second time in 1800. Mr. Wardenaar, who brought good order into the chaos he had encountered upon his arrival, sent an American ship hired by our government that year, the *Massachusetts*, to Batavia with a good cargo of copper and camphor. On board was Mr. Leopold Ras, who had to account for the chaos in Deshima.

In 1801, I was promoted to warehouse master to replace Mr. Ras, and Mr. Maarten Mak replaced me as scribe. Mr. Wardenaar had already asked for his discharge the previous year because of *engborstigheid*[50] and had proposed me as his successor, but the High Government in Batavia would not as yet accede to this. They were extremely pleased with the way Mr. Wardenaar had handled the situation on Deshima, though former chiefs were not pleased *at all*. They now had to give an accounting of their administrations to the *Visitateur-Generaal*[51] of the Indies Government auditor's office. I do not know what the end result was. In the same year, a small Portuguese brig ran aground on the Gotto Islands, which I already related elsewhere in this book.

In the spring of 1802, Mr. Wardenaar made the trek to the Court in Edo, and during his absence I was in charge. Then, two ships arrived in August: one was a Dutch Company ship, the other one a hired American ship which brought us the news of the Peace of Amiens.[52] The sugar we received that year was so bad (the dregs of the warehouses in Batavia) that we had to sell it one *tael* below the usual price. Nevertheless, the two ships returned home with a good return cargo. With the arrival of the American ship *Rebecca*, James Deal captain, I received my appointment to succeed Mr. Wardenaar as chief on August 22, 1803. Mr. Mak became warehouse master and the accountant, Age Iges, became our scribe. At that time, we knew nothing as yet of the renewed war in Europe. At the end of his administration, an ample supply of goods had allowed Mr. Wardenaar to send a substantial quantity of copper held over from previous years' quota to Batavia.

Shortly after the arrival of the *Rebecca*, we learned that a European ship had sailed into the harbor where it soon dropped anchor under the American flag. At the request of the governor of Nagasaki, Mr. Wardenaar, accompanied by a commission of chief banyos, boarded the ship. To his great surprise, he discovered that the captain was William Robert Stewart.[53] This man, hired by our government for the Japanese route in 1797 and 1798 had been put under house arrest in Batavia for having lost his ship, as well as for other suspicious dealings, but he escaped. The Japanese suspicion about all ships appearing on their shores doubled the necessity to investigate in this case. Questioned by the commissioners, Stewart claimed that he came from Bengal and Canton, and that the cargo was purely American and belonged to him. To the question of the Japanese, "who is the king of America?" Stewart replied, "President Jefferson." "What had he come to Japan for?" "To request for himself and for his compatriots free trade in Japan," Stewart replied, whereupon the delegation returned to shore. Wardenaar quickly gathered that the cargo did not belong to Stewart but to someone else who was called "doctor." He also suspected that both the ship and its cargo were English. Two days later, Wardenaar and I, accompanied by a Japanese commission, went out to sea in a big ship from which a smaller Japanese boat was launched to invite Captain Stewart to come and see us. Once on board, a translator told him in Dutch, which Stewart understood very well, that his request could not be fulfilled and that he had to leave immediately and never return to

Japanese shores again. Stewart still requested a supply of water which was granted, but the Spanish pepper and oil he also requested were denied by the Japanese. When I was able to prove to the Japanese that the oil was necessary to read the compass by at night, it was finally supplied and, like the water, at no cost. After two more days, Stewart left and did not return.

The circumstances surrounding the repeated loss of Stewart's ship contain some noteworthy peculiarities. As his trip with the ship *Eliza of New York*, had been very satisfactory to his employers, the Dutch, his ship was again hired in 1798. Then, after Chief Ras had provided him with a return cargo and he had all his papers already on board, Stewart weighed anchor at night *when there was no wind*, ran ashoal on a sunken reef where it took on water and sank. Japanese divers attempted to retrieve the copper, but the camphor had melted and its noxious gasses killed two divers. These retrieval efforts had to be abandoned, and other ways were sought to lift the ship and put it on shore so it could be repaired. All efforts failed until a simple fisherman, Kiyemon from Hizen, promised that he could do it. He would only charge what it would cost him and would not take anything if he failed. This man, who perhaps for the first time in his life saw a European ship, was met with derisive laughter. This did not perturb the man in the least. He fastened to either side of the sunken ship 15 or 17 small boats similar to the ones used to tow in our ships and connected them with each other by props and stays. When it was high tide, he came with a Japanese cargo ship which he fastened in a similar way to the stern of the sunken ship. When the tide was at its highest, he hoisted the sails on the small boats as well as those on his own. The heavily loaded, deeply immersed ship rose from the sunken reef and the skillful fisherman then put it on a flat piece of beach where it could easily be unloaded and repaired. Kiyemon not only received compensation for his costs, but the Prince of Hizen granted him permission[54] to carry two swords and to bear as his coat of arms, a Dutch hat adorned with two Dutch tobacco pipes. From this it is clear that even the Japanese of the lower classes are not devoid of ingenuity and intelligence.

In the meantime, the crew of the stranded ship was not at liberty to come to us on Deshima. The moment a European ship has passed the imperial guards[55] (the last outlook post beyond the harbor), it cannot re-enter the harbor in that same season. On Kibatsi, a place near the ship, stockaded quarters for the crew were made out of the stalls which are built for us on Deshima every year. Although the crew was not allowed to come to Deshima, once in a while the Japanese surreptitiously allowed the captain or the carpenter, who was also the navigator, to come provided they did not stay overnight. Unloading, repairing, reloading, and equipping the ship required vast sums of money, for which Stewart was responsible. Our government in Japan advanced this money to Stewart. When the ship was ready, around May 1799, Captain Stewart left again for the open seas in June *against* everyone's advice and despite the bad *mousson*[56]. Just when I arrived here for the first time in July 1799, his ship had drifted toward the Japanese shore after having lost all its masts. One day after me, he entered the harbor. Stewart had lost all his masts in a terrible three-day storm below Formosa (Taiwan), a storm I had also encountered.[57] It was the worst storm I ever experienced. New expenses and new costs were now required, which Chief Ras once again advanced. In November, Stewart was ready to sail again. As mentioned elsewhere, I too was about to depart for Batavia at that time, and I tried to persuade Stewart as well as Captain Devereux, whose ship I was to board, to make the trip jointly, but to no avail; Stewart left on November the twelfth, twelve days before us.

When I returned to Japan in July of 1800, I was very surprised to again find Stewart there. According to Chief Ras, Stewart had *once again* lost his ship, this time with cargo and all. After this total loss, Stewart arrived in Manila, the capital of the Philippines, where a friend enabled him to buy another small brig[58] as well as another cargo with which he had now come to Japan *to pay his debts*. When Mr. Wardenaar asked him why he hadn't immediately gone to Batavia to account for the loss of his ship, Stewart only replied that he intended to do so *after* he had paid his debts in Japan.

The whole story sounded suspicious to Mr. Wardenaar. On board the small brig, they found a galley which they recognized as coming from the ship *Eliza of New York*; when a ship goes down, the last thing one would try to salvage is a galley, yet Stewart maintained that he had not been able to salvage *anything*. Therefore, his intentions and actions could not have been above-board. I myself am convinced that Stewart thought that Batavia would not send a ship because of the war and thus tried to persuade Mr. Ras, whose lack of character he was well aware of, to give him a return cargo of copper with which he most certainly would not have returned to *Batavia*.[59]

However, Stewart's intention failed. Mr. Wardenaar sold his cargo and from the proceeds paid part of his debts. He then sent him to Batavia on the *Massachusetts,* under the surveillance of Captain Hutchings. A navigator and several sailors of that ship were put in charge of Stewart's small brig which, after a stop in Manila, arrived in Batavia shortly after Captain Hutchings arrived in Batavia. While being investigated, Stewart was ordered not to leave Batavia or its environs, but he fled to Bengal. Once there, he was undoubtedly able to present himself to the English as a man of experience and influence who could persuade the Japanese to grant them free trade. You know how he made out.

That the English availed themselves of the American flag, while Stewart reported Jefferson to be the king of America, is strange. However, this would not be the only English undertaking. Three or four days after this ship's departure in 1803, we again were notified that a foreign ship was in sight. We thought it would be Stewart who, because of adverse winds, had to stay close to shore. To our surprise this was not the case. Again, Mr. Wardenaar and a Japanese committee sailed out to investigate to which country this ship belonged. I accompanied them. At first, its flag was unknown to us, but soon it turned out to be the flag of the English East India Company. The Jack that normally showed the cross had been removed and the red and white stripes just went straight across. We learned that the ship[60] came from Bengal. When the translators learned that it was an English ship, they asked us to *warn* the captain to say only that *the ship came from Bengal* in order *to prevent serious problems*. From this it is clear how little Japan was inclined to allow the English to enter.

Not quite reassured that we had indeed delivered this warning, the translators gave that same warning to a German who spoke a little Dutch. He appeared to be the scribe on board. The captain's name was James Torry. He was very young but seemed to be a calm person. Despite the fact that Torry claimed not to know Stewart at all, it was quite clear that they belonged together. Whenever Torry heard Stewart's name, he had a hard time suppressing his anger and seemed to curse the fortune hunter who had thus misled him and his masters (the English Government in Calcutta) by misrepresentations and false promises. Torry also requested free trade, and it appeared that the American (Stewart) had been sent ahead because, if the Japanese had granted him who was known to them free trade, they could hardly have refused it to the English flag. After two days, Torry's request was denied, and he was ordered to leave and never sail to Japan again. After having been provided with drinking water, just as Stewart had been, this ship also set sail again.

Wardenaar left in 1803, ending his administration on a profitable note. He was able to get an additional 2,520 *pikols* left over from previous years' quota, as well as 1,000 *pikols* camphor on top of the regular quota of 6000 *pikols*. With this cargo on board, the ship set sail carrying Mr. Wardenaar, who left me in charge as the new chief. My administration started at a very unfavorable[61] time in history, a period full of obstacles for this far flung trading station as well. After only one year of peace, war with England had resumed, adversely affecting the Japanese trade. On August eight and eleven, 1804, two Dutch ships, the *Maria Susanna* under Captain Gerrit Belmer, and the *Gesina Antoinette* under Captain Arend Musquetier, brought the news of the shattered peace. The cargo of those ships did not at all contain the same assorted merchandise that the Japanese used to receive before the peace fell through in 1795.[62] This didn't only happen in 1804, but during the whole time, from 1803 to 1817, that I had the honor of being the Dutch chief in Japan. In all that time, I never received a cargo that was sufficiently assorted and geared to Japanese taste. It caused me endless difficulties to make these unwanted goods palatable to the Japanese, which I had to do in order to be able to send back substantial cargos of copper. I considered this to be one of my first duties, as I had been notified by the High Government that the shortage of copper coins in Java had put it in a serious quandary, as the war prevented the import of copper from Europe. I was lucky indeed to have been able to accomplish this to such extent that it brought me from year to year the approbation of my superiors.

This year, an abundance of so called *polemieten*, fabrics consisting of a mixture of wool and goat's or camel's hair, caused me a lot of trouble. This material, once used a lot in Europe, had fallen out of favor, but was still coveted by the Asians, whose taste and dress do not change as often as ours. This material, mostly made in Leiden, was widely exported to the Far East and also to Japan, but this year the import exceeded the usual quantity. When it arrived in small quantities, we got a good price for it, but now that the market was flooded, it caused a big fall in its price. If I wanted to get a good cargo of copper, I had to sell it below the usual price. I was in a quandary and wrote to Batavia that it seemed better to me to sell the material at the prices offered, which still gave us some profit, than to send it back and thus get far less copper. By doing this, I still got both ships a reasonable cargo of copper.

Those two ships also brought me the High Government's notification that I could expect the arrival at any time of a Russian Embassy to Japan. Newspapers also reported that news. I immediately notified the Japanese Government. On October 7, when both ships were already partially loaded, I received the news that a European ship had arrived in the harbor. The governor of Nagasaki, Fita Bungo No Kami, asked me to accompany the Japanese commission, or rather follow them after they had been on board for some time, to investigate the reason why this ship had come. I complied with this request the next day. After the commission had been on board for some time, I had Captain Arend Musquetier, whom I had asked to accompany me together with Captain Belmer, ask permission to board the ship as well. Permission granted, I boarded. I was greeted on deck by Captain Krusenstern and led to the ward room. According to Japanese custom, I first greeted the commission representing the *shôgun* while standing up before I paid my respects to the Russian ambassador who showed me due courtesy.

The questions I asked, such as how long the trip had been, from where they had last departed, and what the ambassador's intentions were on this trip, are of little interest today. Of interest is that the commission asked the translators to inform the ambassador that it was the Japanese custom to show respect to the representatives of the *shôgun* by standing up, and that they fully expected the Russians to do so. The ambassador, Mr. de Rezanov, refused to do this, giving the excuse that his high rank forbade him to do so. Despite the remark of the translators that even the highest ranked Japanese, when arriving in a foreign country, had to and *would* most certainly conform to the prevailing customs, de Rezanov persisted in his refusal. We and the Japanese commission thereupon took our leave and returned to Deshima. Mr. de Rezanov had handed me letters of the Government, the Council of Asian Possessions, and the Dutch ambassador to Russia, all strongly recommending that we treat Mr. de Rezanov in a friendly fashion and assist him in every way. I considered these recommendations carefully[63] and decided to extend to Mr. de Rezanov as *Russian* ambassador all possible friendship. As to the second recommendation, however, I had to consider the state of affairs in Japan, which I knew better than any European government, as well as the instructions I had received from Batavia concerning all foreigners in general.[64] I was Chief from the only *European* nation permitted residence in Japan, and I knew that laws and ancient customs strongly forbade the entrance of other European nations. What would the Japanese have thought of us Dutchmen if we had stood up for the Russians? Wouldn't we have drawn the suspicion of the mistrustful Japanese? They certainly would have had even more reason to deny the Russians' request, as they would have undoubtedly thought that we supported it because we had joint designs on the empire of Japan. For those reasons, I felt strongly that I had to stay clear of any intercession between the Japanese and Russians and the intentions of the latter.

The next day, I asked permission from the govenor of Nagasaki to send the Russian ambassador some fresh provisions. A reply came, stating that the governor himself had already done so, but that I could send some the following day. With this reply also came the request that I go on board again in order to witness the questions of another Japanese commission consisting of an accountant and a secretary. One can find the questions asked at this meeting in detail in Langsdorff's book, *Journey Around the World*. To the Japanese, it really seemed absurd that the ambassador refused to give up his rifle yet was willing to give up the gunpowder. The ambassador was in this matter as intransigent as he had been in regard to the Japanese ceremonial custom of standing up, a custom to which the translators again asked him to conform. Muskets were kept on board, and the officers kept their side arms, but the gunpowder was taken away and kept in the Japanese gunpowder depot. The ship was then allowed to anchor closer to shore. With my party, which included Mr. Van Pabst, a captain of the army in Batavia who was making a trip to Japan to recuperate from a serious illness, I stayed for dinner with the ambassador. The conversation was very affable and we only left the ship after it anchored outside the Papenberg,[65] when we bade a friendly goodbye to the ambassador, his retinue, and Captain Krusenstern. Since that encounter, we were not able to speak with each other again.

The account Langsdorff[66] gives of this meeting is in certain respects not accurate, and in other respects a misrepresentation.

He implies that I had omitted to adhere to Japanese customs and had to be reminded of these by the translators. This was truly unnecessary. I had become so well acquainted with the country's customs during my five-year stay that no translator needed to point them out to me. Neither I nor Mr. Van Pabst[67] deserve to be depicted in such a preposterous light by the Russian legation. According to Langsdorff's *own* admission, I did the Russians a real service by prevailing upon the Japanese accountant to allow the Russian ship to anchor elsewhere that very same night, as the previous place was so dangerous that the ship would have come aground on the reef called the *Rooster* at the first heavy wind gust. In addition, Captain Musquetier's dedication was such that he stayed the whole evening on the fore-castle in order to get the ship to a better anchoring place. In his report, Krusenstern commits the same impropriety as Langsdorff.

In addition to these two writers, many others chide the Dutch and consider it demeaning that they conform to the Japanese customs and ceremonials. I can't understand what is so demeaning about this. The ceremonial acts we engage in, in regard to the Japanese, are the same they engage in among themselves. Japanese rulers do not require of *us* more signs of respect than they require of *their own citizens*. These are simply their customs, and wherever you go in this world, you either have to conform to the local customs or ceremonies or stay home. After all, you cannot expect that a nation whose friendship *you* seek should conform to the customs of its *visitors*! I feel that there is nothing offensive in conforming to these customs and ceremonies, provided one is not obligated to show more signs of humility than the subjects of such a nation show each other. To paint something as ridiculous — even if it is far from the case — is easy, and one could perhaps in the same manner ridicule the ambassador. In doing this, one does not so much deride the ambassador as the one who sent him, and respect for His Majesty, the Emperor of Russia, requires that I keep silent.

But let us go back to our story. The next day I sent as

refreshments to the ambassador some chickens and ducks, a pig, and some fresh vegetables. Several days later, his Excellency asked me for some sugar and butter. With foreknowledge of the governor of Nagasaki, I sent him 500 pounds of sugar but I could not provide his Excellency with butter as we had not received any that year. In the meantime, the new governor of Nagasaki, Narusa Inaba No Kami, had arrived, but this time the retiring governor was not allowed, as per usual custom, to depart for Edo. He had to stay with the new governor until the Russian matter was resolved. As the anchoring place of the ship was still not a safe one, the ambassador had requested a better place and received it.

On the 16th of October, the Russian ship anchored in the bay of the Papenberg, at the same place where our ships, upon leaving the roadstead of Nagasaki, usually anchor to pick up the last part of their cargo. The departure time of our ships for the Papenberg which always had to be on the 20th of the Japanese month of *Kuguats*,[68] was now approaching, and the governors informed me that our ships could not drop anchor at their usual place below the Papenberg nor have any contact with the Russians. We had to do this just past the imperial guard post. I wrote the governors that I would obey their order but that I wanted it in writing, which they supplied to me. On October 25, our ships left the roadstead of Nagasaki for their designated spot, where they dropped anchor. It was customary for our ships to shoot one cannon volley in the morning and one in the evening. After several days of this, the governors had a request sent to me to stop that custom this year, because some burning wads had fallen on the roofs of houses due to the ships' proximity to the imperial guard post. This request seemed perfectly reasonable to me, and I gave the necessary orders. I did not know however, that the request was made on the insistence of the Russians, as Langdorff's story tells it. In the meantime, the Russian Ambassador requested via the governors that I send a letter in duplicate, addressed to the Russian Emperor, to Batavia on board our two ships, and ask the Governor General to send them on to Europe. I granted

RECOLLECTIONS OF JAPAN

this request. Now it was time for our ships to set sail. The governors had instructed me that our ships had to sail in complete silence past the Russian ships and not call out to them. When Captain Musquetier received my order, he only responded to the Russians' loud greetings and wishes for a good journey by taking off his hat and waving it. However, I wrote Mr. de Rezanov to apologize for the fact that the crew of our ships had not responded to the Russians' good wishes in a way that is common among civilized nations, but that I had been forced to order them to act in this manner. His reply was friendly, and from that time on we started a correspondence (in French) which the translators secretly allowed. They even allowed me to provide Mr. de Rezanov with the newspapers I had received from Batavia that year. Several times already, the ambassador had asked to be assigned a residence on land so that the ship could be unrigged and repaired. The governors were not at liberty to accede to that request without orders from the Court in Edo. However, to accommodate the ambassador as much as possible, a bamboo stockaded place was provided for the ambassador and his retinue on Kibatsi, where in 1798, Stewart's sunken ship had been repaired, and where the Russian ship could also be repaired. But the ambassador hardly availed himself of this place. Before instructions from Edo were received, no cargo was allowed to be brought on shore, but in this respect also the governors were accommodating. They offered to request a junk from the Chinese for Mr. de Rezanov to stay on while his ship was being repaired, and also have the cargo transferred to it as well.

A Chinese junk came but was sent back as being inadequate, because the Chinese had left only the hold open for the Russians but had nailed shut the captain's and officers' quarters. A long time passed before anything was heard about allowing the Russians to come ashore. At the end of November, I learned that the warehouses for dried *tripang*[69] and *klipzuigers*[70] were being readied for the ambassador and his retinue. These warehouses stand on a place called Magasakki, which lies slightly to the east southeast across from our island of Deshima.

Pending a decision by the Court in Edo, the ambassador had to take up residence in these warehouses. This decision surprised me ever more since the Japanese had sounded me out earlier as to whether *I* could lodge the ambassador and his retinue on Deshima. My reply had been that this would indeed be possible, but that I had to lodge them in my own house situated in the garden of the chief's residence which had burned down in 1798. This would be the *only* place becoming the rank of an ambassador of the emperor of Russia. The Japanese did not take me up on this, but talked about readying a temple for the embassy, in which case they would have been lodged as splendidly as is possible in Nagasaki. I was dumbfounded that instead of a temple, the Japanese were now readying a warehouse for dried fish to house their foreign guests. The new quarters were ready on December 16 and, to avoid any contact between the Japanese and Russians, a high bamboo fence was put all around it. The next morning, we saw a tender of the Russian ship head to Magasakki and then return to the ship. In the afternoon, the ambassador and his retinue came on shore on the big ship belonging to the prince of Hizen. Aft of the ship, where the Russian grenadiers stood with their rifles, the Russian standard fluttered, and the Japanese accurately noticed that in this standard, the eagle carrying the globe in one talon lacked the usual sign of the cross. Several days later, the Russian ship came within the imperial guard posts and anchored so close to our island that it sat in mud by low tide. From time to time, they put the presents the ambassador had brought with him ashore, and I kept up an increasingly lively correspondence with him via the translators. I did my very best to provide Mr. de Rezanov with the few European vegetables that grew on Deshima, such as cabbage, endives, celery, and so on. Now and then I added a freshly killed wild boar or deer, all with the foreknowledge and permission of the Japanese government, which did not wish me to send anything they could provide, such as a quilted dressing gown for the ambassador who suffered from gout. I myself already had one made, but permission to give it to him was denied, as

RECOLLECTIONS OF JAPAN

they wanted to provide Mr. de Rezanov with one themselves. With the permission of the governors, the ambassador sent me a big mirror, two yellow marble slabs for pier[71] tables, a green and gold French porcelain tea service for one, a set of steel jacket buttons and forty-eight bottles of assorted wines. With my thanks, I sent him a beautiful black Japanese lacquered desk inlaid with mother of pearl and several other now forgotten small presents in return. Due to the shipwreck of the *Admiraal Evertsen,* in which I lost all my belongings and papers, including the original letters of the ambassador and copies of my letters to him, I cannot give an exact accounting of all the presents I sent. Mr. de Rezanov's presents to me also perished in that shipwreck, except for the mirror, which pirates probably stole from another ship.

In the meantime the year 1805 arrived, and nothing as yet had been heard from the Court regarding a decision about the Russian Embassy. The ambassador's impatience was certainly very understandable, and the translators and banyos had a hard time keeping the ambassador in good humor when an answer did not seem to be forthcoming. It took us Dutch a long while before we got used to these many time consuming customs which are inseperable from any interaction with the Japanese. Imagine how it must have been for someone who was sent as ambassador of a powerful emperor to have to wait six months for an answer? But the strictest adherence to all the institutions and laws of the land established by Gongen prohibit the Japanese from circumventing these even in the slightest, especially in a matter of such importance. I personally think that de Rezanov's refusal to give up the muskets was the cause that, first, his ship wasn't allowed within the imperial guardposts earlier and, second, that he was lodged in a warehouse for dried fish at the very tip of Nagasaki. Since even the country's ruling princes cannot have guards of honor with rifles, pikes, or exposed side weapons, the governors of Nagasaki couldn't possibly permit this. They most certainly consulted Edo over this matter. The fact that this was later permitted for just a short while can be ascribed to the fact that a decision had been made not to negotiate with Russia. This permission was also granted more readily because the Russians' quarters on Nagasaki were totally separated from the rest of the city, and very few ordinary Japanese citizens could observe the Russian soldiers march with their rifles. In the meantime, the ambassador asked me to provide him with lacquered goods, *chatouilles*[72] such as tobacco and snuff boxes and trays. He also requested fans, silk materials, crepe, and wallpaper, and other things, all together amounting to a not inconsiderable sum of money. I immediately gave orders to gather the requested articles. When we finally got the word in February that an envoy from the Court in Edo was coming to grant an audience to the Russian ambassador, the governor of Nagasaki asked me for the loan of my *norimon,*or palanquin,[73] which I gladly gave to him.

The arrival of the envoy did not take place until the end of March however, and the audience was not held until the fourth of April. On this occasion, the Japanese authorities' mistrust of foreigners manifested itself very strongly. All the houses on the route the ambassadorial delegation would take had to close their blinds, and abutting side streets were boarded up so no one could see the procession. Citizens of Nagasaki were strictly forbidden to be in the vicinity of the procession. No one was allowed to show his face other than those who were on duty. The Russians therefore could see absolutely nothing of the city or its people. All these measures indicated to me, that the ambassador's request for free trade had been denied. On the morning of April fourth, we saw the ambassador, accompanied by several officers, sail past our island on a ship belonging to the prince of Hizen, which carried the Russian imperial standard on its stern post. We greeted the company, and once on land, the ambassador climbed in my palanquin while the others proceeded on foot. Some time later, we saw the procession return to Magasakki in the same order. According to the translators, the ambassador was only asked a few questions about the papers he brought. The next day, the ambassadorial procession again passed us in the same order. Since it rained, *kagos*, smaller palanquins, were needed for the officers, which delayed the procession for about an hour. After a while, the ambassadorial procession returned the same way. The translators told me that at this audience the ambassador had received a negative answer to his proposals. The governor of Nagasaki passed on a request to me that together with the translators, I translate the papers the Russian ambassador received from the Court from Japanese into Dutch so that the Russian Court could then also understand them. I would have much preferred not to have to do this — the transmission of a certain refusal — but I could hardly refuse. However, I took this task upon me only under the explicit stipulation that after the papers had been translated, I would receive a certificate stating that my translation was completely correct and corresponded exactly to the Japanese version.[74] This request was granted, and the translation took me and the translators two days, as every single word had to be translated. As these translations also had to be sent to Edo, I was asked not to concern myself at all with Dutch linguistic style but adhere strictly to the Japanese one. This forced me to delete even the auxiliary verbs necessary to complete a sentence. I will give a rendition of the peculiar translation of this answer, done to please the translators and to prevent any objections, as it must have come across in Edo. The intention was to give it to the Japanese doctors, who were fluent in Dutch, to be looked over. On top of this reply (from Edo), I will give a verbatim translation of a separate warning from the governors of Nagasaki to Mr. de Rezanov, which they transmitted in writing to his Excellency:

"Warning of the governor of Nangezacky by order of his Imperial Majesty.

Over ten years ago, a Russian ship arrived in Matsmay,[75] at that time were warned by us that friendship and trade could not happen as written in Japanese on paper, was anyhow not understood, not permitted to come to Japan; most of all, Matsmay is not a place from which to inform the Court of the affairs of foreign lands, when there are some Japanese in Russia, and, want to sent to Japan, or request other such matters, in Matsmay cannot happen at all, but if want to do again, then must come to Nangazacky, because Nangazacky is a place where affairs of foreigners are dealth with, therefore a permit letter is given that Russian ship may sail to Nangezacky. Preceding the reasons, has been warned already, but this trip again from Russia brings a letter written in Japanese, which make think Russia not understand very well the warning of that time, this because of difference of character and unfamiliarly of country's way, therefore once again by order of the Japanese Emperor, previous warning is repeated. Whatever the ship needs, stoking wood and water will be delivered. After leaving here will soon set sail for open sea and not stay close to shore, and shall not anchor near the islands surrounding Japan. (Understood) Japan at Nangezacky *Bunka nengo*,[76] second year of 7th *Sanguate* (on top stood) A big red imprinted Japanese seal.

Agreed.

(was signed) Age Iges . Scribe Conformable to the original. The 1st clerk of the General Secretariat charged with safeguarding old government archives.

(was signed) D. A. Temples. "

"The translation of the Japanese imperial order to the Russian Ambassador de Rezanova:

"It was in the olden days usual in Japan to associate with quite a few foreign nations, but no virtue was found in this, therefore a strict interdiction made, that no Japanese to trade can go to foreign countries, just as foreign nation is also not permitted in Japan to come, whoever come anyhow against that interdiction, cannot not permit anyhow, but directly must again depart, except of the people of Asia, the Chinese, Korea, Leques,[77] and of Europe the Dutch alone, these peoples are permitted to engage in trade here, but this is not alone to seek profit, but because of olden days for exceptional reasons is permitted, but with Russia from olden times to now not have relation, but over ten years without thought some shipwrecked Japanese brought to Matsmay, and, like then, made request to trade, and now in Nangezacky again arrive to get token of friendship and request trade, which not only ten years ago in Matsmay was asked, but now again in Nangezacky is repeated, thus appears much affection Russia for Japan wants to have.

"Yet the requested friendship attitude and trading cannot enter into, for reason that the association of Japan with other foreign nations for a long time not has taken place. Though not unaware, that with neighboring country friendship will keep, but the different character and ways do not permit, to make ties of friendship, and so would a lot of trouble, and the sailing back and forth useless be, and, that is why the attitude of friendship cannot happen, and, the existence in our land of long standing established laws according to which our land is governed, and how can such old laws (for which we have a lot of esteem) change? and, be it that other countries seek our friendship, the rituals and ceremonies would on each side trouble cause, when as example from another foreign country presents to us are send, and accepted, and, from our side no reciprocal honor made, then could be spoken of our country, as if our country did not ceremonies know, and, even wanting to mutually pay respects, it would because of far away country not be possible, and, therefore it is better it not be permitted than yes. Concerning the trade on both sides with exchange of many products, of which each is short, so seems possible advantage, but we have carefully weighed and experienced that if our useful merchandise for other merchandise traded, then would be possible for us to get shortage of our useful merchandise, and, thus it would be, as if we in our country not know how to govern; in addition if more trade is engaged in, than for some people who always seek profit more opportunity to break Japanese ways and laws, and which thus is detrimental and unpleasant to govern our citizens, and even it be that without trade only new friendship will bind, this can however not happen anyhow, because our country's laws cannot break, and because of that cannot enter into a relationship, this is the *Imperial* decision, and therefore must not to sail on waters to Japan any longer engage in. (Understood). Japan in Nangezacky Bunka nengô second year of the seventh *Sanguats* (stood above) A big red printed Japanese seal.

Agreed

(was signed) Age Iges, Scribe

Conformable to the original

The 1st clerk of the General Secretariat charged with safeguarding old government archives.

(signed)   D. A. Temples."

For those who know Japan reasonably well, the refusal to deal with the Russian Embassy and thereby engage in closer relations with Russia came as no surprise. The laws, customs, and manners of this nation, as I have often brought to the fore and which is also clear from the Court's answer, do not allow them to engage in friendly negotiations or trade relations with other nations. Barring the repeal of the laws of the land under which, for two centuries, the Japanese have experienced such well-being, all requests that any nation makes will be refused. If it hadn't been for the fact that we Dutch were already settled here, we would never have been allowed entrance, and were we not covered by the pass given to us by the great Gongen, author of our present day laws, the Japanese would long ago have gotten rid of us. It can also not be assumed that the Japanese keep permitting us to be in this realm solely on the basis of the profit we bring them. This profit, to put it generously, cannot amount to more than 100,000 *tael*, about 150,000 *guilders*, and what does such a sum mean for a country like Japan? Besides, the only ones who profit are the governors and inhabitants of Nagasaki. Anyhow, Japan does not need imports from abroad. The main import we bring them, sugar, grows sufficiently in the province of Kyûshû. Japan is also self-sufficient in tin. Instead of pepper, a Japanese could easily content himself with *kosho*,[78] and the lord of Tsushima, who oversees Korea, sends the pepper we import there. The Japanese have cotton thread but no sapan wood, though they do have all kinds of dyes. They use tin instead of lead, which they do not have. The amount of cloves we bring in is small, and the Japanese only use them now and then as medicine. They could well do without such luxury items as elephants' teeth as well as wool, silk and linen, glass work, clocks, and other knick-knacks; the more so since, with their country cut off from the outside world and they themselves not allowed to travel abroad, they are not familiar with many luxury items we in Europe can't do without, and that they wouldn't even miss. It is with reason, therefore, that in their reply to the Russian ambassador the authorities implied that Japan could very well do without all foreign imports, which my 19 years' residence there has convinced me is true.

I may now ask the following: can the failure of the Russian Embassy[79] be rightly blamed on the Dutch, and thus mainly on me? Surely, it must be acknowledged that it would have been ridiculous on my part to intervene with the Japanese government in order to block the admittance of the Russians, since I knew and had already experienced the previous year, that the country's laws forbade trade with foreigners, as corroborated also in Golownin's *Adventures*, Vol. II, pp. 206 and 243[80]. One can not therefore assume that the Japanese government would allow in 1804 what they had declared not allowable in 1803, as it was against the fundamental law of the land. What could my intercession have done for or against? Would the Japanese have found it in their country's interest to break the rules and enter into a trade relation with Russia, they would hardly have heeded me. Neither orally nor in writing did I meddle in this matter but remained totally on the side lines as I knew very well that, even had the Russians been admitted, it would not have been detrimental to the Dutch, with whom the Japanese had lived in friendship for close to two centuries now. Rumors have it that letters were sent with a certain ship sailing from Batavia to Europe, indicating that the Russians had been denied entrance into Japan through Dutch intervention. Whatever may have been written about this from Batavia, I do not know. I myself never reported anything to this effect. When I sent my day registers to the High Government in Batavia, I only wrote these words, *"That since the Japanese had denied trade to the Russians who are their closest neighbor, no other nation would ever have any prospect either."* If the previously stated letters were indeed written from Batavia to Europe, it is possible that, contrary to the truth, the refusal of the Russians was ascribed to my efforts in order to do me a good turn, something I totally reject. The above also makes clear that Mr. de Rezanov's refusal to conform to Japanese customs, such as giving up his muskets, could have been a reason for the refusal, as well as the belated permission for the ambassador to come ashore and the subsequent allocation of a strange and unsuitable residence. Even had Mr. de Rezanov submitted himself reasonably to everything, the main purpose of his trip would not have been achieved anyhow. After the ambassador had received the long awaited answer, some other difficulties arose concerning the acceptance of the counter-gifts the Japanese government intended to give the Russians. They consisted of 2,000 packages of silk wadding (not raw silk as Langsdorff wrote), 2,000 straw wrapped packages of salt and 100 bags of rice. At first, the ambassador refused to accept these gifts since the Court in Edo had not accepted his, but one of the translators convinced him to do so. For this, the translator received permission from the governor and the chief spy sent from Edo to take for himself several of the presents which surely still remain, untouched, in the governor's mansion. If the governor and the chief spy from Edo had not been able to have the ambassador accept the gifts — as was their specific mandate — they would have been guilty of disobedience. Then the only thing left for them to do was to cut open their bellies to prevent the dishonorable punishment which they could not have avoided. They clearly had reason to be happy when the ambassador[81] accepted the gifts. The Japanese paid for all the living expenses incurred by the Embassy, and even provided the ship with six months worth of provisions of the Russians' choice. For quite a while during this time, the ambassador maintained a friendly correspondence with me. On a certain occasion when I had sent his Excellency something or another, he thanked me in the name of all Russians with these words (written in French): *"When I return to Europe, I will most certainly mention you to my august Master."* Later on, he also wrote about the end result of the embassy literally these words: *"However bad the outcome was, nothing shall be attributed to our Batavian[82] allies."* Indeed, he wrote this with such a heartfelt conviction and in such a gracious manner that it truly hurts me that I cannot incorporate here the original letters which were lost in the unfortunate shipwreck. However, Mr. van de Capellen and Mr. Elout have read them; the former in 1818 in Batavia, the latter on board the *Admiraal Evertsen*. In addition, copies of these letters must be among the secret letters from Japan sent to Batavia in 1805. Would these copies have been lost during the English administration, there should still be other copies in existence among the secret papers of Japan. As stated, Mr. de Rezanov asked me to have certain goods be made for him as well as for the Russian Court. Whatever goods were ready, I sent to him before his departure, but the majority of goods were not yet ready. The ambassador therefore requested that these goods be shipped at his own risk and for his own account to Batavia with our first available ships, and then be sent on from there to Russia on Danish or other ships. His Excellency wanted to pay for this in hard currency, namely Spanish piastres, but the Japanese government did not allow this. The ambassador then wrote me that he would deposit this money for my account with the Russian ambassador in the Hague as soon as he arrived in Europe. Since then, however,

I have heard nothing more about this. Mr. Langsdorff also wrote me a note asking me to send on some things via Batavia to Amsterdam. I sent all the goods, amounting to 300 *rijksdaalders* for Mr. Langsdorff and 2,850 for the ambassador, to my proxies in Batavia in 1805 on the ship *de Resolutie*.

Because of the war, however, the goods remained in Batavia until my proxies, fearing the goods would totally spoil, as white ants had already invaded them, sold them at auction, where they did not get nearly the amount of money I had advanced. In his *Annales des Voyages* (journeys' annals), chapter XXI, p. 263 and on, which deals with the Russians' journey around the world and reports written by Mr. Horner to Mr. Depping, Malte Brun says:

> *"It was also very unfortunate for the Russian ambassador that the drafts that the American Company had given him were not accepted at the Dutch trading station in Japan. The Dutch chief (Doeff), a very cautious man, answered that he did not dare pay such large sums as long as the government in Batavia had not authorized it."*

Again, I have to contradict this account. Such drafts were *never* shown to me; indeed, the Russian ambassador never even mentioned anything about them. If he had asked me for an advance, I would not have hesitated for a moment to give it to a man of such a high position, and who acted in every thing in the name of the Russian emperor. After all, I did not hesitate (though it was a lesser amount) to advance the ambassador the price of the described goods. Most likely, Malte Brun confused this matter with the Japanese government's refusal to let Mr. de Rezanov pay me ahead of time in piastres for the goods. Shortly before his departure, the ambassador once again asked permission from the governor of Nagasaki to pay us a farewell visit on Deshima, but this was also refused just like my request to visit the embassy on Magasaki. We had to content ourselves with greeting each other from a distance when the ambassador and his retinue sailed past our island on board the ship of the prince of Chikuzen. The Russians gave us the most unambiguous signs of being satisfied with us and of friendship.

After a stay of six months, the Russian Embassy finally left Japan.

On the 14th of August, 1805, we received notice that a European ship was close to shore. We were very worried that the long awaited ship might be torn to pieces on the reefs, as that afternoon a heavy storm had come from the south, which worsened during the night. Our joy was therefore great when we learned the morning of the 15th that the ship was sailing in. It soon passed the corner of the Papenberg and anchored close to shore. It was the ship *de Resolutie,* whose captain had died and said ship was now under the command of Mr. Hendrik Voorman, Captain-Lieutenant in the colonial service. Once again, the cargo on board was not very varied, just like the previous one had not been, and again it had a much too large quantity of *polemieten* fabric. The High Government's strict orders not to send any goods back to Batavia, but to sell them for the highest bid offered, spared me the embarrassment of having to send back what was least desirable. Trade this year proceeded very quietly, and the ship returned without any mishaps and with a good cargo (including the goods of the two Russian gentlemen) to Batavia.

The year 1806 had arrived, which was the year when the chief, in person, had to make his trek[83] to Edo. I will describe this trek as well as those I made in 1810 and 1814 in the following chapter.

inazuma no   Lend me your arms
kaina wo karan   quick as lightning
kusamakura   as pillows on my journey

Haiku by Hendrik Doeff[1] [2]

CHAPTER III

The Trek to the Royal Court In Edo

When the trek to the court is about to take place, luggage is inspected and repaired if needed about six weeks to two months ahead of time. Our government takes care of all bills. As previously mentioned, our government reimburses the Japanese treasury in the amount of 12,000 *tael*. For years, this trek started on the 15th of the Japanese month of *shoguats*[3] (the first month of the Japanese calendar), but since my first one, this trek was scheduled earlier, on the 7th of *shoguats*, which corresponds to the end of February. The reason for this is that the trek has to proceed without hitches if we are to arrive in Edo before the 22 or 23rd of the following month *(niguats*[4] *)* in order to be able to appear at the emperor's audience on the 28th, the *rebi* or day of compliments. If we arrive too late, the audience is postponed for a whole month. Since our gifts to the court were almost destroyed once in the great fire of Edo, a story I'll get back to later, a new arrangement is now instituted, whereby our gifts, at the very moment we arrive in Edo, are sent to the emperor's palace under the supervision of one of the governors of Nagasaki who, at that time, is stationed in Edo. This arrangement releases us from a heavy responsibility. The governor who is stationed in Nagasaki assigns us a chief banyo, who has to accompany us during the whole trek, facilitate it by removing all obstacles, and procure for us the help of the domain lords whose territories we traverse. The chief banyo has three lower ranked banyos under him who assist him. A chief and lower ranked translator accompany us as well, with the first paying all the expenses with which the chief therefore

RECOLLECTIONS OF JAPAN

doesn't have to concern himself. When previously he (the chief) held the purse, paying bills caused endless troubles, especially at the post stations[5] where they wanted to force more horses on us than we needed. The chief translator shared in the profit of this transaction, but the new arrangement has eliminated this extortion completely. The chief translator now gets a fixed sum from which he has to pay everything. The lower ranked translator is only in charge in the absence of the chief translator. From among the Dutch employees, the scribe and the doctor accompany the chief. Several days before departure, the chief, accompanied by the person who must replace him on Deshima during his absence, visits the governor of Nagasaki to say good-bye.

The journey itself proceeds in three stages: first, over the short country road, then over water[6], and thirdly over the long country road[7]. Heavy luggage is not transported over the first road, but is loaded 10 or 12 days before our departure on a Japanese barque which flies the Dutch flag with the Company's coat of arms and is festooned with the Dutch colors (red, white, and blue) while off shore.[8] The barque sails along the west coast of the island of Kyûshû where Nagasaki is situated, while the procession of the chief crosses the island on land to its north side. On the day of our departure, our cooks go ahead first with all their kitchen utensils so they can prepare the meals at our rest stops. Next to go are the gifts, trunks filled with our clothing and bed linen, and two crates filled with the most indispensible everyday household effects, as well as silk waist-cloths in the Dutch colors with the Company coat of arms in black, with which our overnight lodgings as well as our noon rest stops are decorated. This same custom also applies to the domain lords when they travel, and we are therefore put on the same footing as they are.[9]

The procession itself is also very carefully arranged and set up according to the Japanese way. Heading the procession are two train masters or guides who also make a path in case a crowd surrounds us. They are followed by two lower ranked banyos, each traveling in a small palanquin *(kago)* with two carriers, the lower ranked translator in a somewhat bigger *kago* with four carriers and accompanied by a servant on foot. Then comes the doctor preceded by his medicine chest. His palanquin is bigger than the previous one and already carries the name of *norimon*[10] . With some minor difference, it is similar to the *norimon* of the chief and of equal size. The doctor's *norimon* is also carried by four men, and accompanied by a servant who does not go on foot the whole way, but rides a horse in the afternoon while he is replaced by another servant on foot. By contrast, the carriers are never spelled and have to walk the whole length of the short country road, which takes seven days, and then do the same on the long road to Edo, which takes 15 to 16 days. They sometimes walk 15 to 16 hours per day! It seems inconceivable that they can endure this without days of rest. Yet I have noticed that, barely arrived in their night quarters, they bathe in hot, almost boiling water, and wash their feet with camphor brandy and hot water. Then the next day, at the crack of dawn, they walk the road again without any trouble.

The *norimon* and the office equipment of the scribe who follows the doctor is identical in every aspect to that of the physician. Next comes the office equipment, which consists of a kind of black lacquered, scarlet-red cloth covered table with silver inlay. It has a drawer that once, years ago, contained the imperial free trading pass that had been given to us. This is noted in writing on a tablet which, when Japanese crowd[11] around us, is shown to them. Invariably, the crowd will then respectfully give us room to proceed. Nowadays, this famous pass remains on Deshima and the chief uses the drawer for some other necessities.

The chief follows behind the office in his state *norimon* carried by eight men in dark blue uniforms emblazoned with the company's coat of arms in white. Two servants walk on each side of his *norimon*. In addition to his *norimon*, a small *chabentô*, or chest, is carried which has everything in it to serve tea, and it always includes boiling water. Warm tea is Japan's national drink to quench thirst, but the tea is very bad, nay almost undrinkable, in the inns. This tea is made in the morning by throwing some handfuls of the worst quality tea into a big iron *qualie*, a pot with a wide mouth and wooden lid. Water is then poured on the tea and left to boil the whole day long, after which it tastes more like a medicinal drink than a refreshing quaff. Only domain lords and rulers are allowed to carry a *chabentô*, which, like the coat of arms on uniforms, indicates the rank of the one carried. This again shows that the representatives of the Dutch nation in Japan are considered to be of the same rank as princes. The *norimons* that carry the chief and the other Dutchmen are the biggest ones available in Japan. They are about four to four and a half feet long, three to three and a half feet high, and very light. The inside is covered with gold paper, the ceiling is lacquered in black, and the two sides have sash windows of fine plaited bamboo. The sliding doors also have black lacquered sash windows, which are normally papered with fine Japanese paper, but for the *norimons* used by the Dutch they are made with Moscow glass. One can sit and rest comfortably in this *norimon* but not lie down. You can also write and smoke in them, and they are so well constructed that no implements can fall down when descending a mountain. The pole above the *norimon* which is borne by two men, one in front and one in back, is bent more or less, depending on the higher or lower rank of the occupant. Behind the chief, the strong box of the chief translator carried by two men follows, and behind them that official himself is carried by four men in a *kago*. Then come the lower ranked banyo and the chief banyo whose *kago* is the same as the chief translator's.

Beside the chief banyo, two men carry a small chest called a *yoroibako*. Normally it should contain a suit of armor but here it contains travel gear. Each evening, his Dutch fellow travelers and the Japanese officials await the chief at the entrance door of that night's rest stop. The chief banyo comes later, and is obligated to ask the chief whether he enjoyed the trip, or if he had experienced something disagreeable. It is also left to the chief at what time he wants to leave, and how far he wants to travel. During the journeys I made, I never had any quarrels with the Japanese officials, though that wasn't always the case in the past with previous Dutch chiefs. Some contend that the decrease in the Japanese trade of 1790 was due to the heated quarrels chief Romberg had during his Court trek. In my opinion, that is not correct as the decrease was caused by another chief.

The accommodations of the Dutch when they travel to the Court in Edo are the same as those given to the rulers and domain lords of the realm. The Japanese call these accommodations *honjin*[12]. The Japanese in the procession stay in small inns called *yadoya*. However, in the big cities of Kokura, Osaka, and Miyako, chief and lower banyos stay the night with us in the same inn, but the translators do not. Only in Edo does everyone in the procession stay together at night in the same place. When no *Honjin* are available to us, as sometimes happens, we are housed in temples, but never in *Yadoyas*. The daily treks are long. I often left three hours before day break and travelled until eight or nine in the evening before we arrived at our inn.

We travel this way until we reach Kokura, where we have to cross the strait that separates the island Kyûshû from the main island Nippon.[13] We usually do this on the day we arrive and then land in Shimonoseki. When the weather is bad, we cross from the little village of *dairi*, where the crossing is only a half mile wide. Our *norimons* are left at Kokura until we return, except for those of the translators and lower banyos which are loaded upon the barque. When in Shimonoseki, we are not assigned to an inn but stay at the house of one of the two regents then residing in town. They live in the most beautiful homes built in the Japanese taste and are sometimes wrongly called *hospes* (in the sense of innkeeper). They meet us as soon as we arrive on the beach and accompany us to their homes where they do everything to make our stay comfortable. Normally we stay there for a couple of days of rest, until the barque from Nagasaki that had left ahead of us joins us here. The luggage carried overland is then put on board and after the ship is made ready to accommodate us, we set sail.

Sometimes, strong head winds delay the departure for eight

days as happened to me once. We then amused ourselves and passed the time visiting some temples. Contrary to our custom, the Japanese consider the front end of the ship the best one. The chief's room is here and is very comfortably appointed. Across is the room of the physician and scribe, in which we eat together at noon. Only three rooms are available for the Japanese officials of which the chief banyo has one to himself.

Adverse winds frequently force the ship to go into a harbor between the islands of Kyûshû, Nippon, and the smaller island of Shikôkû, usually the harbors of Kamenoseky, Mitarai, or Tomo, and Muro[14]. If the weather cooperates, it takes six or seven days to reach Fiogo,[15] but once it took me seventeen days!

Upon landing, we find the *norimons* and the chief banyo's *kago* that will transport us over the long country road to Edo. Here too, the ancient custom requires that we do not arrive in the major cities late in the evening but in the afternoon. This is the reason why the journey from Fiogo to Osaka takes two instead of one day which would be possible. So we stay overnight in Isnomia[16] and arrive the next day in the early afternoon in Osaka, where our entry takes place with full pomp and ceremony as all the carriers are dressed in new outfits. We customarily stay three or four days in Osaka[17] and pass the time ordering different household goods for Deshima, to be picked up on our way back.

Each of the two governors of the city receives a gift from our government, usually a piece of cloth and some *Patnasche chitzen*.[18] Most often these gifts are presented when we're on our way to Edo, but the governors do not dare show these gifts publicly, but wait to do so when we return from Edo. In Osaka, there is also a guardian of the castle who ranks higher than the governor but who has nothing to do with city governance or us and therefore does not receive a gift from our government. He is solely in charge of guarding the famous castle where, in 1616, as I mentioned earlier, the *shôgun* Gongen was victorious over his pupil Fideiri, son of the famous Taiko and, according to some, killed him; others believe he fled to

Satsuma.

From Osaka, all our luggage is transported by boats on the river to Miyako, but we travel in our *norimons* to Fushimi and from there to Miyako[19] the next day.

In Miyako, the governor and the great-judge (as we call him) are notified of our arrival by the chief translator. We request a pass from the Great-Judge in order to get through the two big guardposts, in Arai and on the Hakone mountain. These three high officials also receive gifts from our government, but they only accept them openly upon our return from Edo. I mentioned once before that the palace of the Great-Judge stands right across from the gate of the *dairi's* castle and that he basically lives there to keep a very close eye on the *dairi*. The official pretext for this is to expedite any news that the *dairi* may want to impart to the *shôgun*. Here in Miyako, all luggage is again inspected and new sleighs are put under crates and wardrobes as the long country road starts here.[20]

We stay three or four days in Miyako and then move on. In *norimons* we go to Quana[21] where we have to cross a bay to Mia.[22] This crossing is sometimes so difficult, either because of low tide or bad weather, that it takes three hours to get to Saya, from where it is still seven miles overland to Mia. If tide and weather are favorable, the crossing straight to Mia takes four hours, which we of course prefer. From there, we go overland to Arai where the big guard post is situated which no one can pass without getting out of the *norimon*. Weapons and women (especially the latter when they come from the Edo side) can absolutely not pass without having very secure passes. I mentioned before the reason for this, as wives and daughters of princely rulers who are in the provinces have to stay behind in Edo as hostages. The most thorough inspection takes place here to see if there are women disguised as men among the travelers. The people of this province's prince (who is usually one of the government's councils), man this post and are under the command of one of the prince's highest officials. We normally stay overnight here in an inn close to the post and then leave the next day for a half mile boat trip across a small

RECOLLECTIONS OF JAPAN

bay. The boat is magnificent, red lacquered on the inside, black on the outside and besides, as fancy as our tent yachts.[23] The chief usually pays hommage to the commander of the guard for his ruler's courtesy. After crossing the bay, we land in Maisaka[24] from where we continue overland several days away from Arai. There we face the river Oigawa which is not navigable because of its strong currents. We are carried over this river by people who are trained to do this and who would surely pay with their lives if they had the misfortune to have one of their travelers drown!

After crossing the river, we arrive at the foot of the famous Mount Fuji which has a year around snow capped crown. A hamlet called Missima is there where we camp overnight . At six in the morning, we are carried up the mountain, arriving at the top only at two in the afternoon. We have lunch here in an inn that has a fantastic view over a big lake situated at the top of this mountain. The air here is very thin which is not good for the traveler who is not used to this.[25]

On this mountain top, not far from our inn, is the second imperial guard post. All our Japanese travel companions, even the chief banyo, have to pass this post on foot, but we Dutch can stay in our *norimons* and greet the guards by sliding the window back and forth as we pass, just as one would do in Europe by lowering the window. We stay overnight in Odowara, on the east side of the mountain and, after two days, we arrive in Kanagawa[26] where the host of our inn in Edo meets us. The next day, the chief translator leaves again ahead of us to notify the governor of Nagasaki in Edo and the two commissioners for foreigners of our impending arrival. We leave an hour later and usually arrive at about three in the afternoon in our inn[27] in the capital. We are carried into the city through a big gate and and adjoining passage that is very wide at the beginning but then narrows so much that our *norimons* can barely pass.

The rooms at the upper level of the house where we stay and from which we may not leave, only look out on a narrow street. There are two rooms for the chief, one each for the doctor and scribe, a common dining room where we also receive people, one room for the servants, and a small bathroom. The somber view and the idea that we *have* to stay inside, except for the days of the audience, make our stay not a particularly pleasant one. Everyone who is part of our retinue, even the carriers of our *norimons* and *kagos*, stay with us in the same inn and are basically, like ourselves, under house arrest until the *shōgun's* audience. Even the chief banyo, always a resident of Edo and a court official, may not leave the inn to see his wife or other family. Even his son, if he has one, can only come to him on the sly. After the audience however, he may visit his family two or three times a day but has to make sure that he's always back at the inn at night. After we have barely arrived at our lodgings, an official of the governor of Nagasaki visits us briefly to inquire whether we had any unpleasant experiences during our journey. The next day, the gifts are unpacked. The chief translator is responsible for all damage and would be jailed, if not dismissed from his job, would that have happened. Several years before, it happened that some *chitzen* got more or less wet, and because of that, the chief translator spent three months in jail! He requested this punishment himself in accordance with the custom of all officials in Japan. Whenever they make the slightest mistake in their jobs, whether through their own fault — inattention or mishap — or not, they immediately confess it fully to their superiors and request that they be jailed, fully convinced they would only make their case worse by blaming it on happenstance or accident.

As soon as the fabrics, like *chitzen*, sheet material, etc. which are not offered as gifts in bolts, are cut in pieces and the company's coat of arms is put at each end in red lacquer; as soon as the other presents are put in order and the display boards on which they must be presented are ready, everything is transported to the castle where they remain under the supervision of the governor of Nagasaki until the day of the solemn audience. That same day, we are officially welcomed in the name of the commissioners of the foreigners, by two gentlemen belonging to their household, and we request of them an expeditious hearing. Our forced residence at the inn is enlivened by the many people who come to sell their wares since we are totally free to buy here. One should however not buy lacquerware as it is much cheaper in Miyako, but silk and transparent crepe are the best here, especially the purple colored ones, the quality of which one cannot find anywhere else in this country. I don't believe their brilliant colors can be equalled in Europe. There is a prominent silk merchant here, a Mister Itsigoya, who also has shops in all the other big cities of Japan. When one buys something in his shop and takes it to another city, say Nagasaki, one can, if it is no longer desired and given that it is not damaged, return it to his shop there and get all the money you paid for it in Edo back without any deduction. Mr. Itsigoya sent us some five or six big chests with silk from which to chose. According to the following story, this man's wealth must be astonishing.

During one of my stays in Edo, there was a big fire, three hours in length and one and a half miles in width, which burned to ashes everything in the area, including our inn. In this fire, Itsigoya lost his shop and its inventory, as well as a warehouse with over 100,000 pounds of spun silk. This was a total loss for him as the Japanese know nothing about insurance. Nevertheless, he immediately sent us forty of his servants to assist us during this fire and they were indeed of great help. The second day after the fire, he was already rebuilding and paid every carpenter's help two *boontjes*[28] or about six guilders daily.

Talking about this fire, it may be of interest to give a short description of it. On April 22, 1806 at ten in the morning, we heard that there was a fire about two hours away from our inn. Nobody paid much attention, as here in Edo one is used to hearing the fire alarm. When the weather is nice, there is a fire somewhere every night and because there are less fires when it rains, the citizens of Edo are in the habit of congratulating each other when it does rain at night. However, the fire started to get closer and closer, and by three in the afternoon, the hard wind that blew the sparks in our direction caused fire to break out in four places around us. At around one o'clock we had already started to pack our belongings to be on the safe side, so we could now flee immediately as we were in imminent danger. Entering the street, we saw everything on fire. It seemed to us that walking ahead of the wind with the flames was very dangerous. We therefore walked obliquely into the wind through a street already on fire and thus managed to get behind the flame into an open field called *Hara*. It was everywhere staked out by little flags of the princes whose palaces had already burnt down and whose wives and children had taken refuge in the thus delineated areas. We followed their example and equally delineated an area with the little Dutch flags we use when crossing rivers. We now had an unimpeded view of the fire and I never saw anything so horrendous. The awful scene of this sea of fire was made worse by the heart-rending cries and moans of the fleeing women and children. We were safe here for the moment, but we had nowhere to stay. The governor of Nagasaki, Fita Bungo No Kami, who was staying in Edo, had been fired, and the house of his successor who was named that same day, had already been reduced to ashes. We were billeted therefore in the house of the governor now stationed in Nagasaki which stood way at the other side of Edo.

We arrived at half past ten that night and were very graciously received by the governor's son who supplied us with everything we needed. The next day around noon, heavy rains doused the fire. We learned from our innkeeper who visited us that only five minutes after we had left, the flames had reached his house and destroyed everything, as he had not been able to salvage any goods or household items. To help him out, our government sent him as a gift twenty *kanassen*[29] of sugar for three years. The innkeeper also told us that 57 palaces of princes were destroyed and that 1,200 people, including the small daughter of the ruler of Awa, were either burned or drowned. The latter happened when the *Nippon Bas*,[30] a big and famous bridge in Edo from which distances to several places in the realm are calculated, collapsed under the weight of the fleeing masses. Those still on land were unaware of this and in their

RECOLLECTIONS OF JAPAN

frantic efforts to escape the fire, they pushed those ahead of them into the water. Truly a terrible day![31]

No matter how politely we had been received in the house of the governor of Nagasaki, the fact was that we were less free there than in our inn, and therefore we tried our very best to find another suitable one. After four days, we thanked the governor's son for his hospitality and departed for our new residence which was situated in a very agreeable spot indeed. The back of the house came out onto the big river which bisects Edo and it was the fourth house of one of the bridges *(Riokoki-bashi)* which spans this big river and on which many people pass. We really gained in cheerfulness by having such a view! From a projection or balcony built behind our inn, we frequently looked down upon a constant coming and going of people. Their numbers were augmented by the many who were curious about us,[32] but given the distance, that didn't bother us. However, it caused consternation with some people. The governor of Edo, by way of the subtranslator Saiyemon, sent word to me that, from now on, we were not to show ourselves on that spot again, because it attracted many curious people who wished to see us. I immediately requested to see the chief banyo who had accompanied us on our trek and conveyed to him my surprise that I had received such a message from the governor of Edo and not from the governor of Nagasaki.[33] The latter was really the only one to give all orders and messages to the Dutch during the whole trek, as he alone had the right to do so. The chief banyo, on behalf of the governor, had told me this numerous times, adding that I should not obey any other orders. I therefore made an urgent request that the governor of Nagasaki be informed of this. Appealing to the latter's authority turned out to be fruitful indeed. The next day already, the governor of Nagasaki, through the same chief banyo, sent word that he totally approved of my behavior and granted me and my compatriots the liberty to use this balcony without being disturbed, and ever since we have done so without incident. The governor even increased our comfort and pleasure by having a certain square cleaned up! From this, you can really glean how necessary it is to know Japanese customs well. Had we immediately obeyed the governor of Edo, we would not only have deprived ourselves of a pleasure, but perhaps offended the governor of Nagasaki which, given the need for our many relations with him, could have been detrimental to us in the future.

Several days after this, we learned that the solemn audience with the *shôgun* would take place on May the third, the 28th day of the third Japanese month *Sanguats*[34]. This occasion requires a prescribed attire; velvet for the chief, cloth braided or embroidered in gold or silver for the doctor and scribe. The chief also wears a velvet cloak, the doctor and scribe black satin ones which they only put on when they enter the palace's inner sanctum. Only the chief has the privilege of having his sword carried behind him in a black velvet pocket.[35] No one else, neither the doctor nor the scribe, nor any other official or ship's officer, can keep his side arms in Japan. As soon as they arrive by ship, they have to hand them over as well as their rifles. Thunberg, in his book *Voyages* (Volume III, pg. 125) is mistaken when he writes: "le ceremonial exigeait que nous cussions nos épées" — the ceremony required that we sheath our swords. At six in the morning on the designated day, we went to the palace in order to be there before the arrival of the government council. We were carried in our *norimons* into the castle and to the gate of the palace where also all the rulers have to step out of their palanquins. Only the three royal princes, the rulers of Owari, Kyûshû, and Mito are carried to the gate in front of the hundred-men strong guard post. We reach this guard post on foot and stay there until the arrival of councillors of state. We had to sit on small benches covered with small red tapestries, and we were offered tea and materials for smoking. We then watched the governor of Nagasaki, accompanied by one of the chief snoops or commissioner general of foreigners enter the palace, after he has congratulated us with the impending meeting with the *shôgun*. The commander of the guard post also comes to pay a visit to the chief. It is necessary here to stand rigidly upon one's rank. He wanted me

RECOLLECTIONS OF JAPAN

to move from the back room which is considered to be the most honorable one, to the front room adjacent to it since his lower rank did not permit him to go into the back room. From my side, I claimed that it was not possible for me to leave my designated highest place. The commander thus approached me at about a distance of two *mats* (about twelve feet) to greet me. By sticking to my guns in this matter, which one always *has* to do in Japan when in the right, I ensured the observance of the old customs, the restoration of which would be exceedingly difficult if, by agreeing, one ever gives in.

After all the government councillors had entered, we also were asked to enter the palace where we were received by several people, all with shaven heads who could be considered pages called *boosen*[36] by the Japanese. These *boosen* brought us to a waiting room where we sat down with our legs on the floor in a diagonal direction, and covered our feet with our cloaks, as it is extremely rude in Japan to show them. After a short waiting period, I was escorted by the governor of Nagasaki and the commissioner of foreigners into the audience hall where I first had to rehearse the required ceremonial acts because, if something didn't go right, the governor would pay the penalty. Then I was escorted back to the waiting hall. A short while later, I went for real now with the governor to the audience hall from which we had already seen several grandees return. Through a wooden gallery, I was escorted to the *hall with the hundred mats*,[37] so called because it is truly covered with a hundred mats each six *ikje* (six feet) long and three *ikje* wide. The mats are made of straw, around two thumbs thick and over them are laid other mats of a finer texture. All the halls have these mats. Leaving the chief translator in this hall, I went alone with the governor of Nagasaki into the audience hall where I found the presents at my left hand side. The *shôgun*, or emporer, whose clothes were almost indistinguishable from those of his subjects, was there. I paid my respects in the same manner as all the princes of the realm do, whereupon one member of the government council introduced me by calling out: *Oranda Kapitan*[38]. After this, the governor of Nagasaki who stood a few feet behind me pulled at my cloak to indicate that the audience was over. The whole ceremony took at most one whole minute. As we still had to stay for a while in the palace, we took the opportunity to look at the interior. There is no splendor whatsoever, no furnishings; all the halls have sliding doors, painted and papered with gold in the Japanese fashion, and provided with gilded handles to open and close them. These handles are the only luxury in this big hollow palace. The vastness of the halls and the whole building, the prevailing aura of gloom and the unreal silence amongst such a vast number of people; all this inspires a reverence far more spine-tingling than in more sumptuous palaces. From the palace of the shôgun, we went to the one of the crown prince which is built in the same style as that of the *shôgun*. As the crown prince wasn't home, we were quickly admitted for an audience by the government councillors especially designated for this purpose. The ordinary and extraordinary government councillors whom we also went to visit to offer our gifts were not home, but everywhere we were very politely received by a secretary who offered us tea and sugar pastries. The latter are presented on small wooden plates, but you do not touch them; they are wrapped in paper and closed with a silver or gold cord and then carried home in lacquered boxes (which the under translator and innkeeper did for us). Behind the paper screens, we heard the wives and children of the councillors who espied us out of curiosity. That they do not show themselves in the room is not because women in Japan are not allowed to show themselves as in Turkey, but because this could cause too much fraternization with the foreigners.

The next day we visited the temple guardians (the fact that these persons reside in Edo is again proof of what I mentioned before; namely that the *shôgun* also has authority over religious matters). We never found the guardians at home, but we were received in the same way as we were by the council members, albeit in a less grand style. Next, we had to pay a visit to the governors of Edo, but we were exempted from having to pay a visit to the commissioners of foreigners. The former, of

RECOLLECTIONS OF JAPAN

whom one governs over the eastern, and the other over the western part of Edo, received us in person and treated us, according to Japanese custom, to a warm meal and *sake*, a rice wine. This time, we traversed a big part of Edo, but it is difficult to establish how big Edo really is. Thunberg, who estimated it to be twenty-one hours walking in circumference, did not exaggerate. The number of people constantly coming or going is unbelievable, and the constant bustle assaults sight and hearing. The castle which I, like Thunberg, estimate to be five hours walking in circumference, lies above this big city and is surrounded by canals. The inner part is composed of the palaces of the *shôgun* and the crown prince, the rest is inhabited by princely rulers and government councillors. Their wives and children are kept there in perpetuity as hostages.[39] Before the audience with the *shôgun*, no Japanese, other than those who have official dealings with us, can visit us, but afterwards, the personal physicians and stargazers of the *shôgun* usually ask us for an appointment individually three times. Those visits are very cumbersome because of the pomp and ceremony, but one cannot help but admire the patience and attention with which they anticipate the answers to their multiple questions which give evidence of great eagerness for knowledge. Their craving for everything that concerns medicine and knowledge of medicinal plants knows no bounds, and our physician has to have all his wits about him on such an occasion, as they frequently ask him questions which they have prepared way in advance and which he has to answer immediately. The questions of the astronomers were immediately directed to the chief, which was often very difficult for him, because he couldn't answer their questions since he was not trained in that science. It is indeed admirable that one can find among the Japanese, people who learn as much as they do about astronomy. A Chinese can at least find teachers among the missionaries in Peking, but a Japanese has barely any source except some Dutch books like the translation of LaLande's[40] *Astronomia* from which he is able to calculate very accurately the solar or lunar eclipses. In 1810, I came to know and became very friendly with the first astronomer Takahashi Sampei. All these men usually come around two in the afternoon and stay until the evening. We receive them as politely as possible and treat them to liqueurs and candied fruits.

The farewell audience is seldom postponed more than three or four days after the first audience. The ceremonies are completely the same as the first ones, except for the fact that this time the government councillors and not the *shôgun* receives us in the hall of the hundred mats. The governor of Nagasaki reads the usual orders to the Dutch, which mostly consists of this:

'From times gone by, the Dutch are allowed to come to Japan; if they want to continue coming, they have to abstain from proselytizing the Christian faith in Japan. Would they learn of any attacks or enterprises of foreigners against Japan, they should immediately inform the governor of Nagasaki. They will not accost Chinese junks sailing to and from Japan, but let them sail freely. They will equally let the *Liqueers*,[41] as subjects of Japan, sail freely."

After the reading of this order (which otherwise, when the chief is in Nagasaki, takes place every year at the government house when the ships are ready to depart), the chief leaves for a while. When he returns to the hall, he receives a counter gift from the *shôgun* consisting of thirty silk ceremonial dress coats; he then leaves again and comes back to receive twenty dress coats from the crown price, whereupon he crosses the waiting hall and goes home. In the afternoon, officials for the government councillors, the temple magistrates, the governors of Edo, and commissioners of the foreigners present us, in the name of their masters, with several silk dress coats which are of lesser quality than those of the *shôgun* and crown prince and only quilted with cotton. The first mentioned royal coats were traditionally sent to the High Government in Batavia; the others are for the chief who gives most of them away to the

Japanese officials who accompany him on the trek to the Court. He only keeps a few for himself. The counter gifts for the officials who come to bring these dress coats are candied fruit, a paper with Dutch tobacco, and two Gouda pipes.

After all these audiences and visits, we did not stay much longer in Edo, where we were more or less sequestered. Before starting on my story of our return trek, I need to comment on the notion of some people that we gave Dutch names to several Japanese, our innkeeper and his servants among them. The case is thus: neither the innkeeper nor his servants carry Dutch names; the name of the former is Nagasakaya Gennemon, but some other Japanese have indeed jokingly received Dutch names from us.[42] During my first trek to Edo in 1806, I met a man in Miyako who spoke a bit of broken Dutch. He told me he lived in Edo where he always was in the habit of paying his respects to the Dutch. There, chief Romberg had given him the nickname of Adriaan Pauw.[43] Feeling that he had carried that name long enough, this man asked me for another name. I fulfilled his desire and called him Frederick van Gulpen, a name that pleased him no end.

During my second trek to Edo in 1810, I met a Dutch translator[44] in Edo who had been my pupil in Nagasaki but had been summoned to Edo by the Court in 1808. This very alert young man's name was in reality Baba Sazuro, but he had received the nickname of Abraham from the Dutch on Deshima. This made several people in Edo who were studying Dutch eager to also get a Dutch nickname, and it was this Abraham who requested that I give nicknames to some of his friends. The first one for whom he requested a nickname was the first court astronomer and scholar Takahashi Sampei under whose administration Abraham was at that time. I met this astronomer for the first time that year. He visited me daily in secret as a friend. Although his personal appearance was on first sight less than fetching, I soon got to know him not only as a very capable, but also as a kind and soft-hearted man with whom I forged an even closer friendship in 1814. He in turn gave me, when I left Japan in 1817, clear indications of his affection. His gracious and at the same time solid character gained him so much respect at the Court, that he was sent to Matsumae as *Ginmiyak* (commissioner or investigator) into the Golownin affair. In the writings of that Russian sailor, Takahashi Sampei, as well as Abraham (Baba Sazuro) are mentioned. I felt embarrassed to give such a distinguished gentlemen a nickname, but he himself insisted for such a long time, that I finally chose for him the name of Johannes Globius[45]. At his own insistence, I couldn't think of a better name to give one of the first personal physicians of the *shôgun*, Katsuragawa Hoan, who assiduously studied not only our language but herbal medicine as well,[46] than Johannes Botanicus. In his book, Thunberg mentioned his grandfather. I bestowed the name Pieter van der Stolp on the secretary[47] of the ruler of Nakatsu, second son of the old prince of Satsuma, father-in-law of the *shôgun*. In turn, his master, the aforementioned ruler of Nakatsu, did not stop insisting, yea literally forced me to give him a nickname as well. I finally gave him the name of Frederik Hendrik.[48] These are all the Japanese people with Dutch names when I left Japan. The above story shows sufficiently both *how* they got those names *and* how wrongly such a minor thing gets so blown up.

Even less credible is the story of Golownin, in his book *Adventures in Japan* (Vol. I, pg. 262), that a certain Dutchman by the name of Laxman would have settled in Edo for a certain amount of money and decided never to return to his country. During my three visits to Edo, in 1806, 1810, and 1814, nay during all my nineteen-year residence in Japan, have I ever heard the name Laxman mentioned. Never during our period has a Dutchman decided to stay in Japan, and never would the Japanese have given such a permission to a Dutchman. Let us now return to our story.

On our return trek, we followed the same route as when we came, observing also the same ceremonial acts at the imperial guard post at the Hakone mountains, as well as at Arai. The next day or two days after having arrived in Miyako, we solemnly offered our gifts to the chief judge and the two governors which they, just like the governor of Osaka, did not dare accept openly during our procession. We were received in the same way as by the government councillors and governors in Edo. As a return gift, the chief received from the chief judge three silk garments and from each of the governors three silver *schuitjes*,[49] each worth four *tael* and three *maas*. We usually stay about four days in Miyako in order to buy merchandise best found there.

Although not as big as Edo, this city is nevertheless quite substantial and is considered the healthiest city in all of Japan. On the day of our departure, we usually visit some temples on route. Among the most important is the temple of the 33,333 idols[50] and also the temple *Giwon*. In small tents erected at the latter, we were treated to finely chopped white beans called *toof (tofu)*. At first, it doesn't taste good, but you get used to it. The crowd of curiosity seekers who gather at such an occasion to see the Dutch is unbelievably big, and I have never, not in Europe nor in the Indies, seen such a crowd of people at any ceremony.[51] In olden days, one could also admire there the big and famous temple *Daybeets*,[52] but a raging fire destroyed it.

From Miyako we go to Fushimi, from whence we go to Osaka in a flat bottomed boat. This boat neither sails nor is pulled, but just drifts with the rapid current. The doctor and scribe leave at night in another boat in which beds are made ready for them. Very early the next day we arrive in Osaka where, just as in Miyako, we only now present our gifts to the governors who treated us in return to a splendid meal. We also visited there the race track of one of the governors and a copper refinery which Thunberg also accurately describes. At the end of the audience, the chief throws a merry party for the Japanese officials in a tea house called Wukasimi. It always was a party full of joyful gaiety which I still remember with pleasure.

Osaka, which is not nearly as large as Edo but no less busy, is correctly considered to be the staple-town and the center of trade from all the regions of the realm. All that we or the Chinese import is brought here, and there is an abundance of everything to be had. Osaka is also where the most money is, and where most of the biggest merchants live. However, it is not a very salubrious place, and the water is not considered safe to drink. In Osaka, we receive several articles which we already had ordered when we first passed through and which are far cheaper here than in Nagasaki, especially a daily need such as rice. After three or four days here, we float down the river in the same boats to Amagasaki, and from there in our *norimons* over Isnemia to Fiogo[53] where all our purchases are put on board. That same day, we leave to go over Shimonoseki to Kokura. If we arrive in the afternoon in the former place, we stay overnight and often purchase charcoal, one of the prime needs in Japan, which is cheaper there than in Nagasaki. From Kokura, we take the same short land road previously described and, close to Nagasaki and Deshima, our translators and acquaintances come to meet us and welcome us back. Once back in Deshima, the chief banyo immediately congratulates us on our successful trek.

In 1806, I was unfortunate enough to get sick while on the long land road. A severe colic caused me the most accute pain. On the strong insistence of the Japanese, I decided to have them stick me with needles as they are used to doing. When one sees a representation of this procedure in Kaempfer's book, one would really be scared of this cure, but I, who underwent it, must confess that this mode of treatment has nothing terrifying about it. A needle made of the purest gold and as fine as a hair is deftly pushed through a sheath with a finger there where it is deemed necessary. As soon as the needle slightly penetrates the skin, the sheath is removed, and the needle is coaxed in deeper with the finger. When deemed deep enough into the skin, the tip of the needle is rotated back and forth between the fingers. This causes a prickling in the nerves, which is all one feels. The sticking of the skin and the needle being coaxed in deeper are hardly felt at all, and it does not leave a wound or scar, nor does it draw blood. Although this procedure did not take away the cause of my colic, it nevertheless gave me relief for quite some time.

I never had any quarrels whatsoever with the chief banyos

who accompanied me during the three times I went on this trek. With those that accompanied me on the last two treks, and until the death of one (*Sanise Tozuro*), I forged a strong bond of friendship that lasted until my departure from Japan.

Several days after our return, the barque carrying our goods also appears and is unloaded. At this occasion, the chief once again entertains the chief banyo. Several days later, the chief pays a visit to the governor of Nagasaki, which ends all the ceremonies attached to the Court journey.

Doeff was chief from 1803-1817.
Keiga Kawahara (c. 1786-c 1869)
Kobe City Museum, Kobe, Japan.

CHAPTER IV

My Further Stay in Japan Until My Departure in 1817

Shortly after my return from Edo in 1806, the hired American ship *America* under Captain Henry Lelar, as well as the Bremer ship *Visurgis* under Captain G. Herklots arrived. Due to the continuing war, I again had a much unwanted cargo on my hands for which I still (but with great difficulty) received a rather decent return cargo. In June of 1807, news arrived that a ship had been sighted. It was too early in the year for the arrival of our ships,[1] but we soon received from a Japanese ship a note written in very broken Dutch from which we gleaned that the ship requested water and other provisions which it lacked. Subsequently, as is the custom, a note from the governor of Nagasaki requested that I, together with a commission of chief banyos, go out to the ship to gather the necessary information. It soon turned out that the ship flew an American flag, and we went on board. I do not remember the name of the captain, but the ship, if I remember correctly, was called *Eclipse*.[2] The captain asked me to intercede with the Japanese Government in order to get water and wood for stoking. On his way from Canton to the north-west coast of America, the captain had struggled with adverse winds for 43 days, and was in need of those provisions. On my urgent intercession with the Japanese and strong affirmative answer to their question whether it was truly an American ship (which, from the papers I had read, left no doubt), his request was granted the next day. He was then ordered to leave the shores of the realm with the utmost speed. The captain wanted to pay for the provisions, but the Japanese refused to accept anything. The next day, the ship set sail for the open seas. There was a woman from the Sandwich Islands on board this ship whose name was Cariabo. She had quite a presence and was not at all bad looking were it not for the fact that her whole face was tattooed, something that surprised the Japanese who came on board quite a bit.

On July 22, 1807, the American ship *Mount Vernon*, which we had hired, arrived under the command of Captain John Davidson. On board was Mr. Hendrik Voorman, sea captain in the colonial service. Before the American ship, another hired one, the Danish boat *Susanna* under the command of Captain Ditmar Smit, had already arrived and had brought us the news that Louis Napoleon had become King of Holland.[3] I immediately informed the Japanese of this. In this year, I had the pleasure of receiving in the cargo genuine Leiden sheets, which had not happened since 1795. As the natives ascribed this arrival to my good care, the regents of Nagasaki, out of gratitude, offered me a hundred gold *kobans*, which they themselves handed to me. Apart from the troubles I had with the always drunken and difficult captain Davidson, and with the previously mentioned Captain Stewart (of whom I still have doubts that he was an American), I recognize with pleasure that the American captains with whom I had dealings, J. Devereux, W. V. Hutchings, S. Derby, G. Stiles, J. Deal, and Lelar (who was, however, Dutch born) always presented themselves as honest and very decent men who brought honor to their country.

That year, the *Mount Vernon* brought three Japanese whose boat had been shipwrecked east of Japan. They and three other compatriots had been picked up by an American ship sailing from the north-west coast of America to Canton where they were put ashore. The Chinese, however, did not want to have anything to do with these people, nor were they willing to send them to Japan, claiming that there was no navigation between the harbor of Canton and Japan. The Dutch chief in Canton then shipped these six people to Batavia, where three of them died; but the other three arrived in Japan from Batavia. One of them died the same night the ship anchored in Japan; I myself delivered the two others to the chief banyos, who put them under strict supervision, just like they had done with the Japanese Mr. de Rezanov had brought.

Once the trading season was over, I sent both ships back with a good cargo of camphor and copper at the usual time. Captain Smit arrived safely in Surabya, but Captain Davidson suffered a leak in his ship, had to throw copper over board, and finally managed, although with great danger, to enter Macao in China. There, other misfortunes befell him. An armed sloop of the English war ship *Discovery* boarded his ship[4] and wanted to confiscate it as the cargo was Dutch owned. Hendrik Voorman, Maarten Mak, and Age Iges, the Dutch officials who happened to be on board, immediately called for the help of the Portuguese government, as the ship had already passed the batteries. That government did us a great service at that time. It sent a contingent of soldiers on board which forced the English to let us keep the cargo which, as the ship was declared unseaworthy, had to stay with Dutch officials in Canton.

1807 was the last year that hired ships entered Deshima. At this point, I should mention that we truly had a lot of difficulty in the beginning in making clear to the Japanese that the Americans were *not* English because, years ago, they had learned that North America was an English colony. As they had never heard the news of their declaration of independence, they could not understand that the Americans were not the same people. Once we gave them an exact account of this event, their objections disappeared. Golownin is greatly mistaken when he writes in the first part of his book *Adventures in Japan* (pg. 305), that the cargo brought us by the Americans had to be sent back again. He's also wrong in stating that it was English cargo, and it is equally untrue that those American ships were turned away from the harbor by the Japanese. I've not been able at all to find the motive for this fairy tale.

Some time before the departure of our ships, rumors reached us about hostilities committed by Russian ships on the north-east coast of Japan. Several days later, the governor of Nagasaki officially informed me of this, and also asked me what my thoughts were. I answered that I could not understand it. After all, the answer Mr. de Rezanov received after six months — quite a long time according to custom — had been so mild and diffident, that I could not believe it could have lead to hostilities on the part of the Russians. I assumed therefore that this whole matter had probably been a mistake, that something had happened, perhaps between the crew of one or another Russian ship and the coastal people. However, the translators claimed that they were *armed* ships, which captured several Japanese and also several cannons, etc. They also left some papers behind, the content of which was not known to them. However, the governor speedily dispatched two translators to Edo. After several days, other translators showed me a paper written in Russian with the flags of the Russian navy and merchant fleet drawn on the bottom. As I didn't know Russian, I could not translate this paper, but the next day I received another paper written in French which was not signed, and was directed to the governor of Matsumae. Since the Japanese knew that I understood French,[5] I could not very well decline the request of the governor of Nagasaki that I translate this paper with the utmost accuracy, and as verbatim as possible.[6] I proceeded to translate it into Dutch, but attenuated the expressions as much as possible. I found my translation in the second part of Golownin's book (pg. 105) and thus am able to put it here. The letter goes as follows: "The close proximity of Russia and Japan gave rise to the wish to establish closer trade relations between these two countries which could benefit the subjects of Japan in particular. With that goal in mind, an embassy was sent to Nagasaki, but the insulting and negative answer as well as the expansion of trade by the Japanese on the Kuril and Sachalin islands which are considered Russian possessions, forced the ruler of Russia to take steps that will prove without a doubt that the Russians can harm Japanese trade for however long it takes until the inhabitants of Grup or Sachalin shall be informed that the Japanese seriously want to engage in trade with us. By these mild measures against Japan, the Russians only want to make it known that the northern part of Japan is always exposed to their arbitrariness, and that the Japanese could lose these territories if their government continues its refusal to trade."

I'm truly sorry that the original French document is not published in Golownin's book; from that piece one could have gleaned the mild terminology I used in my translation. There is one sentence though, at the end, which I remember in its entirety: "Et qu'un plus long entêtement du gouvernement du Japon leur peut faire perdre leurs terres." If I had translated this correctly I should have used the word *stubbornness*[7] or *willfulness* of the Japanese government. Fearing that this could only engender more bitterness and do more harm than good, it seemed better to me, provided every thing in the sentence remained the same, to chose the mildest expressions to calm rather than rile Japanese sensibilities, and thereby prevent misfortunes as much as I could.

The translators left with my translation and informed me that the Russian paper had been translated by other Dutch translators who, during de Rezanov's stay in Japan, had learned Russian, and that their translations corresponded to mine. I was also consulted about the two flags drawn at the bottom of the Russian letter. I expressed my ignorance, but told the Japanese that I thought they meant to indicate the difference between Russian war flags and merchant flags. The translators kept coming back to say how puzzled they were about the Russian government's actions, as the answer on their part had been so polite. I answered that it possibly came about because of an altercation between the Russian coastal people and Japanese fishermen. The Japanese decided to accept this explanation, even though they couldn't correlate it with the papers that had come from higher up. Because of my good offices in this as well as in the case of the Russian Embassy, I received as a token of gratitude from the Japanese government a gift of thirty silver *schuitjes* in April 1808. At the same time, the wish of the Court was conveyed to me; that I investigate in Europe whether the Russian hostilities, which I had mentioned before, had been ordered by the Emperor of Russia.

In 1803, I had been allowed to export another 2,520 *pikols* of copper on top of the allotted 6,000 *pikols*. I certainly took advantage of this extra allowance at that time and now once again, at my request, an extra allotment of 1,466 *pikols* was granted for the next three years.

Otherwise, the year 1808 was a very fateful one. No ships of ours arrived, but the arrival of a foreign frigate caused many difficulties, and finally the death of the governor of Nagasaki and many other Japanese. Let me explain what happened.

In the beginning of October 1808, authorities in Nagasaki learned that a European ship was within sight. As the time of arrival of our ships had long passed, I assumed that when our Japan bound ships were ready to depart at the normal time, enemy ships close to Batavia had perhaps held up their departure. As is the custom, the governor of Nagasaki requested that I delegate two commissioners to go with the chief banyos to investigate that ship and see if it was Dutch or not. I complied, and the two commissioners left that same afternoon at two o'clock. I was quite indisposed that day and in bed, but great curiosity and worry compelled me to leave my bed and go into the gardens of the house I was living in. From there I saw, towards the evening, a ship sail around the Papenberg and anchor shortly thereafter. Going out into the street, I could only gather that it was a Dutch ship, as the Dutch flag was flying at its usual place, and *not* a Russian flag, as Golownin falsely claims (op. cit, Vol. I, pg. 104). Soon, two translators brought me the results of the commissioner's report. From afar, they were already convinced that it was a Dutch ship, which really pleased them. The ship lowered its sloop, which was rowed to our boat. The quarter master spoke in Dutch to our delegates, Dirk Gozeman and Gerrit Schimmel, and invited them to step over into his sloop to be rowed to the ship. Barely had the accountant Gozeman (later warehouse master) answered that they would do so as soon as the chief banyos, who were still a bit behind, had arrived, then an unintelligible call was heard. Immediately thereafter, the rowers of the sloop, revealing swords that they had hidden in the boat, grabbed the Dutch delegates by force (Schimmel even lost his hat), and brought both of them in the sloop to their ship. One can imagine the consternation of the translators and chief banyos when they witnessed such a treatment of the Dutch in Japanese territory by a ship carrying the Dutch flag. I now was sure that it was an English ship, even though I couldn't imagine the reason why an English ship sailing under our flag would come here to commit hostilities. I immediately had the chest that contains the imperial pass brought to me, and had all the government's silver packed in order to safeguard them quickly if necessary. In the meantime, I received news that the governor of Nagasaki had not kindly received the chief banyos who had sailed out with the Dutch delegates, and had ordered them to immediately go out to sea again and to not come back unless accompanied by the two Dutchmen. The governor asked me if I thought the ship was Dutch, and if I saw a way to get the two Dutchmen freed. I had to respond negatively to the first question, and tell him that I thought the ship was an English one. Concerning the second question, I replied that I would notify the commander of the ship in a letter that the two men were not soldiers but civil employees, and that I requested their immediate release. I had no doubt that this would happen. I then heard confused cries that boats were approaching the island and that the Dutch had to go immediately to the government house in Nagasaki. We obeyed, bringing the above-mentioned items with us. In the city, everything was in a state of terrible confusion and chaos. The governor was in an indescribable rage, specifically aimed at the chief banyos, because they had come back not only *without* our compatriots, but also without knowing what kind of ship they were dealing with. Before I could ask him yet another question, he told me, full of fury: "Don't worry, chief, I will get you back your Dutchmen." The translators also assured me that the governor fully intended to keep his word even if, in doing so, he would have to go against the laws of the land. I observed that everyone was being outfitted and armed to defend themselves or, if need be, to capture the ship. To his immense chagrin, the governor learned that the imperial guard posts between the Papenberg and Nagasaki, which were supposed to be manned at all times by a thousand men (who the prince of Hizen had to deliver), at this moment had only sixty or seventy men. Even the commanders were not at their posts. This terrified the governor, because he could predict from this the fate that awaited him. Around eleven in the morning, a short note written on board in the well known hand of assistant Schimmel arrived containing only this: "A ship has arrived from Bengal; the captain's name is Pellew, and he requests water and provision." In the name of the governor, I was again consulted whether it would be alright to fulfill this request. My answer was that I was now sure that the ship was English, and that I could therefore not fulfil this request of the captain, as we were still at war with England.[8] (I understood however that the governor would have liked to have seen this request granted.) Not until midnight did the governor finally respond. His first secretary summoned me and informed me that he had an order to get the Dutch off the ship. To my question as to how he envisioned doing this, he replied, "Just as the ship treacherously imprisoned the Dutch, so I will try alone, without any retinue, to board the ship with the strongest expressions of friendship, and ask to speak with the captain in order to get the Dutch back. If the answer is negative, I will, with a hidden dagger, first stab the captain and then myself." He added that assassination basically went against the Japanese character, but that he considered the captain worthless because he had treacherously and surreptitiously committed hostilities on their territory under the Dutch flag. For this reason, he (the first secretary) would gladly sacrifice his life. Astonished by such a courageous but also desperate decision, I made the secretary understand that he not only forfeited his life if he did this, but that the Dutch, on whose behalf he would do this, would without a doubt be hanged by the English. The secretary could not understand why I advised against him doing this, and stuck by his decision.[9] Worried over this, I sent word to the governor that I wanted to speak with him. Informed of my objections, the governor was convinced like I was that this plan could not provide freedom for our compatriots. The plan, then, was no longer a consideration. I rather extensively write about what transpired between me and the secretary only to show how prodigal a Japanese is with his own life when it is a question of following an order.[10] Without a doubt, the secretary would have executed his intention if I had not persuaded the governor otherwise.

The governor's plan now was to keep the ship from sailing away until all the ships and people summoned from the neighboring princes had arrived, and then to forcefully capture the English ship. The night passed, and in the morning one could see goods being hoisted onto the ship. Later on, I learned that they were the cannon balls with which the armed sloops that had sailed in the bay to look for Dutch ships the night before had been provided. Around nine in the morning the English flag was hoisted, confirming my suspicion.

In the meantime, the Japanese put everything in a state of defense[11] and also occupied our island, Deshima. Everything was a bit confused, however, which is quite understandable for a population that for two centuries now had lived in peace. During this time, the two chief banyos *who could not return without the two Dutch hostages*, sailed around the English ship in a small vessel and tried, in polite words, to achieve their freedom, but it was to no avail. Around eleven in the morning, a sloop with four sailors on board sailed from the English ship to Nagasaki. Later I learned that the captain himself was in that sloop. If this crew fell into my hands, it would be easy to arrange an exchange with our people; if, however, they fell into Japanese hands, their lives would be in jeopardy given the state of excitement the Japanese people were in and that, in turn, would probably also cost both of our compatriots their lives. I was therefore much relieved when the sloop, sighting a Japanese vessel, rowed back to its ship.

Finally, at around four in the afternoon I saw my bookkeeper Gozeman again. He told me the following: As soon as they had been brought on board the English ship, they had asked to see the captain. A young man, about 18 or 19 years of age, was pointed out to them as the captain. He first brought them to his cabin and then asked, *under threat of death* if they didn't tell the truth, whether there were Dutch ships in Japan. They had truthfully replied that no Dutch ships had arrived this year, but the captain didn't believe them, as a Portuguese ship coming from Batavia had informed him otherwise and said that *the Dutchmen were lying*.

The captain then told them that he would investigate this himself and that, if the contrary appeared true, their lives would be finished[12]. Thereupon, the captain left, leaving the two men behind with two guards. The Dutchmen learned from some English officers that the captain was rowing around the bay to look for Dutch ships. They also learned that Mr. Daendels was now Governor General in Batavia. Back on board, the captain told his two prisoners that they were lucky he had found them to be telling the truth. The two prisoners now insisted upon being released, but they were instead shown a place to sleep. The next day they again asked for their release, and the captain then sent Gozeman to shore to request water and provisions. Gozeman asked to be authorized to do this in writing. Everything that transpired between him and the captain had to be translated by a sailor by the name of Metzeler, who spoke Dutch. This man also translated the note the captain dictated to him, which in essence contained the following: "I let Gozeman be put on shore in my own sloop to get water and provisions and if he doesn't return with them on board *before nightfall*, then I will sail into the harbor at the crack of dawn and set fire to Japanese ships and Chinese junks." The note was signed by the captain, Fleetwood Pellew. In addition, Gozeman received an oral warning from the captain to get back with or without provisions *otherwise Schimmel would be hanged without mercy*! Gozeman was then put by boat on a cliff from which he hailed a Japanese boat to come and get him.

Fortunately, Gozeman had a good enough command of the Japanese language to make himself understood, because otherwise no native would have dared to take him. He came to shore, and I brought the note to the governor, who jumped up in rage and regret after reading about the threat. He asked me if I could give him assurance that the Dutch delegates would be freed if the demands of the English were satisfied. My reply was that I could not give him a *sure and certain* answer but that it would be probable, as one has to take an officer at his word, and the captain *had* given his word to Gozeman. The governor then decided to send the requested provisions, but very little water in hopes of retarding the ship's departure. He also did not want Gozeman to return immediately to the ship "as he now had at least retrieved one Dutchman from the power of the perfidious enemy and had to take care of only one more."

It took all my power of persuasion[13] to make clear to the governor that Gozeman *had* to return at all cost *because he had given his word*. I also did not believe that even the procurement of provisions, but without Gozeman, would bring about Schimmel's freedom. Finally I was heard; Gozeman was sent back on board with the provisions, and after the governor had spent the evening suspended between hope and fear, both Gozeman and Schimmel returned to shore around nine in the evening. They assured the governor that, after the delivery of the provisions, the captain had treated them very politely, even forcing them to take some sustenance, but that they had declined this and hastened to come ashore as they were aware of the deadly predicament the governor of Nagasaki was in. No one was happier than the two chief banyos who had been held responsible for the return of the Dutch commissioners. Without their release, the two banyos would have had to fight to the death or cut open their bellies or die another shameful death, which meant that their offspring would have been considered dishonored. The return of the Dutch was like a release from the death penalty for them. In due time, they left for Edo, but never returned to Nagasaki. Though afterwards I was in Edo twice, I never heard from them again.

It was now the task of the governor to make sure that the English ship did not escape him, because his mandate is that if a foreign ship appears on the horizon and engages in hostilities, he detain this ship until the Court tells him what to do. On the other hand, the governor can, when foreign ships enter the bay because of lack of water, stoking wood, or rice (provided they act in a discreet manner), give them all these articles for free after having consulted with the Dutch chief. After a consultation with me, this was done in 1807, with the American ship *Eclipse* which was sailing from Canton to the north-west coast of North America. With the *Phaëton* (which was the name of this English ship under Captain Pellew[14]), this was not the case. He had engaged in hostilities on Japanese territory by taking the Dutch prisoners, and by making threats of an even more serious nature: to set Japanese and Chinese boats on fire. It was therefore of the utmost importance to the governor that the ship be detained. In the middle of the night, he asked me again if I had any advice to give on how to prevent the ship from leaving. I did not consider the Japanese strong enough to do this, as the frigate was well armed, and I told him that frankly. But I advised him to detain the ship for as long as it took to sink a multitude of ships, recruited from various small Japanese harbors and loaded with stones, in the smallest passages between the Papenberg and the so-called Cavallos.[15] These passages are so narrow that no ship could then possibly pass. As the following day would certainly be needed to prepare for this, it meant that the plan could only be executed the next night. The Japanese harbor master who was present at this consultation, immediately proved the feasibility of this project by making a drawing and he was ordered to proceed instantly and obtain all the necessary boats. In the meantime, I warned the governor that the eastern wind which was blowing since the previous night, might entice the Englishman, for whom it was favorable, to set sail. But the governor trusted that he would wait for more fresh water which he had promised him for the next day. The governor also thought of another way to detain the ship. At the crack of dawn, a commission of chief banyos would board the ship and tell the captain in confidence that, since no Dutch ships had arrived this year and that this could possibly happen again during the war, they would like to engage in negotiations with him concerning the sending of

English ships. One of the translators told me that this was a deception that did not agree well with the honest nature of the Japanese, but the governor of Nagasaki understood that deceivers like Captain Pellew deserved being deceived. The commission had barely left at the crack of dawn when the prince of Omura arrived in Nagasaki with his troops. He immediately proposed to the governor that three hundred small vessels, each manned by three rowers and filled with dry reeds and straw set fire to the *Phaëton*. He reckoned that fifty vessels were the absolute minimum necessary to accomplish this, because about two hundred vessels would probably be sunk by cannon fire and the men, if possible, would have to swim to safety. This would leave a hundred vessels, and they could surely manage to accomplish this. He himself would lead this expedition. While we were consulting about this, the *Phaëton* weighed anchor before the commission had even reached it and, with a fresh easterly wind, sailed out of the harbor. As nothing could be done now, we Dutch returned to Deshima.

All plans were now for naught and the governor found himself in a state of disobedience, as he had not fulfilled the definitive orders of the Court. Besides, he was not totally free of guilt, since he had omitted to man the imperial guard posts adequately and had been entirely unaware of how denuded of manpower they had been. He was also so sure of the fate that awaited him that he sacrificed himself for his family and cut open his belly about half an hour after we left.[16] The commanders of the imperial guard posts (not really government officers but subjects of the Lord of Hizen), followed suit, thereby safeguarding their relatives from an otherwise unavoidable state of dishonor. It is clear that the Court would have punished their laxity with the utmost severity, since the Lord of Hizen himself, though not in residence in his domain but in Edo at that time, was punished with a hundred days of imprisonment because he had not made sure that the attendants he had left behind in his domain would accurately execute the given orders. In contrast, the young son of the governor of Nagasaki, who was totally innocent in this matter, immediately attained a high regard in the Court and received a very lucrative post.

When I was at the Court in Edo in 1810, I heard the following story about this young man. The Lord of Hizen, fearful that *he* for the most part would be held responsible for the death of the governor of Nagasaki, as the absence of men at the imperial guard posts had mainly contributed to this even though that wasn't his fault, asked the Government Council permission to give the son of the unhappy governor a present of 2,000 *kobans*.[17] Not only was he allowed to do this, but in addition he also got the unexpected and unrequested favor *of repeating this gift yearly until revoked.* This permission, *which equals an order*, cost the Lord of Hizen a yearly stipend to the orphans of the governor!

Because no ships arrived in 1808, there was no merchandise in the spring of 1809, and therefore no gifts for the Court. The same situation had occurred in 1719, when three ships coming from Batavia perished; in 1782 when no ship set sail from there; in 1791 when the ship *de Goede Trouw* (the Good Faith) had perished; and in 1796 when again no ship had set sail from Batavia. With those years as precedents, the Court was not offered anything this time either, and we didn't even have to pay our dues of the previous year to the city of Nagasaki.

That spring, I moved to the big residence which was started in 1808, to replace the chief's residence which had burnt down in 1798. During all that time, the chief had had to content himself with the garden house. On July 28, 1809, the Dutch colonial ship *de Goede Trouw,* under the command of Captain Voorman, arrived. On board was the new warehouse master Jan Cock Blomhoff, a replacement for Maarten Mak who had left for Batavia in 1807. We also learned that in April, the American ship *Rebecca*, with Mr. Hendrik Tielenius Kruithoff on board, had sailed for Japan. This man was supposed to replace me as chief as my normal time in office, five years, had passed. In addition, the new Governor-General Daendels had a system not to let any official stay in office longer than was absolutely necessary.

Party given in the residence of Chief Doeff on 2-28-1809 to commemorate 200 years of friendship between Japan and the Netherlands. Keiga Kawahara (c 1786-c 1869). Netherlands Maritime Museum, Amsterdam, the Netherlands.

As the ship *Rebecca* hadn't arrived yet, we feared the English had captured it which was later confirmed.[18] I therefore had to stay on as chief. *De Goede Trouw* was the smaller of the two ships sent out, and hardly brought enough to cover our debts made in 1808 and in this year. The absence of ships the year before, plus the capture of one and, on top of that, the arrival of an English ship in search of Dutch ships, were not auspicious signs for our credit by the Japanese who now had to advance money to us. Yet I had received an urgent recommendation from Batavia to be sure to send both ships back with a good cargo of copper (camphor was not necessary). The letter of the Government informed me that there was such a shortage of copper coins that tranquility, especially among the soldiers, depended on it. I tried my utmost to get, if possible, 5,000 *pikols* of copper but was informed that only 2,500 *pikols* could be had. This put me into a terrible predicament. I knew that Batavia counted on 8,000 *pikols*, and that less than a third would not do. This time, I decided to show muscle and see if I could press the matter through daring firmness. I summoned the translators and charged them, in the presence of Commander Voorman, to tell the governor that the ship could not sail with only 2,500 *pikols* copper, as it had brought in sugar alone more weight than that, and that, therefore, I *had* to receive 4,500 more *pikols* of copper. In the meantime, the normal day of departure[19] arrived and the governor firmly asked whether or not I intended to let the ship sail that day. My answer was that I would fulfill to the letter the orders of the Court which required the ship to go to the Papenberg, but that it would then wait there for the favorable decree of the governor before its final departure.[20] I then received another 500 *pikols*, but 3,000 *pikols* were still not enough. I thanked the governor for his favor, but submitted yet another petition, which I brought to the governor myself, and I also made oral recommendations to the commissioners of foreigners. The next day, I was given little hope, as the governor who had stepped down had wound up everything that had to do with trade, and the new governor could not change that. I had not received an answer to my last petition yet, but the translators now offered me 700 or 800 *pikols* of camphor. I answered that Batavia did not need camphor but copper, and that if my request could not procure it, I would have to use a supply of scrap iron still laying around or even stones to get the required weight which certainly would not go over well with the Court. A cargo of 4,500 *pikols* of copper was the absolute minimum necessary to give the ship adequate balance, the more so as it was 1,500 *pikols* below the usual export quota. I stuck to my guns. Several days passed before I got a reply. Finally, the translator-messenger reported to me that my request had been denied and that, if I so wished, I could load the stones. I realized that this was only a trick to assess my stance, and I therefore cold-bloodedly replied that in that case I was asking permission to do so the next day. He then left, but the next day I did not as yet have the desired permission to load the stones. Two days later, I received an altogether different message; namely, that another 1,000 *pikols* of copper had been granted, making the total 4,000 *pikols* of copper for export. I can only ascribe this as a big favor to me personally on the part of the new governor. Although I did not receive my full request, it was short of only 500 *pikols*, and I contented myself with this amount, as I could not possibly detain the ship any longer. To validate my contention that the ship had to have 4,500 *pikols* of copper in weight, I filled in the missing weight with the above-mentioned scrap iron, even though it had no value.

The unpleasantnesses that happened in 1808 with the English frigate *Phaëton* made the Japanese think of ways to avoid being duped again by that flag. I was charged with writing up, in Dutch and in French (for foreign countries), an order which, as soon as a European ship came in sight, would be brought to the ship by a Japanese rowing boat. The ship then had to immediately drop anchor close to the north island of the Cavallos.[21] In doing this, they wanted to assure themselves that the arriving ship was indeed sent from Batavia because, if it did not obey these orders, they could be sure it came from elsewhere. When the ship did anchor as ordered, two hostages had to be delivered to a Japanese boat, then be brought to the authorities and examined by myself. Only after this would the usual committee members go on board. The procedure was followed this year, but it took, because of the Japanese ceremonies, a good five hours. This could possibly cause a ship to capsize because of the strong winds at that dangerous spot.

It was then decided that it was preferable to choose a secret signal flag[22] with which our ships that showed this flag could sail on to the Papenberg, and there deliver their hostages. In a secret letter, I informed the High Government in Batavia of the agreed upon secret signal flag and gave special orders to commander Voorman to get rid of this letter in the best possible way in case he unexpectedly met English ships. The governor of Nagasaki also had issued an order on how we had to conduct ourselves when a foreign ship with hostile intentions arrived. I was especially mindful in that scenario of the safety of the trading pass. Two Dutchmen would immediately carry it on land to Nagasaki, and I would personally stay with the governor in order to be readily available should something happen. With this, the year 1809 ended without anything further of importance happening.

In the spring of 1810, I made my second trek to the Court in Edo[23], and at the farewell audience in the imperial palace I received a public commendation for my actions in the case of the English frigate *Phaëton* in 1808. I made many new friends in Edo, even among those who were well regarded at the Court. This happened through the mediation of the previously mentioned Baba Sazuro, whose father was under-translator in Nagasaki. He himself had been my pupil, but had been called to Edo in 1808. Amongst my new friends was also the esteemed Takahashi Sampei and others who, later on, rendered true services to me.

At the normal time, I arrived back on the island but waited in vain for the arrival of our ships. No English ships arrived either, as they perhaps understood that the Japanese would now be better prepared to receive them! When none of our ships arrive, the chief always has to give a reason for that. We could now reasonably ascribe it to the war, but I did not give this as the sole reason, adding that the ship could also perhaps have perished. As this was not an uncommon occurrence, the Japanese were satisfied with that answer, but not before endlessly questioning me.[24] When the year 1811 dawned, we focused with almost certain hope on the end of July and the beginning of August, the normal time for our ships to arrive, but we waited in vain. From the crack of dawn until sunset, our eyes were focused on nothing but the signal posts,[25] which immediately announce the approach of a ship once it has been espied. Such a sign sometimes made us happy for half an hour, but then we were even more distressed to learn that it was a Chinese junk. No one who has not experienced this personally can imagine our emotional state. Cut off from all society, stuck on a place where, so to speak, ships never pass and so is much less visited; not knowing nor hearing anything of what was transpiring in the rest of the whole world around our tiny island; not sure whether we would ever see, next year, yes, in ten, twenty years or never, a Dutch ship again, and would thus perhaps have to end our sad careers here, far from our fatherland; living under the intense scrutiny of a very suspicious nation which, I must admit, treated us in the best possible way and did not deprive us of anything it could provide us with, but which never considered us or could consider us fellow citizens — this was a sad outlook on the future! In such a tragic uncertainty, it would even have been a consolation had we known that this state was to last five years until we were liberated.

In 1811, the time of arrival of our ships passed again with not a ship in sight. At that same time, I received a visit from the great-comptroller and accountant of the government, who had served on a commission that was sent to the island of Tsushima to receive the ambassadors of Korea, whom I have mentioned earlier. These gentlemen again asked me many questions concerning the arrival, or lack thereof, of our ships.

I gave the previously mentioned answers, and I had to do this in writing (as in the previous year). I really stressed the war as a reason, but now it was the *second* year in a row that no ships had arrived, which had never happened before. At the end of September, I was informed that some time ago, a Russian ship had appeared on the north coast of Japan, from which the Japanese had taken several sailors as prisoners. What truly transpired remained a mystery to me for quite some time. Finally, I learned that the ship in question had not engaged in hostile actions like those in 1807, but that the Japanese, in revenge for the acts of outrage committed by the Russians at that time, had imprisoned several sailors of that ship who had come ashore in a sloop, whereupon the ship had sailed away. The prisoners had declared that the hostilities had not been committed by order of the Russian government at all, but had been the result of the arbitrary mischief of a Russian merchant ship. The governor of Nagasaki asked me what I thought of this, and I let him know that this agreed perfectly with what I had already expressed as my thoughts in 1807. Once again, hope focused on the year 1812, but alas, this year too ended without any supplies and without any news from Europe. All our supplies from Java had been used up; since 1807 we had not seen butter, as the ship *de Goede Trouw* did not bring any in 1809. To the credit of the Japanese, I have to recognize that they did everything they could to supply whatever we lacked. Our daily nutritional needs and other necessities were paid for monthly by the treasury on orders of the Court. Two or three times a week, the governors of Nagasaki had their emissary ask whether we were in need of something or whether the suppliers took proper care of our needs. To state it simply: The Japanese did everything to make our miserable circumstances bearable as much as they were able to. For an example, the snoop Sige Dennozen went out of his way to stoke *Jenever*[26] for us, for which I loaned him a big distilling kettle and a tin tube which I happened to have. He succeeded reasonably well in this, but could not get rid of the resin like taste of the Juniper berries. But the grain brandy that he also knew how to stoke was excellent. As we had not seen red wine since 1807, except a very small quantity brought in that year by *de Goede Trouw*, he also tried to make wine from the grapes of the wild vineyard, but that didn't work too well. He did manage to produce some red liquid which also fermented, but it certainly wasn't wine! In this manner everyone diligently tried his best for us. I myself tried to brew beer at that time. With the help of the home economist dictionaries of Chomel[27] and Buys, I indeed succeeded, insofar as getting a whitish liquid tasting of *Haarlemmer Mol*[28]. However, it only remained good for three or four days because I could not make it ferment enough. I also did not have hops to give it a bitter taste and keep it a bit longer.

Each and every one of us thought about doing something for our comfort, but our greatest shortage were shoes and winter clothes. We had straw slippers made which were covered with Japanese unprocessed leather across the front end of the foot. With these, we shuffled through the streets. We made long pants from an old carpet I still had. In this way, we provided for ourselves as best we could. No one had any special privileges; we were all equal. Whoever had some supplies shared readily with everyone else. We literally lived in communion of goods.

In this quiet monotony, the year 1812 had passed already into November, when we woke up one night in great fear, as a raging fire was spreading through Nagasaki. I was already in bed at 11:30 at night when I heard the fire alarm. I immediately sprang out of bed and, opening a window, saw a terrible fire. We were *above* the wind, thus not in danger for the moment. Nevertheless, I had the trading pass, silver, fifty silk dress coats of the government, and all our own goods packed in crates and brought to the square near the watergate in order to be ready to transport them if the winds changed. I also sent a request to the Japanese Government asking to be allowed, when danger threatened, to bring the goods destined for the Court trek onto the barque, which was anchored outside the watergate. At two in the afternoon, two chief banyos arrived on Deshima, who had the express order of the governor to take care of us and our goods. All the servants were also given direct orders to make sure that *the Dutch thereby would not suffer any loss, as they were already unfortunate enough due to the non-arrival of their ships*. This was touching proof of the humanity of these people, even in regard to foreigners.

In the afternoon, the fire seemed to diminish, but as the wind turned by eight o'clock that evening, it raged even more fiercely than before and gained so quickly in force that, in a split second, the streets close to Deshima were aflame. As we now could not escape through the land gate, we had to go through the watergate which was opened by the chief banyos who were on the island. With the warehouse master Blomhoff, I sent the women, children,[29] servants, and goods to the barque, while I myself, the clerk Gozeman, and the servant Paschen remained on the island to see how the fire would end. I did not want to leave Deshima before it would be destroyed. What a terrible situation! Cut off from the fatherland, we now were about to lose our last refuge as well. But Heaven brought deliverance. The winds died down and were replaced by a rain which got the fire under control by the afternoon of the *second* day around five in the afternoon. Nevertheless, a warehouse with 100,000 pounds of sapan wood kept on burning the whole night and created raging flames. Fortunately, this warehouse stood by itself as all the houses around it had been destroyed, and it therefore did not do us any harm.

This being the case, I had warehouse master Blomhoff with all the others and their goods come back on shore around seven in the evening. The destruction caused by the fire was horrendous.[30] Eleven streets of Nagasaki were totally burnt to ashes, and six more partially so. The so called fireproof warehouses[31] of Japan have to provide the merchant with some protection for his goods, as fires are so frequent here. Their fireproof warehouses consist of posts standing three feet apart between which bamboo canes are plaited. The space in between is then filled with a mixture of earth, cut straw, and water, about a foot thick, and the posts themselves are also covered with it. Next, these walls are left to thoroughly dry out and then they're plastered with chalk mixed with a lot of oil. The doors, made the same way as the walls, are very heavy and hang from heavy hinges. Hatches and windows which are made in the same fashion open inward. The windows are covered with copper blinds, and when there is a fire, the crevices of the doors as well as the hatches are covered with a loam specially made for this purpose, which is kept in the warehouse in a vat and always has to be on hand. Experience shows that these precautions are adequate to safeguard the warehouses from fire, except for the raging fire which I experienced in Edo in 1806. A so called fireproof warehouse of the wealthy merchant Itsigoya was consumed by flames.

This same year, I also learned that the captured Russians had tried to escape but in vain, as one can well imagine. The translators also assured me that they would be freed if it appeared that the hostilities did not take place on orders of the Russian emperor. As this eventually became absolutely clear, they were let go. One of them, Golownin, wrote about their adventures, and I have quoted from his work from time to time.

In all of this, I faithfully took care to keep the books every year and to close them out at the normal time. I then sealed the book as well as my daily register, addressed them with an accompanying letter to the High Government in Batavia, and thus made them ready to be sent out. In doing this, it would always have been possible, in the event of my demise, to see how much had been consumed each year and how much the office had gotten in arrears every year. At this time (in 1812), the debt of our government amounted to 80,269 *tael*, which included the advance the Japanese extended for the return cargo of 1809.

In 1813, we entered the fourth year of our total separation from Batavia. One can understand how eagerly we looked for ships coming from there. In July, we were notified that two ships were in sight. No one can imagine our happiness, as finally, we had well-founded hope of deliverance. Everything confirmed this, the Dutch flag was in its normal place, the secret signal decided upon in 1809 was given, and finally, the *verpraai brieven*[32] were received, which took away my last doubts. The letters informed me that Mr. Willem Wardenaar, former chief in Japan and at that time council member of the Indies, was on board one of the ships. He had the function of a commissioner and was accompanied by a secretary, a scribe, and a doctor. On the other ship was Mr. Cassa, slated to be the next chief. He was accompanied by three assistants or clerks. As this had not in the least aroused my suspicion, I decided that peace must have arrived. Therefore, the High Government had sent Mr. Wardenaar as commissioner in order to help improve the trade with which, from his own experience, he was familiar, while Mr. Cassa had come to replace me as chief, as I had already overstayed my term for so many years. The scribe and the clerks were not superfluous either, as the previous scribe had left for Batavia in 1809, and I had only two clerks left in Deshima. All this led me to have no suspicions. Then the warehouse master Blomhoff, whom I had sent to the ship with one of the clerks, came back. He informed me that, although he had seen the commissioner Wardenaar as well as Captain Voorman who had already made several trips to Japan on board, something seemed strange. Mr. Wardenaar had told him that he would *personally* hand me the government papers he had on board.

In the meantime, the ships sailed into the harbor, and as all the officers spoke English, the Japanese assumed that the ships were American ships hired by our government, something they had gotten used to since 1795. To ward off any suspicion, I went on board to welcome Mr. Wardenaar as is the custom when a commissioner or chief arrives. Just like Mr. Blomhoff had reported to me, everything did indeed seem strange and peculiar to me. Mr. Wardenaar; my old friend and protector, under whom I had served as scribe until I became chief, a job he had recommended me for when I was just 25 years old; Wardenaar, in whom I had the fullest confidence and who, as my proxy, was entrusted with all my worldly goods in Batavia; this man invited me to come into his room where he handed me a sealed letter and requested that I read it. Often, I still thank the Good Lord in Heaven that I kept my head at that moment, as in contrast Mr. Wardenaar appeared very ill at ease.

I asked him to accompany me on shore where I would open the letter. Mr. Wardenaar and his scribe, Mr. Hinen, indeed accompanied me to land shortly. In the presence of both these gentlemen and the warehouse master Blomhoff, I then opened the aforementioned letter in my house. Its content was mainly this; "that two ships had been sent to Japan, on one of which was Mr. Wardenaar under whose orders I was to put myself immediately." It was signed by Raffles, *Lieutenant-Governor*[33] *of Java and its subjects.* When I asked who this Raffles was, the answer was that *Java* had been taken *into custody* by the *English* in order to protect it against the French;[34] that *Holland* no longer existed as an independent nation but had been annexed by *France*, and that he, Wardenaar as well as Mr. Ainslie, had been sent to Japan as commissioners by the present English Government. Because I had not received any news to speak of since 1809, when Governor-General Daendels was still in Batavia, and I could only conceive of myself as being a Dutchman, I only barely believed in the conquest of Java by the English, but not nearly as readily in the annexation of Holland by France. This could very well be a story spread by our enemies in order to persuade me to cede the office to the now English Commissioner Wardenaar, in accordance with the instructions of Raffles. In the presence of Mr. Blomhoff, I declared, "... *that I could not nor would not submit myself to the orders stated in the letter, as it came from the administration of a colony now in the power of enemies.*"

The English Commissioner Wardenaar had not expected this reply. He had only counted on our old friendship and on my feelings of obligation, as I owed him for what he had done for me in the past. Therefore, he was shocked by my candid declaration. He wanted to make it clear to me that it was incumbent upon me to follow the fate of Java and Batavia, as *the capitulation*[35] had also been signed in the name of its dependencies. I then asked to see a copy of that capitulation, but Wardenaar did not have one. I nevertheless stood firm in my refusal, as I considered the office in Japan *not* as subject to Java but as an entity unto itself.[36] It was my understanding that when one capitulates a place with its dependencies, it only subsumes under those the fixed points or places that can be considered necessary for the defense of the capital, like Java in this case. In addition, I had never considered myself a French subject (it is not the question here whether I ever would have). I had also never, officially or otherwise, received any news about our country's annexation by the French empire, so that it could very well be considered a fabrication to make me decide to capitulate. As a *Dutchman*, I could not, just like that, consider myself instantly a French subject and consent to a *capitulation* concluded by a French[37] general (Janssens). I therefore continued to refuse.

Mr. Wardenaar now took another tack. He reminded me of our old friendship and his help in my promotion years ago. As this too did not do him the least bit of good, he stooped to the baseness of promising me substantial monetary advantages, while he promised warehouse master Blomhoff that, in the case of my departure, he would leave him as chief. To defend accepting these two propositions, we could easily find spurious grounds. However, both of us indignantly refused these enticing but humiliating propositions. My answer to Wardenaar was that, though I had considered him my friend in the past and had paid tribute to his, at that time, honest character, I could never have imagined that he would ever invoke that friendship to pull me away from my duty but that, in any case, he would never succeed.

Only now was Wardenaar convinced that his own carefully planned scheme had failed. The scribe, Hinen, let slip that Mr. Governor in Batavia had already heard that I would not obey his orders lightly and, to that end, he had managed to bring over to his own side, my oldest and most faithful friend.[38] But now he could convince himself that making me into a scoundrel was not happening. Regardless of the fact that Wardenaar (whom I now had to consider my enemy) had power over all my assets, as he was my proxy in Batavia, and regardless of the fact that my refusal could cost me all those assets, I nevertheless felt it necessary to put all of this in the balance, rather than break the oath of loyalty I had sworn to my lawful rulers. The weight of such an oath is only felt, as in this case, when the interest of one's country clashes with one's own interest. But my decision was quickly made. In breaking my oath, my honor, which no one could compensate me for, would also be lost. By holding my honor steady, I kept the esteem of all decent people even if I had to lose my fortune. At the same time (and I don't want to deny this), I was convinced that my country would compensate me at some point in time.

I now confronted Wardenaar with how ill-advised his undertaking was; how he, though arriving under the Dutch flag, had exposed himself and his crew to the ultimate danger had the Japanese government learned that they were English ships and subjects. He alone was responsible for this ill-advised action as he, former council member of the Dutch East Indies, could not be unaware of the *Phaëton* affair in 1808 of which I had informed the government in 1809 in a secret letter; only he could know the secret signal agreed upon in 1809 for our Dutch ships which he now had used to bring English ships into Japan and to mislead the natives; he, as former chief in Japan, had to know the Japanese character well enough to realize that, given what happened in 1808 (the death of so many important people), the Japanese would take revenge on the English most severly if, like now, the occasion arose. Hereupon, Wardenaar for an instant adopted a firm tone, even threatened to tell the Japanese the whole truth and, to this end, summon the translators. I replied that *I* would call in the translators to inform the government that it had become evident to me how both ships had deceived the Japanese by sailing into the harbor under the Dutch flag, just like the *Phaëton* did in 1808, while misusing moreover the signal that only Wardenaar could have known.

I didn't leave it to words alone but immediately sent for the five most important translators[39] (though without the spy which I considered to be the prudent thing to do). Wardenaar now became extremely anxious. He urgently requested that I speak to him one more time before the arrival of the translators.

Subsequently he beseeched me, tears in his eyes, to protect him and his men. He now clearly realized in what a fix he had gotten himself and in how much danger he had put so many people. He implored me to save him. I answered that that was impossible;[40] that the translators were already waiting for me in another room, and that I had to speak with them first before I could give him any hope. I then left him with his scribe, both in deathly fear, and again ordered Gozeman to let no one near them.

The five chief translators then appeared. In the presence of Mr. Blomhoff, I explained to them that "*Batavia* had been conquered by the *English*, that both ships were English and that I didn't want to have anything to do with them." I ordered them to immediately inform their government of this.

It is impossible to describe the surprise and astonishment of the translators when they heard this news. They could not understand at all how this was possible; especially how Mr. Wardenaar, himself a Dutchman and whom they themselves had known when he was chief, was now in the service of the English and even came here as the main player. Finally, convinced that what I was saying was true, they asked if they could deliberate among themselves for a moment. When we came back into the room, they pointed out to me the consequences if, as I desired, they explained this situation to the government. Within a half hour, the English ships would be in flames and no crew member would escape death. Everything to accomplish this was ready. All the Japanese warships were still anchored in the bay. However, was such a drastic step really necessary? The ships had entered under the Dutch flag using the secret signal established in 1809 Mr Wardenaar was known as a Dutchman in Nagasaki; he had come on those ships and had a good reputation in Nagasaki, so no one would harbor any suspicion against him. Moreover, no Japanese would ever believe that the English, enemies of the Dutch, would ever take a Dutchman in their service. I made no bones about the difficulties that were inseparable from such a step and told them that, should this ever come to light, I could always call upon the fact that I truthfully told them the whole story that was to be conveyed to the government in the presence of the warehouse master Blomhoff,

The translators stuck to their opinion that there was no risk at all, if everyone treated this matter with circumspection and pretended that both ships were hired *American* ships. Once again, I refused all responsibility and told them that I would always declare that *they* had been fully informed. "Chief," their answer was, "if it becomes known, only we are guilty and then most certainly we must die, but believe us, there is no suspicion nor will there ever be: it could only be dangerous if Mr. Wardenaar was not present, but since he is, no one will have any doubts."[41]

Secretly, I was very happy with this turn of events, because I, as Dutch chief, could now maintain my independence from the English government without facing the necessity to sacrifice so many people who had come without violent designs against the Japanese, but whose government had only tried to alienate me from my duty. I therefore agreed to the translators' proposal, but commanded them to not ever accept any orders from anyone else, but from me only. This they promised, and they entirely kept to their word in 1813. What happened in 1814 I will relate at the appropriate time.

At this point, I had to settle this matter with Wardenaar, but I wanted to take advantage of his troubles for the benefit of the Dutch office. As has been stated earlier, we had not received any ships in 1810, 1811, and 1812. When the ship *de Goede Trouw* left in 1809, we had gotten the whole return cargo of copper through an advance of the Japanese. When the books were closed in 1812, our debt, as I mentioned before, amounted to 80,296 *tael*. I considered it to be my first duty to relieve my government of this debt through proper means. Consequently, and always in the company of Mr. Blomhoff, I went to see Commissioner Wardenaar and promised him that I would keep quiet about his reckless step *if* he immediately ceded to me the cargos of both ships. I would then sell this in the usual manner and, in return, deliver to him a return cargo of copper with the proviso that he would then pay me twenty-five *tael* per *pikol* in taxes instead of the usual twelve *tael*, three *maas* and five *conderin*. Mr. Wardenaar was beside himself with gladness, yet asked me to lower the price somewhat as he couldn't pay it. Finally, after some negotiations and not without threatening to reveal everything[42], we came to an agreement to deliver the copper for the regular price on the condition that he (Wardenaar) paid all the debts the Dutch government had in Japan. He asked me to put this agreement in writing and he would then sign it. He also brought to my attention that Dr. Ainslie, who was still on board and had been assigned as his co-commissioner, had to sign this agreement as well. Mr. Wardenaar guaranteed me that he too, would not cause any difficulties. The next day (before he could talk to Mr. Wardenaar), I called for Dr. Ainslie to come ashore and confronted him with the great danger in which he found himself. I also made him aware that Wardenaar had counted too much on the influence of his old friendship to seduce me to engage in a dishonest act and had thereby misled the English government; that he had now entered into an agreement with me which had to be signed by both of them today. Ainslie was flabbergasted upon hearing this news and, though he did not acknowledge this openly, that he had been misled by Wardenaar, but he did give sufficient evidence that he had grievously miscalculated. Yet he was very friendly, and we promised each other secrecy. I assigned Ainslie and Wardenaar the little garden house as their quarters. That same day, the agreement between myself and both gentlemen was signed. It went as follows:

"Agreement between Hendrik Doeff, chief of the Japanese trade and other transactions with Japan, and Willem Wardenaar, former council member of the Dutch East Indies and Daniel Ainslie, chief of surgery in Batavia, both part of the present government of Java. The first signer giving notice to the second and third signer of his refusal to obey the missive of Mr. Lieutenant-Governor of the island of Java and its dependencies dated June 4,1813, in which first signer was put under the

RECOLLECTIONS OF JAPAN

direct orders of the second signer even though this missive irrefutably shows that our colony has been invaded by the enemy, the first signer explains why he cannot obey this order and also shows the second and third signers the dangerous situation in which the here anchored ships *Charlotta* and *Mary* and all the members on board find themselves in case the first signer informed the Japanese (no matter in how white washing or complicated a manner), to which nation those ships belonged and in whose name they came; that these ships without much ado would certainly and immediately be burned, killing all members on board, and that the first signer could not do anything to prevent this, as the Japanese have acquired such a hatred toward the English nation (mainly due to what happened here in 1808 with the English frigate *Phaëton*) that they're only waiting for the opportunity to thoroughly avenge the brutalities that that frigate wrought here; this is very understandable given the fact that, because of this incident, the governor of Nagasaki and five vice regents of the prince and ruler of Hizen who were commanders at the imperial guard posts, had to cut open their bellies and died; that the above-mentioned prince of Hizen himself was arrested and, with the doors nailed shut, locked up in his house for a hundred days without being allowed to shave and that this prince as well as countless others of his Japanese subjects have sworn to kill all Englishmen who come into their hands, and that today these subjects of the prince keep guard everywhere. The first signer, without feeling in the least allied or obligated to the present Government in Java, but considering himself still the chief of the Dutch trade in Japan, and having considered the dangerous situation potentially causing so many people, who came here after all without any hostile objectives against the Japanese, to become the victims of the vengefulness of the Japanese if the first signer informed them of the true state of affairs; that he could not bring himself to be so inhuman as to deliver these innocent souls to the Japanese and thus to a certain death, and that he had decided to enter into an agreement for their sake. This agreement entails that, in order not to give even an iota of suspicion to the Japanese, the cargos of both *ships be delivered to the first signer who will trade as per custom and give an accounting to the second signer. In addition, the two last signers, at their government's expense, will take care of all debt and charges accrued since 1809, including this year's which will be paid from the profit made on the cargo; in return for this, the first signer commits himself to buy, with the remaining funds if these are sufficient, as much copper as is allowed this year for the export, namely 6,766 Japanese pikols for the ordinary price of twelve Tael three Maas and five Conderin, with in addition the 700 pikols due the first signer, which will be paid in Batavia to his proxy for the sum of twenty-four silver rijksdaalders per Japanese pikol which comes to the sum of 17,500 rijksdaalders; in addition also the 500 pikols camphor due him if the funds permit this. Understood. Thus agreed upon in Japan the 26th of July 1813.* Was signed: Hendrik Doeff, Willem Wardenaar, and Daniel Ainslie in the margin. *Occurred in my presence* was signed: J. Cock Blomhoff"

By these actions, I believe I did a lot of good and prevented major disasters. I disobeyed the orders of a commander who was the enemy of my country. I stayed on in Japan, not as an *English* but as a *Dutch* chief, and under the Dutch flag. Yet I rendered a service to the English, because I saved the lives of the crew of both ships (pawning even my honor, since otherwise they would have been killed to the last man). I also kept their ships safe, averting even more hatred and resentment of the Japanese against the English; and I promoted peace in their realm by preventing the revenge and the war that undoubtedly would have broken out between England and Japan because of the murder of the crew of the two ships. Both Wardenaar and Ainslie, after reading the detailed account in my day registry of the *Phaëton* incident in 1808, were also convinced of the absolute necessity of the step I took, and understood very well the bitterness of the Japanese when I showed them the written threat of Fleetwood Pellew to set fire to the Chinese junks and Japanese ships. I thus obtained the thanks of both commissioners and the assurance of their eternal obligation to me.

While I took care of my country's interest and the payment of its debt which amounted to some 112,000 or 114,000 *tael*, I did not ask for anything more for myself than what I could in this case expect from my own government, namely my share of 700 *pikols* of copper to be paid to me in Batavia. In doing this, I wanted to show my enemies that self-interest had not been my motive. Raffles informed me in 1814 that this sum had been paid to my proxy. Yet later he confiscated this sum and also, after 1814, withheld from it the share he had assigned, as per agreement, to Mr. Cassa.

The cargo, now assigned to me on the orders of the commissioners, was unloaded and brought on shore by me. Caution however was taken to remove all English coats of arms and other signs of English origin from the fabrics. I now had to present the Japanese government with a well thought out pretext as to why on the one hand, Mr. Wardenaar who had come as commissioner, and Mr. Cassa who had come as chief on the other hand would immediately depart again with the same ships. It was easy to give a reason for Wardenaar. I pretended that he had come this time to bring about the export of all the copper that had not been picked up from 1808 to 1812, according to the augmentation of the copper quota established at 1,466 *pikols* per annum for three years in 1808; that I had pointed out to him how untimely such a request was at this time, as the Japanese would surely first like to see exported the copper granted in the spring of 1808, and that they would not allow additional export of copper before peace had come about, and that Mr. Wardenaar had accepted these reasons. The Japanese did not only believe this, but my feigned concern for their interests pleased them greatly and earned me praise. The five translators who were in on the secret and had put everything in my hands, most faithfully supported mc in all of this. It was more difficult to varnish over the nomination of Mr. Cassa as chief. I pretended that the High Government in Batavia had appointed him just in case the Japanese insisted that I (whose normal term of five years as decreed in 1793 had

passed, and by now had already doubled), be replaced, but that it would rather see that I would be allowed to stay in my post for another year to compensate me for all the losses I had sustained while no ships arrived in Japan, in which case Mr. Cassa would return. Would the first one fail, the second reason I had ready was that Mr. Cassa had also injured his leg on board and could not possibly make the Court trek in 1814. All of this had to be requested on paper and be signed by Mr. Cassa. Twice, an investigative commission came to Deshima, but everything turned out well, and I obtained my desired permission to stay.[43]
Finally, the special gifts destined for the Court and declared as such in the beginning, had to be explained, as we could not deny them now. On the surface, they could be considered as an incentive for the request of Mr. Wardenaar to get a bigger copper quota, but then one would have to be totally ignorant of Japanese customs. Mr. Wardenaar, who himself had been chief, knew very well that to offer gifts to the Court in order that a favor be granted would be just the way to have that favor denied. I pretended that those presents were a token of gratitude for the way the Japanese had shown us their friendship during the four years (from 1809-1813) that no ships had arrived and for the way they had seen to it that we didn't starve, but, on the contrary, had done everything to ease our unhappy circumstances. These special gifts were composed of a box with two pistols, a rug fashioned in the style of a tapestry, two big mirrors, a set of nine serving platters with gold rims, a desk in the form of a barrel-organ, four beautiful telescopes, a table clock in a glass dome, and a live elephant. The latter two objects were not accepted; the clock because it was decorated with images from Greek mythology and all images are forbidden in Japan; the elephant[44] out of fear that problems would arise in its transportation to Edo.

All the other presents were accepted, and I was elated that I had thought up this excuse. I sold the wares imported from England without arousing suspicion, passing them off as Dutch wares, but the Japanese did not like them as well as ours, at least the woolen fabrics, though in reality they were finer and better. The price we got for them was a disappointment, as was the price we got for that part of the sugar that was brought in sacks.

It began to be noticed that Mr. Wardenaar had a foreign doctor instead of a Dutch one with him, an American, as that was what Dr. Ainslie had to pretend to be. He did take care, however, not to mention that he was a commissioner. I saved myself again by saying that the Dutch were more interested in skill than in nationality. This was certainly nothing new. The Japanese had only to remember the Swedish physician Thunberg. The rest of the questions which were not infrequently asked, as is wholly in the character of this nation, we obligingly answered with the help of the five translators who were in on the secret.

The export of copper this year, the usual allowance of 6,000 *pikols* plus the extra quota of 1,466 *pikols* amounted to 6,766 *pikols*, after deducting my share. After having paid our old and present debts, the remaining monies of the goods I had sold were not sufficient to cover the whole cost of the copper. I didn't feel like advancing them the monies even though it would have been easy for me to get a credit from the Japanese government. Instead, I made another agreement with Wardenaar and Ainslie. They would transfer into my account, and payable in Batavia, another 700 *pikols* of copper in addition to the aforementioned amount, for my services in 1812 — when no ship had arrived and I had no profit sharing — and at the same price as this year, 25 silver *rijksdaalders* per *pikol*.

It could well appear that I took advantage in this instance of the embarrassment of the English commissioners to gain for myself a bigger profit than I could get from my own government, but this was not the case. I had also received my 700 *pikols* under the Dutch governor Daendels for the years 1808 and 1809, when no ships had arrived either. Clearly, I did not require more from the English than from our own government. Despite all this, there was still a cash shortage for 7,466 *pikols* copper, my share included, and 500 *pikols* camphor. I could not send less without making the Japanese suspicious.

Mr. Wardenaar would also have liked to have received more copper on my credit worthiness. He said that the ships would be too light with such a meager return cargo and thus be at risk. This was true, yet I had already decided not to put myself into debt for him, and to give him no more copper than was absolutely necessary to remove all untoward suspicions of the Japanese. I told Wardenaar and Ainslie that I would deliver to them the allowed amount of copper, as well as camphor, and would advance the required money (about 5,000 *tael*). If the ships were not then heavy enough with cargo, they could take on ballast. I stuck to my guns despite all further pressure.

The ships were loaded with 6,066 *pikols* of copper, and 500 *pikols* of camphor, with in addition, 1,500 dunnage boards, 10 *pikols* pitch, and 2,000 *pikols* ballast. All this made for an advance of 5,806 *tael* in addition to the 35,000 silver *rijksdaalders*[45] which were to be paid to my proxy in Batavia for my share of 1,400 *pikols* copper. I now thought a bit about my situation in the days to come.

Completely ignorant about the state of affairs in Europe as well as in the Indies, I understood that it could still be years before we would get any news. What would ultimately become of us? At least for now we were out of debt, but we would again incur debt from year to year. What were our prospects? According to what we were told, the French, conquerors in Europe, had now penetrated Russia. What would the outcome of all of this be? Java was in the hands of the English, and I had to assume that since my refusal to hand over Deshima, all further attempts to trade with Japan would be scuttled. Trade from the East Indies could only be conducted from one place, Batavia. In order to be able to maintain myself in Japan without incurring debts, I proposed to the English commissioners that they enter into a trade agreement with me as Dutch chief in Japan, whereby the English, as long as they would be in possession of Java, would yearly send me ships under the Dutch flag. I would sell their cargo and then deliver a return cargo, but *only* on the condition that the ships' commanders obeyed *my* orders. Both commissioners declared that they did not have the authority to do this. That disappointed me but did not make me give up my plan. I asked them if they would grant a room on one of their ships to someone whom I could send as my deputy. They readily agreed to this, and I nominated my warehouse master, Blomhoff, to be this man. To give more force to his mission, I nominated him (contingent upon the approval of my legal masters) as chief-in-reserve. In doing this, I had in mind that, should the Japanese at some time insist so strongly that I be replaced that I had to give in, I could then hand over the post of chief for a year to Mr. Blomhoff, make a trip to Batavia, and then come back the next year. I instructed Mr. Blomhoff to board one of the ships and go to Java to conclude the proposed agreement[46] with the English government. Before doing this, he had to require as a condition, that the English government would continue to recognize me as chief of the Dutch in Japan, and had to negotiate with Mr. Blomhoff as my deputy; and also that all the Dutch now residing in Japan would be allowed to visit Java in full safety of life and goods. Would the English government not agree, Mr. Blomhoff had to break off negotiations immediately. Would the English government agree to this, he then had to negotiate further about sending cargo under the Dutch flag. I also gave Mr. Blomhoff a letter addressed to Lieutenant-Governor Raffles, which dealt with the appointment of Mr. Blomhoff and requested that he be recognized as my deputy and to enter into negotiations with him. I also had agreed with Mr. Blomhoff upon a secret signal. He then left on the ship *Charlotta*. We put all our hopes on a successful result. In order to send a report of all this to Holland (as I didn't know whether the annexation by France was true or not), I also gave Mr. Blomhoff[47] a letter to be sent to Europe from Batavia. This letter was addressed to Mr. van der Heim, who, according to the last we heard in Japan, was minister of the navy and the colonies. In this letter, I recorded all that had transpired between 1809 and 1813 and specifically what had happened in that last year, adding that we were now totally out of debt.

And so the commissioners Willem Wardenaar and Daniel

Hendrik Doeff showing the English Commissioners Wardenaar and Ainslie the door. Family property.

Ainslie, as well as Antoni Abraham Cassa, the chief appointed by the English, the secretary of the commissioners, Abraham Wardenaar, and the appointed scribe, Hinen, left, their mission a failure.[48] To eliminate any suspicion in the Japanese, I took into my service two clerks, Gratiaan and Hartman, born in Ceylon and Batavia respectively. It was in the beginning of 1813 that both ships, the *Charlotta* under Captain Brown, an honorable man, and the *Mary* under Captain W. Wood, took sail and to my great joy, as all had ended without any unpleasantness. The English[49] had paid all the debts of my country, and I had managed to maintain the Dutch flag on Deshima.

After the return of the ships to Batavia in the beginning of 1814, Lieutenant General Raffles gave a report of what had happened to his superiors, the Committee of Directors of the East India Company in Calcutta. I will give an excerpt of this letter as an addendum to this book, but I will refute here some of what he says in that letter. The expressions in question would, in a clever way, give people the impression that the English, at least in part, had achieved their goal. But if one considers how disappointed Mr. Raffles was in the enterprise which he undertook of his own accord, it is easy to understand that he would, if need be, try to cover up this failure which certainly could not stand him in good stead, with untruths; the more so, as this would have to serve him as an alibi for a second expedition he was preparing in hopes of attaining a better result. Among other things, he says:

> *"I have now the satisfaction to inform you, that the first difficulty is overcome, and if the result of the expedition has not included all the objects contemplated, it has paved the way to a further and more decisive attempt with every prospect of success."*

What Mr. Raffles means by the above, I do not understand. I had rejected his proposals, had been recognized by his commissioners as the Dutch chief, and they had negotiated with me on that basis. Raffles *had* to know this, but he knowingly withheld from the Committee the agreement Wardenaar and Ainslie had made. In addition, the report contains some observations made by Mr. Ainslie in which he claims, among other things, that *"the commercial objects of the voyage have been accomplished."* This, too, I declare not to understand. The English commissioners *had* to cede the cargo to me according to the contract, and they then had no say over it. I traded it as if it were my own, did not give them a bigger return cargo than was absolutely necessary to prevent any suspicion in the Japanese, refused their demand for more copper even though I could easily have gotten it in Japan on credit, and disputed the fact that this copper was necessary for the weight of their ships, which they had to fill in with 2,000 *pikols* of ballast. If their objectives were achieved with that, then they were surely content with little! Mr. Ainslie says mainly that it was of importance that the prejudice against the English character had *been cleared away for the most part. How* that was done is not mentioned. The fact is that the Japanese considered the English, who comported themselves during their dangerous situation with extraordinary submissiveness and circumspection, to be Americans. He further states that "the principal translators and other officials of the Japanese government had known the real state of affairs *long before the departure of the ships from Deglura (Deshima)."* Concerning the five principal translators, this is true *but no one else knew.* The *Phaëton* incident was still too fresh in the memory and feelings about it were, with reason, still too bitter to risk this. If he had known, the governor of Nagasaki would never have dared to keep it a secret, as he did not know how his successor, who was expected to and eventually did arrive during the ships' stay, would have thought about it, the more so since those high officials are rarely friends of each other. At that same time, the son of the governor who had to cut open his belly as a result of the *Phaëton* incident, enjoyed a very strong patronage at the Court. He would have made a governor pay dearly, if he had not brutally avenged the death of his father on the English when he had the opportunity. Also, just this year, the troops and ships of the prince of Hizen kept guard, and the prince himself, by accident also present in Nagasaki, had not forgotten his 100 day imprisonment. Had he gotten wind of this arrival, he would have taken brutal revenge on the English also. Finally, Mr. Ainslie makes it appear as if the *shôgun* of Japan had accepted the English gifts, and sees that as a very favorable sign. The reader of this book already knows that the *shôgun* of Japan was far from suspecting that these gifts came from the English. They were presented in the name of the Dutch government. Not knowing Japanese customs, Mr. Ainslie perhaps erred in good faith in this instance; he certainly did not think of the Russian Embassy attempt of 1804, which was far more of an honor to Japan.[50]

Mr. Raffles himself attached great importance to the fact that the *principal* translators were in on the secret. Mr. Wardenaar undoubtedly had to emphasize this strongly in his report. It was exactly what Mr. Raffles needed to make his impending second expedition palatable to the Committee. However, his conclusion that the governor of Nagasaki was also put in the know, has already been refuted, and it shows that either Mr. Raffles was totally unaware of what really transpired, or, more likely, that he did not want his superiors to know this. Somewhat later, Raffles declares that he does not attach much importance either to the fear of danger which I wanted them to believe, nor to my supposed influence with the Japanese. Of course, he *had* to say this while he was plotting a second expedition to Nagasaki! In the meantime, he was living peacefully in Batavia, but Wardenaar and Ainslie *knew* the reality of this danger.

In that same letter, one can find another excerpt of Dr. Ainslie dated February 10, 1814, in which he claims that the political institutions of Japan are not a real impediment against entering into mutual trade relations with England, and that the Dutch exaggerate this impediment. Mr Ainslie, who spent but *three months in Japan*, implies here that *he* knows the politics of this land better than I who had been here for over fifteen years! Frankly, Mr. Ainslie was not exactly the man who could judge these politics. The gentlemen Blomhoff, Gozeman, Voorman, Sluiter (of whom the second named has died, but the other three are all here now in Holland), and his own landsman, Captain Peter Brown of the *Charlotta*, who now lives in Great Britain, can all vouch for my opinion.

Driven as he was by an exaggerated passion for alcohol to which he had totally succumbed, Mr. Ainslie was incapable of doing anything, let alone engaging in difficult investigations and tricky negotiations. In my extended report on the Russian Embassy's stay in Japan, I showed clearly that Japanese laws and institutions did not permit foreign trade *other* than with the Dutch and Chinese. Raffles' notion that the English, once established in Japan, would be able to expand the trade of certain goods, is totally erroneous when one considers that all trade in Japan consists of barter without any money involvement. The treasury, to which all Dutch government goods have to be sold, always determines before the ship's departure, both the quantity and the monetary worth of the goods it desires the next year, e.g. 100 bolts of fabric, each estimated to be eight *tael* which corresponds to about twelve Dutch guilders per *ikje* (two and seven-eighths old ells[51]); but if the request were to be exceeded and 200 bolts were imported, which Ainslie wanted to do, one can be assured that the treasury would not pay more than four *tael* per *ikje*. As proof of this, a much bigger quantity than requested of *polemieten* fabric was imported in 1804. Previously, this fabric had always been estimated at six *tael* per *ikje*, but it now brought only four and a half *tael*, and the black fabric was even lowered to two and three-quarters *tael*. Normally, the loss of the imported goods (to Japan) is already considerable, even when the requested quantity is not exceeded, but this is covered by the profit on the return cargo of copper, of which there is a quota. We could get a 1,000 to 1,200 *pikols* of camphor, but in Batavia, they can dispose of no more than 200 or 300 *pikols* for the prices they have to get to compensate for losses on the exported goods. We already saw earlier that some trinkets like steel goods, knives, scissors, glass, and such were not for the account of the Japanese government, but for those of officials, merchants, and sailors and for which no copper or camphor can be obtained in exchange, only lacquered goods, wax, flour, *soya*, *sake*, and the like. The other goods mentioned by Ainslie are to be had cheaper in Batavia than in Japan, such as tar, of which a Japanese *pikol* weighing about $120^7/_8$ pounds cost $43^1/_2$ Dutch guilders in Batavia, so it does not make sense to import it. Except for copper and camphor, it is the same for all other goods.

Mr. Ainslie wants to import more luxury items into Japan, but he doesn't realize that, in some instances, all luxury is totally forbidden, even concerning articles Japan itself makes. For example, when silk is in short supply, Japanese women are not allowed to wear silk clothing, and the same goes for head ornaments such as hair combs and quills, for which we import the main elements. Ainslie would have liked to see that the English, once they had a foothold in Japan, be allowed to establish an important intermediary trade between Japan and China. This, too, is a miscalculation, as the Chinese would undoubtedly be able to buy the goods of their own country cheaper than the English could. Besides, they would incur even more losses on these goods if they imported them into Japan, as copper, the only material that must make up for their losses, would be sold to them at a much higher price than to us. Ergo, this plan, concocted by Ainslie and highly approved of by Raffles, is no more than a chimera. Another objection Raffles had was "that he could not understand my refusal to recognize British authority, as it was clear that the trading station in Japan was very expressly included under the capitulation of Java." Therefore, he proposed that his government send to Japan an embassy, with gifts enticing to the natives, in order to establish a British trading station there which would be independent from the trade engaged in up to now between Java and Japan. Here again, I have to refer the reader back to the Russian Embassy story, and point out the remarkable contrast between what happened to the Russians who had not given the Japanese any reason to complain in 1804, and the English who, in 1808, had violated their harbors, threatened their ships with destruction, and driven several of their high officials to commit suicide. How could they possibly imagine that they could, just like that, establish a totally independent trading station in a nation so used to ceremony and so jealous of its rights and independence? Raffles' intention, which he somewhat disguises in his letter to his superiors concerning the result of the expedition, is clearly exposed in an explanatory statement addressed to Lord Minto, at that time Governor-General of British India. This statement, published in a book about English actions in India and made even before the English took over Java, makes clear that an English establishment in Japan was *the* treasured idea of that famous English official,[52] who did his very best to thwart our interest everywhere and in everything. I will quote several passages from this statement to show what means Mr. Raffles wanted to use:

"I feel strongly that there is not an iota of hope for a more favorable reception for us than the one the Russians received, if our attempts are not supported by the Dutch residents of the trading station in Nagasaki. It is therefore my firm opinion that the only hope we have to get the Japanese trade lies in winning over to our interests the present Dutch residents in Japan and the Japanese college of Dutch translators at whatever cost that may entail."

There you have the key to the attempts of Raffles, which succeeded with Mr. Wardenaar but failed with me. It is for that reason that he gave vent to this bitterness against me in that statement by ascribing to the Dutch, but in particular to me, the failure of the Russian Embassy, and the fact that the Russians had been so inappropriately housed. He calls me *"a self interest seeking and avaricious factor who feared the sharing or disclosure of the secret signal."[53]* (My refusal to his envoy surely does not show my self-interest.) Raffles, or the publishers of his memoirs, never fail or rather, even *look* for every opportunity to put the Dutch chiefs in Japan, at whose hands they had sustained such a grievous disappointment, in a hateful light as being "covetous people who sacrificed the general good to their own interest and were therefore not worthy of respect and esteem, and who abased the name of their compatriots in the eyes of the Japanese." Raffles further states that, *"when once an*

RECOLLECTIONS OF JAPAN

English trading station had been established in Japan, the Dutch one[54] *would be abandoned and that their erroneous notions would only serve to destroy their interests and put their character in an abominable light, as it then had to be compared with the character of their successors."*

In another memorandum to Lord Minto written on February 13, 1814, he wrote, "that he is too aware of the diminished and decaying state of the Dutch trading station, to be able to think even for an instant whether it is either honorable or profitable to conduct trade in the same way."[55] In accordance with these stated principles, the English Lieutenant Governor naturally wanted me to be dismissed immediately, as he was preparing to send his second expedition in 1814. *"To relieve Mr. Doeff from his situation, according to established usage"* were his words. This was easier said than done, as the governor of Java soon realized. Raffles really meant to make it appear with these words as if I were his subject, while at the same time also counting on the Japanese custom that no chief could stay in Japan longer than five years. He wanted to take advantage of this but, as we will soon see, he did not reckon without his host. He was also of the opinion that two ships with a duly authorized agent should be sent to Japan in 1815, but not enter the harbor before a friendly understanding had been reached. This was certainly very prudent but nevertheless shows some misgivings about the favorable result of the expedition for which, according to him, the main difficulties had been cleared. The authorized agent was also ordered to threaten that the trade relations between Japan and Java would be broken off if the offers of the English were refused. The Japanese government would hardly have heeded such a threat. No one would really lose if the foreign trade stopped, except for a few lower echelon officials in Nagasaki who cannot live off that trade anyhow (in fact, they are subsidized by the government). All they would stand to lose would be a few special perks. Raffles chose Mr. Ainslie, whom I have already described, for this important expedition. He had to be provided with a letter to the *shôgun* of Japan from the prince-regent[56] of Great Britain. Let me remind you that the Russian Embassy, equally equipped with such a letter, had been turned away. Raffles wanted to see himself placed at the head of this embassy.

While all this was going on, I again had to undertake the trek to the Court in Edo in the spring of 1814, and deliver the special gifts I had taken over from the English. The chief translator of the trip tried to indicate that I had to pay extra for their transportation. I showed him that these gifts were only worth half of those given in 1790, but that the transportation costs had remained the same and that, therefore, I should not have to pay more than I did at that time. Recognizing that I could not be outwitted, the chief translator relented. I offered the gifts in Edo in the name of my Dutch masters and *in grateful recognition of the continued acts of kindness extended to us by the Court during the four years no ships had arrived.* They were accepted in that spirit, and I received in return one hundred silver *schuitjes.*[57] I previously described this trek to the Court extensively, so I will not repeat it here.

While I was in Edo, my friends Takahasi Sampei and my former pupil Baba Sasuro told me that they had gone to the east coast of Japan, the former as commissioner in the affair of the Russians who had landed and been taken prisoner in 1811, in revenge for the hostile acts committed in 1807 on the north-east coast of Japan. These Russians had been released on the basis of a statement signed by the governor of Kamchatka, which said that those acts had been committed neither on the orders nor even on foreknowledge of the Emperor of Russia. Takahashi spoke highly about Mr. Ricort with whom the whole negotiation about the release of the prisoners had been conducted in a most agreeable way. The Japanese gave these prisoners, notably Mr. Golownin, a notification signed and sealed by the commissioners which contained the whole history of what had transpired between the Russians and Japanese since the former first came to Japan in 1791. It also contained the notification that the Russians should no longer consider engaging in any trade with Japan. You can find this story in Golownin's book, and it can serve once again as a confirmation of what I have said in respect to

Raffles' attempts (at trade relations with Japan). The Japanese were very happy to have settled this disagreement with Russia in an amicable way.

In that same book I have read with astonishment that he had convinced the Japanese that they were being duped by the Dutch which, according to Golownin, had raised strong suspiciousness in them against us. He had also informed them that the English had taken over Batavia, which we had kept a secret. Yet it is strange, that I never detected even a whiff of suspicion in my Japanese friends, to whom Golownin had supposedly given those warnings and who were in daily contact with me while I was in Edo. It is also puzzling to me how he could have known, at the time he did inform them, about the English occupation of Java. According to his own account, he had already left Russia, or at least the bay of Awatska in May 1811 when he could not *possibly* have known about this occupation which occurred later[58]. Again, according to his account (Volume II, page 185), he had not had any news from Russia or other civilized countries for two years, from his arrival in Japan until 1813.[59] The only one from whom he could have heard something was the sailor Simonow, but according to Golownin's own testimony, this man was so stupid that he didn't know a Frenchman from a Turk, so it is highly unlikely that this man related to him important political events. I will not even comment on other blatant lies; that the Japanese had told this Simonow that the Dutch had finally confessed their deceit and that the Japanese, until further orders, had imposed an embargo on Dutch ships and cargo, etc. It is even impossible, given the time span, that Golownin who had already left Japan (Matsumae) on October 10 for Kamchatka, could have learned such nonsense from the translators *two months* after the news of the arrival on July 25 of both English ships in Nagasaki which is a more than a month's sailing from Matsumae. This is clearly nothing but fiction.

The time was approaching when normally ships would arrive. I was very eager to learn whether Mr. Blomhoff's mission had succeeded. Finally, on August eight at one in the afternoon we learned that a European ship was in sight. With a southwestern storm raging and a heavy cloud cover, the ship soon came closer. Along with the banyos usually assigned to investigate, I also sent two of my clerks on board. Earlier, I had been informed by a lookout vessel which had been near the ship, that it was the same ship *Charlotta* that had come last year. It was now under the command of Captain Brown, and also had Captain Voorman and Mr. Cassa[60] on board. When the lookouts asked why the secret signal flag had not been hoisted, the answer came that it was too windy. As the lookouts recognized all the gentlemen from last year, the secret signal was no longer discussed. I understood by this that Mr. Blomhoff was not on board. Shortly thereafter, my deputies, who had not been able to get on board because of the winds, informed me officially that they had not been able to find out anything about Mr. Blomhoff other than that he was not on board, but that Mr. Cassa, who passed himself off as chief, requested to be allowed to come ashore. Thereupon I immediately summoned the five translators who were in on the secret. The first thing they asked me was how Mr. Blomhoff was doing. I answered them that I had no more knowledge of that than how the situation was in Batavia, although it seemed to me that it was the same as last year. I added that this did not bode well for our friend. I now wanted to know whether the translators would divulge the true state of affairs or keep it a secret as they did last year. They answered that that would depend on the conversation I would have with Mr. Cassa. I then let Mr. Cassa come ashore. With the most flourishing expressions of friendship, he related to me the joyful change that had taken place in Europe and the defeat of Napoleon,[61] which meant that everything had also changed in Holland, and that the Prince of Orange[62] was now head of state. As Wardenaar had done the year before, he summoned me in the name of the English government in Java, to accept the capitulation of Java and its dependencies since, although Java would most likely be returned to Holland eventually, the capitulation still stood until that time. I replied that I would

RECOLLECTIONS OF JAPAN   139

like to believe him if he could give me any confidential *proof* of what he related to me (which he couldn't); that in that case Mr. Blomhoff would either have returned himself or at least have written to me; that therefore, I could hardly believe him, Cassa, in such an important matter solely on the basis of an oral report and that, in any case, such a turn of events would make me refuse even more since then, on the contrary, I could expect assistance from a friendly power rather than having to surrender to it. Cassa now pretended that Blomhoff was seriously ill which would have prevented him from writing. He then handed me the following letter:

"OFFICIAL

To the gentlemen Doeff and Cassa, chiefs of the Japanese trade.
  Gentlemen!

The Government, after giving approval to let the ship Charlotta, as being very suitable for the Japanese trade and as no other suitable ship is available, once more sail to Japan with the same captains and officers as before; I hereby provide you with these facts for your own report and information and also that Dr. Schaap was put on that vessel as ship's surgeon. In addition, I hereby also inform you that the copper sent to Batavia for the account of chief Doeff has been paid there for a good price to his proxy. The General Directory will send you the invoice and other commercial papers. Having no other important matters to report, I underwrite the information chief Cassa will give his co-chief in regard to the Government.

        Lieutenant-Governor
        (signed) Th. Raffles

Batavia	*At the behest of this Excellency*
July 2, 1814	*Mr. Lieutenant governor as advisor*
	(signed) Du Puy."

  The first thing I asked Mr. Cassa about was the information mentioned at the end of the letter. He answered that he had already given me this information, namely the summons of the British government to submit to the capitulation. I replied once more that he had heard my answer already; that I was not disinclined, however, to conclude a trade agreement with him, as I did last year with Wardenaar and Ainslie *after* having talked to the translators. Cassa claimed that the situation was totally different now and tried to dodge entering into an agreement by means of all kinds of subterfuges. Finally he consented when I threatened to expose everything. The translators also agreed, provided the deepest secrecy was sworn. Before getting back to Cassa, I reread the letter addressed to us both. The Lieutenant-Governor took the stance in that letter as if I were subjected to him, and now sent me as colleague, the same Mr. Cassa who appeared last year only as a projected chief. Raffles seemed to have two objectives in this; first, to make his superiors in Bengal believe that I had made myself subject to the British government last year; second, in the hope that the Japanese government, upon the return of Cassa, would perhaps insist on my departure because the permission received in 1813 was that I could stay *for that year only*. This seemed to me to be an almost insurmountable obstacle, but thank heavens I was also lucky enough to be able to rescue myself from that difficulty.

I was also quite perplexed that I had not received a letter from Mr. Blomhoff nor heard anything about him, as even the letter from the Lieutenant-Governor did not mention him or his mission. All this made me feel that I had to be even more on my guard than the previous year, the more so since I had gotten to know Mr. Cassa, who lived in my house at that time, as someone on whom one could not count very much. He was in reality the man whom Raffles used for his objectives, after he had realized that neither appeals to friendship nor self-interest had been successful in having me shirk my duty. I now truly understood that I had to be doubly cautious.

I went back to Cassa and reiterated my offer to trade with him on the same conditions as the previous year. The translators were also willing to do this, provided Mr. Cassa move with caution on his part. As he showed himself disposed to this, I made an agreement on the old conditions, and in my capacity as chief of the Dutch trade and related subjects in Japan, with Mr. Cassa, nominated by the present Java government as chief. He ceded his whole cargo for me to trade and took on all debts, up until the end of the present year, as well as my advance. In return, I would deliver 6,766 Japanese *pikols* of copper bars for the usual price of twelve *tael*, three maas and five conderin per *pikol*, as well as 700 *pikols* copper for my account, for 24 silver *rijksdaalders* per *pikol*, to be paid to my proxy in Batavia at a total of 17,500 *rijksdaalders*. If there was money left over, I would also deliver for export 300 *pikols* of camphor. This agreement, signed the next day by myself and Mr. Cassa in the presence of warehouse master Gozeman, was followed by the prompt delivery of the cargo to me.

That same evening, I not only had the five translators who were in on the secret come to my house, but also the snoop and all the chief and lower translators. In the presence of Cassa and Gozeman, I notified them that, according to the news I had received from Batavia, very important events had taken place in Europe which could possibly lead to an end to the war and a return to the way it was before the war; that my superiors had given me an absolute order to stay in Japan until peace was signed since the prospects for a general peace were so strong; that Mr. Cassa had been sent for the trading period only but that he had to return directly with the ship. I had this notification put in writing immediately, had it signed by myself and Mr. Cassa, and had it sent to the Court in Edo that same evening. It was clear that Cassa would have liked not to have signed this notification, but he was taken by surprise and did not dare expose himself to a refusal in the presence of the translators who were *not* in on the secret and had the snoop as their head. I fully achieved my objective, as shortly thereafter the news arrived that Edo consented to my continued residence in Japan and to Mr. Cassa's return. As in the year before, the cargo again unfortunately consisted of less desirable goods, which meant that our Dutch fabrics did not receive their full price.

Fearing that it would arouse the suspicion of the Japanese, I did not let Cassa stay in my house that year but put him in the garden cottage. Since I had learned not to trust him, I wanted very much to know what he was up to, which I learned from one of his female housemates.[63]

From time to time, I received notes to the effect that two[64] of the five translators who were in on the secret frequently visited Mr. Cassa in the garden, spoke very animatedly with him, and from time to time received small gifts from him. In regard to these two translators (the youngest but also the most slippery), I had to tread very carefully if I wanted to get to the bottom of what they were up to. Through a certain Japanese, I received accurate information about the rumors circulating in the government, and about the talks these two translators had with Mr. Cassa. On this occasion, I experienced *how* necessary it is in Japan to be on good terms with even the lower echelons of government officials. It was through one of them that I learned that both translators were doing their best to indicate to the government that Mr. Cassa was a very amiable man; that chief Doeff had already exceeded by many years his allotted five-year term in Japan and that he was more knowledgeable about the country's laws and customs than Japanese politics allowed; that also during his residence as chief, there had been several years, especially lately, that no ships had arrived, a situation which perhaps could improve under a different chief. If I hadn't already had the Court's permission to stay in my hands, this could have hampered me quite a bit, but now I considered myself to be safe.

In the meantime, in order to have the translators betray their own disloyalty, I used a ruse which, though going against my grain, seemed to me unavoidable in this case and under the guise of friendship I tried to gain their trust. As my house stood directly across from the street in Nagasaki along which the translators had to come to get to Deshima, I called each separately to come see me one morning. I told the first one I so invited that I had heard bad rumors about his colleague who was trying to give me a bad name with the government. I offered him as my old friend from the time when I first came to Japan in 1791, my silver watch as a gift on the condition that he would tell me the truth about his colleague. The translator, sensing that I knew what was going on and that he thus could not deny it, but also thinking at the same time that I thought *he* was innocent, now tried, at the expense of his colleague, to exonerate himself and said that I was not wrong in suspecting his companion. I thanked him and requested that he notify me if he heard anything else, which he promised. He then left. A half hour after him, the other one came by. I also called him in before he had a chance to speak with his colleague. I told him what had come to my attention, and also that I suspected his colleague, but that I asked *him* with whom I had made the trek to Edo during which we had forged a close friendship, to tell me without detours the truth. He was not any more faithful to his companion than he had been to him, but accused him of having had discussions that were detrimental to me. He promised to let me know instantly should he learn more. I was now convinced of their disloyalty, and the benefit of the immediate signing of Cassa's request to return to Batavia became clear, as without it he would perhaps have tricked me.

Several days later, at the offering of the *Hassaku,* or yearly payment, I discovered another attempt of the two suspect translators. If there are two chiefs, they preside over that ceremony together. Now they wanted to indicate to me that Cassa *had* to accompany me, but I stopped this, though with great difficulty. Three days later the farewell audience took place, and the two suspect translators tried to persuade me to at least take Mr. Cassa with me because it would arouse suspicion if I didn't. I feigned indifference about this matter but secretly devised a plan to prevent it. I kept quiet until the moment we were about to leave for the governor's house. I then pointed out that Mr. Cassa could not possibly go to the audience without a velvet cloak (in Japan they are very strict with the smallest detail at ceremonies). This did the trick. Going to the Court without the required Court attire was a sin for which the translators did not *dare* take responsibility. Had I mentioned this one day earlier, Cassa would undoubtedly have acquired such a cloak.

The moment I was about to enter the government house for the farewell audience, one of the suspect translators warned me that the governor, after reading the usual orders, would convey yet another special one. I felt as if the ground gave way under my feet at that unexpected piece of news. I feared everything; I feared the worst. Maybe the permission to extend my stay had been fabricated by the Court to lull me to sleep, only to then suddenly surprise me with that news. Or did the governors want me to leave on their own authority despite the permission? The first case was possible, but not the second. I had to make a quick decision, which I did, as there was no time for consideration. In the first case, I wanted to immediately reveal everything in the Japanese language to the two governors without the help of the Japanese translators. In that case, I considered myself to be innocent of the blood of so many unfortunate people who would surely have been put to death as a result of the intrigues and machinations of Cassa because, with my departure, the office would be lost for Holland. Finally, the decisive moment arrived. The usual orders were read and then a special one in addition. When that order saw the light of day, nobody can imagine what went on inside me. The order entailed that the Court had granted the old chief Doeff the freedom to stay on for this year while the new chief was allowed to return to Batavia, "but that next year, a competent man familiar with Japanese trade had to come to replace the old chief Doeff." This last addition was very worrisome, and most certainly the result of the machinations of both translators allied to Cassa. The first order of the Court, obtained through the intercession of my friends in Edo, simply entailed that *I* could stay and *Cassa* could return, but it did not mention the next year. If that last order had not appeared, there would have been no difficulty in getting similar permission for next year. Now, however, the matter would become difficult when Cassa returned, because I could not appeal to his ignorance of Japanese trade.

After returning home, I summoned the warehouse master, Gozeman, and the five translators in on the secret. I spoke to them very sternly. Above all, I reproached the two suspect translators for their bad behavior, as they had wanted to have a nation that their country considered an enemy establish a foothold there, and thereby remove me in an underhanded way. They failed this time, but I would be exposed to this possibility next year. I added that it would be futile for them to deny this, as each had accused the other in my presence. The three[65] remaining translators looked upon both traitors with deep disdain. Next, I demanded an immediate declaration, signed by all five translators, that the return of Mr. Cassa next year would be extremely dangerous. The three loyal translators were immediately ready to sign; the two other eventually agreed as well, but not before some hesitation, and after the threat that I would henceforth deal in everything with their three colleagues only and inform the government of what they had done. Now it was their turn to be stumped; they did not hesitate long, and *within* half an hour, the time limit I had set, I had the paper signed by *all* of them in my hands. I did not divulge a word about all of this to Mr. Cassa, but he had already been notified by the two translators. I dealt with the matter accordingly.

The cargo was now sold and delivered, but the sale was not enough to cover the agreed upon 6,766 *pikols* copper and 300 *pikols* camphor. I was not much inclined to a second advance, but I had to do it in order not to arouse suspicion in the Japanese. But I did not do more than was strictly necessary, namely 6,000 *pikols* copper and 300 *pikols* camphor, for which I advanced Cassa about 6,255 *tael*. In addition, as per agreement, I delivered 700 *pikols* copper for my own account, the profit of which had to serve as my yearly salary, payable to my proxy in Batavia for the sum of 17,500 silver *rijksdaalders*. I didn't doubt one moment that this agreed upon payment would be made, as Raffles had assured me in writing that the payment for the first cargo had been made. Little did I imagine that the Lieutenant Governor, out of pique that his expeditions had failed, would withhold the first payment and forcefully take away the last one from my proxy, as I later learned in 1817[66].

The ship, with its cargo on board, was ready to depart, and

Mr. Cassa was also ready to board the ship. To render useless the latest Japanese order, by which Mr. Cassa otherwise could have succeeded me the next year, I wrote a letter to Lieutenant-Governor Raffles which contained mainly the following:

"That the two (failed) expeditions to Japan would by now have convinced him that I did not wish to comply with his desires nor deviate from my duty; that I did not doubt that his Excellency would have acted the same way, had he been in my place; that to my great surprise, I hadn't heard anything from Mr. Blomhoff whom I had sent to Batavia the previous year to enter into a trade agreement for the time that Java would be occupied by the English; that the return of that same ship this year had made clear to me His Excellency's intentions to keep to his previous stance; that I proposed that he let Mr. Blomhoff come back to me the next year and to that end negotiate with that gentleman. Yet I amicably requested that if he chose not to do so, he at least would not send Mr. Cassa or anyone else as chief, but someone who could pass for the ships' doctor or navigator; furthermore that if Mr. Cassa returned, I had to reveal everything to the Japanese government and could then not safeguard ship and crew from the rage of the Japanese, and that he, in that event, could not hold me responsible for the fatal consequences of such an imprudent action against which I hereby had warned the Lieutenant-Governor; that, on the contrary, if he wished to trade with me sincerely and in good faith, he would not be duped by me and that, in that case, I would send him a signal which would do him no good, however, if he sabotaged me."

To convince him of the truth of all this, I also sent him a declaration of all five translators which may also find a place here as a small example of the Japanese Dutch of these men:

"The noble, greatly esteemed governors of Nagasaki have ordered that in the coming year all the requested goods since several years not bring in as much as possible according to the demand of the Treasury, bring in totally by the new chief knowledgeable in

Japanese trade, and he with Doeff exchanged; through which Chief Doeff us told that, as is possible next year no real peace as yet and no Dutch general yet in Batavia, Mr. Cassa nevertheless comes next year, that then cannot replace Chief Doeff, and great madness will come to the detriment of ship and people. Because not yet a Dutch general in Batavia, Mr. Cassa must then not come but possibly have send Mr.Blomhoff to replace Mr. Doeff, as well as the ship or ships under Dutch flag as well as with the agreed upon secret flag signal arrive. If this matter thus acted upon then no madness; but if contrary acted, then cannot keep ship and people from great misfortune; but it does not matter who comes as chief if once Batavia is lasting peace."

I entrusted this letter to be delivered, not to Mr. Cassa but to the ship's captain, Mr. Brown. I also added two other letters. One was addressed to the Dutch Governor-General of the Dutch East Indies who could possibly have arrived in Batavia already, according to what Cassa had stated. It contained a general report of all that had transpired. The other was addressed to Mr. Blomhoff, asking him to do everything possible to have the English government once more enter into trade relations with us, but to recognize us as Dutchmen. I asked Mr. Raffles to have both letters delivered to the addressees. From this, he could see that I was inclined to deal with him in a straight and open way. I think Cassa left in the beginning of December, after having caused me many an unpleasantness, but also the satisfaction that, for the second time, I had disappointed the English in their attempts to have me stray from my duty.

I now had the time to focus on the conduct of the two translators who could cause me an unthinkable amount of harm should the English re-appear. An opportunity to get rid of them could only be welcome to me. That opportunity came in 1815. The *otonas,* or ward leaders, who had little use for these haughty translators, were savvy enough to notice the distancing between me and them. They notified me that the translators charged us more than they had paid for the copper that they received before it was weighed. This had been going on since 1807. I had already mentioned that previously the copper was weighed for us on Deshima on Dutch scales. As this was very costly in terms of labor, and as it often led to disputes, it was mutually agreed upon in 1807 that the copper would be delivered to us as well as to the Chinese, unweighed. This saved a lot of labor costs, but every time the translators-reporters presented me with a bill for 180 *tael* for miscellaneous expenses. As our savings were substantial, I paid these bills without questioning, but now I learned that those translators had illegally taken that money every year since 1807. Once informed of this by the *otonas*, I summoned the snoop and the *otona* of Deshima, told them what I had learned, and requested that they relay this information to the government. This was done. Both men were imprisoned, and I was asked in secret whether I would be content with their dismissal, or whether I desired that they be exiled to the copper mines or even put to death. I contented myself with their dismissal, as that deprived them of the opportunity to cause me further harm.[67] Consequently, they were dismissed from their jobs.

Contrary to our very high expectations, July and August passed that year without any ship approaching. We now started to strongly doubt Cassa's story of what had happened in Europe, and more specifically in Holland in 1813, as we had hoped that we would soon get some more news about these events. We heard nothing. We consoled ourselves with the idea that either Java had not yet been occupied by us in 1815, or that no ships were currently available. But in 1816, nothing like this could be the case anymore; ships now *had* to come, or everything the English had told us was nothing but a fairy tale. Alas, no ships came. In vain, we peered for days on end at the sea in July and August; neither news nor ship appeared. Moreover, we could do nothing else but declare that all that Cassa had related concerning the defeat of Napoleon had been a lie. Our fate became ever more painful. For seven years, we had been deprived of any news from our country, our next of

RECOLLECTIONS OF JAPAN

kin, and our in-laws; there no longer seemed to be any prospect of deliverance! No one who has not been in such a situation can imagine what it is like. Without means of subsistence, we again were at the mercy of the Japanese who generously provided us with everything we needed. Every month, our suppliers were paid regularly by the treasury on orders of the Court, and we were thus spared certain starvation.

While not putting in doubt for a moment that there was peace, I proffered as the reason for the non-arrival of ships the fact that after so many years of waging war, the goods the Japanese wanted were surely not immediately available, but that I fully expected the ships to come with them next year. The natives were satisfied with this explanation. I myself did not dare hope any longer for deliverance.

In this state, we entered the year 1817. Notwithstanding great uncertainty about a renewed connection with our fatherland, I eventually took pains to keep up the daily register, to close the yearly government's accounts, and to prepare a letter with the history of our fate addressed to our High Government (if it existed) so that upon my death there would be no confusion about what had gone on here.

After long and fearful expectations and lookouts, the signal finally came. We learned that two ships were approaching. The joy of our Dutchmen in Japan, of whom only six now remained, was indescribable. At this point, we did not care *whose* ships they were; only that we now surely would hear *something*. How our joy soared when I received the hailing letters that night and learned from them that Mr. Blomhoff was on board. From the depths of our hearts, we thanked the Almighty, who had saved us from the most dismal uncertainty. From the letters, we also learned that Mr. Blomhoff had brought his wife, his child, and its nursemaid,[68] and that a navigator also had his wife on board. The governor of Nagasaki objected to letting these women come ashore as it was against the laws. I took as a precedent the example of 1662, when the Chinese pirate Coxinga had wrested Formosa[69] from the Dutch and when so many Dutch women and children had fled from there to Japan and were admitted to Deshima. I now requested that same favor. The governor answered that those instances were not alike and that *at that time*, 1662, the women had come, *out of necessity* as refugees, but now out of *choice*. In the first case, the Japanese could not refuse a friendly nation a place of refuge; in the second case, it was an altogether different matter. The governor would however present my request[70] to the Court, and refer to the precedent of 1662. In the meantime, Mrs. Blomhoff, her son and the other two women could come ashore on Deshima. But there was one big obstacle. No one who enters Japan can escape a total body search except the chiefs. Even the governor cannot exempt anyone from this. In regard to the women, I took it upon myself therefore to arrange something with the chief banyos on guard on board, as well as those on guard on shore and on Deshima.

The two ships then sailed into the bay; the *Vrouw Agatha,* under Captain Roelof Witsen with Mr. Hendrik Voorman lieutenant-colonel in the colonial service as commander of both ships on board; and the *Canton,* under Captain Johannes Schinderhutte. I went to the first mentioned ship to welcome my friend and successor, and now my liberator, Jan Cock Blomhoff. After our four-year long separation, this meeting was most cordial. He told me briefly how the mission with which I had charged him in 1813 had ended. Against the right of nations, Raffles had sent him as a prisoner to England, and that *after* the people in Batavia had received the news of the turn around in Europe! I myself had a special reason for joy. As a public token of approval of my conduct during the thorny years of 1813 and 1814, his Majesty, our beloved King,[71] had made me a Knight in the Order of the Dutch Lion[72]. My friend Blomhoff was charged with bringing me that mark of honor.[73]

After the first congratulations and heartfelt expressions of a grateful soul, I entered Deshima accompanied by Mr. Blomhoff and his family. The body search could not be totally avoided, but took place with the utmost discretion.

Once again, I had my *own* Government, a privilege of which I had been deprived since the annexation of Holland by France, and the occupation of Java by England. I felt a gratifying self-satisfaction that I had never sworn an oath to either of these two powers, nor had I obeyed them, but that I had the Dutch flag, lowered everywhere else, flap uninterruptedly in the wind here on Deshima.

That very same evening, I sent those tidings to the Court. All the Japanese, the officials attached to the government as well as the inhabitants of Nagasaki, were beside themselves with joy about the news that peace had finally come. One can easily understand that a glass of wine, which, like butter, we hadn't had since 1809, tasted wonderful. We drank it to toast the restoration of our country.

The next day, the unloading of the ships began. The goods were not as yet exactly according to the Japanese demand from before the wars, but now we could easily promise improvements in the future. This resulted for us in reasonable prices and a good return cargo. Once the ships were unloaded, I threw, at my own expense, a party on Deshima to celebrate the restoration of our country. All the ships' officers who could be spared on board, and also all the translators and *otonas* of the island attended the party. The island and the ships anchored offshore were illuminated, which made for a truly beautiful spectacle. This convivial and patriotic rejoicing lasted until the wee hours of the morning.

After two months, an answer came from Edo refusing Mr. Blomhoff's request to keep his wife and child with him. Naturally, Mr. Blomhoff was most unhappy and depressed about this.[74] All our attempts to mitigate this pronouncement were for naught. The governor did not dare address this issue again given the final nature of the *shôgun's* pronouncement. This strictness was not specifically addressed to the Dutch, or in general against foreign women, but to all persons *who were not specifically necessary for the trade*. The general tenet of the Japanese is that no one can enter their country without *cause*. For this reason, no Dutchman gets permission to enter Japan who is not verifiably in the service of the ships or of the trading station. As an example, in 1804 Mr. Van Pabst, an army captain, accompanied his friend Musquetier, commander of the ship *Gesina Antoinetta* from Batavia to Japan. As he was only listed on the muster-roll as a *passenger*, we had to put him on our muster-roll as navigator or writer (I forget which) before he could come ashore, and in spite of all my previous pleadings. Because Mr. Van Pabst had such a gracious personality, they turned a blind eye to his arrival, but he was not allowed to call himself a passenger. This rule is so strict that I am convinced that if the famous professor Reinwardt[75] had also wanted to pursue his scientific research in Japan, he would only have been allowed entrance as a trading station physician or in some similar capacity. One can well imagine that the departure for both spouses, who now had to separate for a long time was very moving.[76] On the second of December, Mr. Blomhoff[77] accompanied his wife, child and nursemaid to the *Vrouw Agatha*, the ship that would bring us to Batavia.

The Japanese Court presented me with 50 silver *schuitjes*[78] as a token of their satisfaction with my administration of so many years. Those Japanese with whom I had by now been associated for 19 years bade me a warm farewell, and each brought me a small gift as a keepsake.

On the 6th of December, 1817, I transferred the authority which I had assumed for 14 years to Mr. Jan Cock Blomhoff, my successor. That afternoon, I boarded the *Vrouw Agatha* and, after having had to wait for favorable winds for a few days and together with the ship *Canton*, left Japan, where I had spent half my life.[79] The *Canton* was a very slow sailer, which was the reason that we only arrived in Batavia after 38 or 39 days, as I wanted to arrive there with both ships at the same time.

Upon my arrival in the capital of the Dutch East Indies, I was most cordially received by their Excellencies[80] the Commissioner-General Elout and the Governor-General van der Capellen but not by the Commissioner-General and Rear-Admiral Buyskes who was on an expedition in the Moluccas at that time. Had I wanted to stay in the East Indies,[81] I would have been placed in a most advantageous position, but having been away from my country for almost twenty-one years, I chose to return and was permitted to do so. For my return voyage, I chose the warship *de Admiraal Evertsen.*

We left the East Indies on the aforementioned ship on February the 16th, 1819, together with the ship-of-the-line *de Prins van Oranje* and the frigate[82] *Maria Reigersbergen.* The *Prins van Oranje* sailed ahead of us and by the end of March, we also lost sight of the frigate, as we were constantly struggling with rain squalls and rough seas, which made us lose our main top mast. Our ship[83] took on water, and we only stayed afloat by pumping continuously. On March the 30th, the water we had taken on had risen so much that everyone had to help pump. Like all passengers, I also had to pump a four-hour shift, after which I was off again for four hours. Every effort was made to discover where the leak was and, eventually, two big leaks were found through which the water forcefully streamed. In addition, several small leaks were also discovered which, together with the big ones, would have been sufficient to send us to the bottom of the sea. Our situation was most precarious, as the rough seas and heavy winds made it impossible to stop the main leaks. Our position then was 15° 31' south latitude and 100° 41' in longitude, which meant we were still about 400 miles from the nearest island Mauritius, or Ile de France.[84] To return to the Sunda Strait or Sumatra was not feasible, given that the south-eastern monsoon was expected to be there. Our rigging was too damaged to hoist enough sails, and not one crew member could be spared to repair the damage without having one or more pumps stand idle, which would only have hastened our demise. Only one option remained; to sail with the wind and try to reach the small island of Diego Garcia, from which we were still separated by some 200 miles. All our efforts went into that option. Sometimes at the risk of losing lives, efforts continued to stop the leaks, but it was in vain. To lighten the ship, several cannons and cannon balls were thrown overboard, but the water level did not go down; quite the contrary, it immediately rose, making only for a shortage of pumps. Fortunately, we had a most able blacksmith on board who repaired the two most important pumps the moment they

Grave of Doeff's son Yokichi Dôfu. Kotaiji temple cemetery, Nagasaki, Japan.

malfunctioned ever so slightly. Without the two pumps which we had taken over from the ship of the line Nassau, it would have been impossible for us to keep the ship afloat for as long as we did. From the thirtieth of March to the eighth of April, we remained in a state of sinking and faced death. A gale, a rain squall — and we would inevitably have perished! Our only hope was the little island of Diego Garcia,[85] but we didn't know if it was inhabited or not. We only knew that it had a place to anchor. How great was therefore our joy and thankfulness to God, when we saw the small island in front of us the morning of April the eighth! Still, our joy increased even more when, upon entering the small bay, we discovered a small brig flying the American flag and sailing toward us. The captain boarded our ship, stepped immediately into water, and was appalled at the shape we were in. To this brig, named the *Pickering* and her decent captain, James B. Edes, whose name I will never forget, we owed our salvation. Because, although we were now in sight of the island, even at the mouth of the bay, adverse winds impeded us, and we could not enter the bay with our half sinking ship and thus also not find a place to anchor. We drifted farther away from the island; darkness fell and now our people started to lose hope. The long awaited island was found, but it also proved to be impossible to enter its bay. Nothing was left but to ask the American captain to take us all on his small vessel. He had seen the dismal state of our ship which kept taking on more and more water. The captain was then persuaded to stay with us on our ship, which helped to reassure us quite a bit, as otherwise the crew would have perhaps lost all heart, and then we would have been lost.

The commander of our ship, Rear Admiral (now Vice Admiral) Buyskes, led a ship's council to see what could be done in these circumstances. Winds and currents pushed us further and further from the island; a change of winds was unthinkable because the monsoon is in that time of year straight from the south-east, with the currents from the north-west. We therefore risked going down between the coral banks situated north-west of Diego Garcia where we would not be able to salvage anything from the ship, and then there would be no provisions to feed the 340 people on board. After a thorough weighing of all these factors, a decision was made to abandon ship and transfer to the *Pickering*.

This brig, which had sailed from America three years ago, had appeared as by miracle for our deliverance. The *Pickering* had put part of her crew on an island in the South Sea for the seal hunt. It was supposed to return after some time and retrieve the crew, while in the meantime, the captain made a trip to Madagascar where it picked up cattle for butchering for Ile de France or Mauritius. To transport these, he needed a lot of water which was hard to come by in Madagascar and very expensive in Ile de France, so that he had come to fetch water in Diego Garcia where it is very good and free. This was the reason the *Pickering*, as if miraculously sent to us by Heaven, chanced upon us.

This ship now had to make room for us. Its cargo consisted of drinking water and coconuts, which are also plentiful on Diego Garcia. They were thrown overboard, and during the night of April 9th we started to abandon the sinking ship. We had to proceed very carefully because, if the *Admiraal Evertsen*, which carried eighty mounted cannons, had sunk all of a sudden, the small brig could, in the resulting swell of the sea, have easily been swallowed up also if it didn't keep a distance. It was one in the morning, when I, with my very pregnant wife who was ill and totally worn out from all the fear and terror she had endured, as well as some ill members of the crew, were ordered to transfer first. As best I could, I wrapped my wife in a hammock, and I will never forget the human compassion and help of Captain Edes. Fortunately, we made it; the sloops went back and forth, and in this way, the last of the crew were on board the brig before eleven in the morning. When the last of our people left ship, the water had already reached the orlop.

The *Pickering* was already quite some distance away, when we heard a gun salvo from our ship. The whole crew was immediately counted and only one man, the gunner, was missing, and therefore clearly still on board. There was no

RECOLLECTIONS OF JAPAN

157

choice; we had to go back to the sinking ship and get the gunner, which we did. Either because of fatigue or of imbibing a bit too liberally from a pick-me-upper, this man had fallen asleep, and thus was forgotten. When he awoke, he shuddered to find himself alone on a sinking ship but had the presence of mind to discharge a salvo which saved his skin.

Once again, we sailed the whole night towards the island, and at the crack of dawn we saw, to our great surprise, heavy smoke arise from the abandoned ship. Perhaps because the gunner had not been too careful when discharging a salvo, our ship perished, not because of water but from fire. In the evening of April tenth, we anchored in the bay of Diego Garcia.

As the order was that no one could take anything with him, I could not save anything except a not inconsiderable sum of cash, which one of the rowers from the big sloop retrieved for me after I had already transferred to the brig. He had the decency to hand me this sum intact. I also saved several shirts which I had put on, one over the other, and several, to me, important papers, which could not take up too much space. Otherwise, I saw everything that I had collected in nineteen years in Japan, rare items and papers, perish with the rest of my possessions.

We were now anchored in the bay of Diego Garcia, and the crew settled on shore in tents. I remained with my wife on the brig. Aside from us, there were some nine other Europeans and about hundred fifty Negroes from the isle of Mauritius on the island. These people made oil from the abundant coconuts, caught fish and dried it, and, twice a year usually, loaded their finished products on a small schooner specially sent for this purpose from Mauritius, to whence it then returned. However, these people are not permanent inhabitants of Diego Garcia, to which they are only lured because of the abundance of coconuts and fish to be found on the island and on its shores. Yet to these people, we, numbering 340 souls, were not a welcome addition. As not all of us could be placed on the brig for a journey that could easily take twenty days, we therefore split up; one half of the crew went on the brig, the other half remained on the island waiting to be picked up later.

For several days we had very bad weather, and once again we were doubly thankful for our rescue; if we had encountered this weather on the open seas, our wreck would surely have sunk. Only on April 22nd did we, with part of the officers and crew, finally leave this island and set sail for Mauritius. I had hoped to bring my so recently rescued spouse to safety there, but my hope was in vain. Already on the fourth day of our sea voyage, I lost her.[86] Her constitution, especially since she was pregnant, had not been able to withstand the shock of our shipwreck. We had only been married ten months; the reader can appreciate my state of mind!

After struggling for a long time with no or adverse winds, and with very few provisions, as none were secured from the warship other than several barrels of hard bread, we finally reached the island of Mauritius on May the 10th. Without awaiting the arrival of the other half of our crew, the Commissioner-General, Mr. Elout, who also had been on the *Admiraal Evertsen*, and I transferred to the English vessel *Belle Alliance* under Captain Rolf who had sailed from Bengal and had stopped in Mauritius on his way to London. On board was the staff of the 25th Regiment of the English Light Dragoons, under the command of Lieutenant-Colonel van Tuyl. After a very long sea voyage, and after spending a few days in London, we arrived safely in our fatherland in October, 1819.

ADDENDUM

$\mathbf{F}$rom the foreword, the reader of this book will have gleaned why I wanted to publish it during my lifetime. In part, this is because of the Dutch-Japanese dictionary I wrote but lost during my shipwreck. I left the original copy in Nagasaki, from where it is possible to get copies or excerpts. Those latter ones are shown off today without mentioning that they are copies and excerpts of *my* work. I would have mentioned this in my book, but only recently was I able, through papers received from Japan, to confirm with irrefutable proof what I had mentioned concerning the work of this dictionary. This book, in which this dictionary is only touched upon, was already too far along in the printing process to still make changes. I therefore resort to this addendum to bring this matter to light.

The experience that the Japanese translators mangled the Dutch language and gave a totally erroneous meaning to many words in the translations, first gave me the idea of preparing a dictionary of both languages. I thought at that time that I had sufficiently mastered the Japanese language to be able to fruitfully undertake this work, of which there was as yet no example. Although there were some small books to help the Dutch officials and translators in getting the main meanings of words, these books were small and faulty. As a guide, I took the Dutch-French dictionary of François Halma[1]. I was faithfully assisted by the ablest of the Japanese translators and one of the district wardens of the Isle of Deshima, who had an excellent command of the Japanese language, something that wasn't always the case with the translators. In addition, circumstances were unusually propitious for me to undertake this work. The otherwise dismal standstill of trade offered me the time to do this, for which no other chief ever had had the time during the busy annual trade negotiations. In addition, my unusually long residence in Japan, by then almost twelve years, had permitted me to make greater strides in mastering that language than most of my predecessors had been able to do. This was the reason why it was now the best time to do this work which previously could not have been undertaken for lack of opportunity.

I was not unaware of the fact that I would not be able to keep this work when I left Japan, even though I wrote the whole work myself. Japanese law forbids that something of this nature be exported, and the Argus eyes of the translators would have spied on me from all sides. I therefore made sure, in secret and without arousing suspicion, that I had a copy which I took with me but which could not escape the general loss of all my papers. I gave my original composition, or rough draft, to the son of the snoop of the Translator College as a farewell gift, thereby eliminating all unfavorable suspicions.

In 1826, I had (as many times before) the honor, as former chief in Japan, to be consulted by the Ministry of Colonial Affairs.[2] This time, it concerned a report from Mr. von Siebold[3] in which, among other things, mention was made that this man had put a treatise about the Japanese language into Latin. He vouched for its authenticity, and was convinced that nothing like it had ever beem published in Europe. In my report, I pointed out what it would take, during as short a stay in Japan as Mr. Siebold[4] had, to be able to write such a treatise. I also made clear that Mr. von Siebold was *not* the first to write something about the Japanese language in Latin. Upon my return from the East Indies, I happened to see in the library of the now deceased Lord Guildford, a Japanese grammar book in Latin, composed two centuries ago by the Jesuits and printed in Rome.[5] In his report to the governor-general, Mr. von Siebold says this verbatim:

"That Mr. Overmeer Fischer, interim warehouse master in Japan, had contributed greatly to the placement and arrangement of the Dutch words *following the dictionary of Halma.* He alone had put in readiness thirteen words of these and had added the Japanese meaning in Dutch characters."

It is quite clear from this that it concerns my dictionary, as it would be truly strange if Mr. Overmeer Fischer, without my involvement, would equally have chosen Halma as a guide. As it is very easy these days to get neatly written copies of the dictionary I wrote, I proposed to the Ministry of Colonial Affairs to officially encourage Mr. O. Fischer to continue this worthwhile work in order to lay hands on the *whole* dictionary which contained *my* introduction. That would most certainly show who the author was. Because of his fame, the return of Mr. von Siebold to Europe was heralded as the opening of a new era for the knowledge of Japan. With bated breath we awaited both these most important results, and the work of Mr. von Siebold, which the government cannot truly consider as a *gift* to science, at least not as far as it is concerned. Perhaps his work would also deal with the Japanese language, because I now wanted to show the nation that during my nineteen years in Japan, I had not been idle. I therefore put in a request to the present chief, Mr. van Citters, to ask the Translators College for a copy of my introductions which was to be signed *and* sealed by the translators. The latter requirement served to confirm the signatures. Recently, I did receive from the chief the requested introduction signed and sealed by fourteen translators. Whoever wants to can see it at my house. The introduction is not written in the correct stylish Dutch that is suitable for our public, but in the Japanese-Dutch of the translators, a small example of which is in this book.

Regarding the dictionary Mr. Overmeer Fischer presented, which is now deposited in the third section of the Royal Dutch Institute, I have the pleasure to report that this man, when I spoke to him about this in my house and in the presence of my family, not only openly declared that the thirteen letters of the dictionary Mr. von Siebold mentioned, as well as the presented dictionary itself were copies of mine, but he even mentioned the translator from whom he had copied it. This man happened to be the one man to whom I had given my rough draft.

After having been allowed to examine the dictionary which is now in the Royal Dutch Institute, I immediately noticed that it was a copy of my rough draft and not a copy of the more extensive and neatly written work that is in the possession of the Translators College. As Mr. Overmeer Fischer, in his preface of the dictionary now in the Institute, did not mention this, I feel obligated to note it here.

At the request of the Institute, I'm now busy to fill in what is missing in this dictionary. In my opinion, I have proven that both the dictionary in the Institute, as well as the one in Japan, are copies or excerpts of my dictionary.[6]

Hendrik Doeff. Charles Howard Hodges (1764-1837.) Capodimonte Museum, Naples, Italy.

EPILOGUE

Hendrik Doeff returned to Amsterdam where he immediately wrote down his recollections of Japan while they were still fresh in his memory.

Clearly incensed at von Siebold's attempt to appropriate his dictionary as well as at the instigation of the minister of colonial affairs, Mister C. T. Elout, who wanted a quick rebuttal to the just published book *The Life and Public Service of Sir Thomas Stamford Raffles* written by his widow, Doeff quickly rewrote his annotations, and had them published.

In Holland, Doeff continued to work for the Dutch Trading Company, successor to the VOC. His interest in Japan, the country he alone at that time knew so well, continued unabated, and he became a much valued advisor on all matters pertaining to Japan to Mr. Elout. Not only a merchant but a man of broad intellectual and cultural interests, Doeff was instrumental in stimulating scientific research in Japan. Most likely, it was Doeff who recommended that von Siebold be sent to Japan to do research, an advice he probably came to rue given the event that also pushed him to publish his recollections.

The loss of all his belongings in a shipwreck, which included not only many valuable papers but paintings and other artifacts as well, was indeed a tragedy, not only for Doeff personally but for history as well. It may also have cost Doeff his rightful place among the luminaries of this unique Dutch-Japanese era. Today however, there is a renewed interest in Doeff and the importance of his contributions which are traceable and traced through many sources.

In Japan, Doeff became renowned among the Japanese

scholars, as his dictionary was widely used and played an important role in the dissemination of Western knowledge in Japan and in the early stages of the opening of Japan.

Once back in Holland, Doeff married his second wife, Sara Frederica Taunay, whom he had first met and fallen in love with when they traveled together to Java in 1798. Her father had been Doeff's former boss. Sara died childless in 1828, and the next year Doeff married Henriette Jacobs, a dark-eyed beauty 24 years his junior. Doeff had himself and his new bride painted by the famous English portrait painter Charles Howard Hodges (1764-1837). These paintings now hang in the Galleria Dell 800 of the Capodimonte museum in Naples, Italy and thereby hangs a tale. For reasons unknown, these paintings were in the hands of Doeff's female descendants, one of whom, his great granddaughter Margaritha Soulier Compagna, Principessa di Marsiconovo, had married an Italian prince. When, shortly after WWII, Margaritha's parents died in Holland, the Dutch government confiscated her inheritance on the basis that she had been a fascist. Out of pique, Margaritha donated these and other family paintings to the Naples museum with the strict proviso that they could never go back to Holland.

In 1829, Doeff also purchased a substantial property built in 1671[7] on the Emperor's canal. His six-year marriage to Henriette produced four children, two girls and two boys, one of whom, Hendrik, died at an early age. Doeff's descendants, from his second son Jan Willem Alexander, continued the tradition of seeking their fortunes in the Dutch colonial empire until it came to an end. Some of them then emigrated to the United States. Doeff himself died on October 19, 1835 at the age of 58 and is buried in Muiderberg, in the province of North Holland.

The little fan-shaped island of Deshima, through which Western knowledge entered Japan and made its rapid development after the Meiji restoration possible, does not exist any more. In 1898, the shallow part of the harbor of Nagasaki was drained, and Deshima was incorporated into the city becoming Deshima-machi. Before its final end as an island, a historical era had already been winding down slowly. In 1850, the last official trek to Edo took place, headed by the last Dutch chief, H. J. Donker Curtius, who later became the first Dutch diplomatic representative in Japan. In 1860 Deshima, no longer needed now that other harbors had opened up, ceased to be a trading station. It remained the seat of the Dutch consulate until 1868, when the long and unique Dutch presence in Nagasaki ended.

In the year 2000, Japan and the Netherlands celebrated 400 years of relations. Crown Prince Willem Alexander of the Netherlands sailed into the harbor of Usuki where the first Dutch ship *de Liefde* had arrived in 1600. He was greeted by his Japanese counterpart, Crown Prince Naruhito.

After many years of effort and seemingly unsurmountable problems, Deshima is in the process of being restored, a project that is scheduled to be completed by the year 2010.

APPENDIX

Engelbert Kaempfer (1651-1716), a German physician and traveler, was an invaluable source on contemporary Persia and Japan. After studying medicine and natural sciences, he went to Batavia in 1690. There, the governor general and former chief on Deshima, Johannes Camphuys, then sent Kaempfer to Japan and provided him with the necessary instructions and guidelines to enlarge upon the manifold observations and discoveries Camphuys had already made during his own stay in Japan. It is often said that Kaempfer managed to see more of the country (he made two treks to Edo) and gathered more information on Japan than any other European before him. Be this as it may, it is also well documented that when Kaempfer went back to Europe via Batavia, Camphuys gave him everything concerning the description of Japan which he had gathered in twenty years. It is known that Camphuys did not like the designation writer and that he had already given the story about the foundation of Batavia to Francois Valentijn who gratefully acknowledged this. Kaempfer, however, carefully omitted mentioning the data and the resources he received from Camphuys. After his return to Holland, he obtained his medical degree at the University of Leiden and then returned to his native Germany. Only one of his works, the *Amoenitatium Exoticarum*, was published during his lifetime. After his death, Sir Hans Sloane purchased most of his manuscripts and arranged the publication of the *History of Japan*, up to that time the most comprehensive description of this faraway and mysterious land. It remained the standard work on Japan well into the 19th century. Some of his other manuscripts were published as well, but many still remain unpublished.

Sir Thomas Stamford Raffles (1781-1826), English colonial officer and founder of Singapore, entered the English East India Company at the age of 14. An ambitious and capable man, he rose rapidly from underling to permanent clerk to assistant secretary, then secretary to the government of Prince of Wales island (Penang, Malaya). Appointed agent with the Malay states, he was the driving force behind the English invasion of Java. After the treaty of Tuntang, he became Lieutenant-Governor of the provisional English administration of the Dutch colonies from 1811-1816. Raffles devoted himself to the task of reforming the Dutch colonial system, which mainly meant to supply England with much needed funds and to open Java to English manufacturers. Like his two expeditions to Nagasaki, he failed, but in founding Singapore, he succeeded where he failed before in harming the Dutch trade, as Singapore became a flourishing free-trade port. Upon his return to England, he was elected a fellow of the Royal Society, published his book The History of Java, after which he was knighted. Shortly thereafter, he returned to the Far East and, firmly convinced that English influence should be extended in Southeast Asia, he continued to be a thorn in the Dutch side, among other things trying to prevent the restoration of the Dutch to Padang and elsewhere on Sumatra. In this, he also failed. Raffles' policy had a decisively anti-Dutch bent, and his dislike of Hendrik Doeff is clear in his widow's *Memoir of the Life and Public Service of Sir T. S. Raffles*, London, 1830. In part, Doeff decided to publish his recollections also to counteract the picture painted of him in this memoir. Raffles left the Far East for good in 1824, and before his death helped found the London Zoological Society, of which he was the first president. The Rafflesia, a genus of six species of plants native to the forested mountains of Malaysia, is named after him.

Nikolai Petrovitch de Rezanov (1764-1808), Russian trader, diplomat, and administrator, was a founder and outstanding executive of the great Russian-American Company, which played a major part in the history of Alaska and of the North Pacific. His correspondence with the company shows clearly that he wished to annex the western coast of North America to Russia. De Rezanov did much to instigate the voyage of Krusenstern, and it was on his ship that he went to Japan on an unsuccessful mission as the ambassador of the Emperor Alexander 1. Sailing, after Japan, to the Spanish settlements in California to trade his wares, he arranged for a treaty for the provisioning of the company's colonies twice a year from New Spain. However, this treaty was never ratified. De Rezanov was one of the ablest and most ambitious man of his time, yet also deeply and humanely concerned for his employees and for the wretched natives who were little more than the slaves of the company. Today, he lies forgotten in the cemetery of Krasnoyarsk, a poor Siberian town, where he died on his way to get Alexander's signature for the California treaty.

Phillip Franz von Siebold (1796-1866), a naturalized Dutch citizen of German origin, was one of the most outstanding physicians in Deshima. He arrived there in 1823 with the mandate to do extensive research, in particular in botany, and teach medicine. Shortly after his arrival, he had a botanical garden built, which eventually contained over 2,000 plant specimen. Many seeds of these, tea for instance, were sent to Batavia. It became the start of Java's tea culture. Von Siebold made the greatest contribution to the advancement of Western learning in Japan with the aid of three Dutch assistants and four translators. He met numerous Japanese scholars visiting Deshima or during his stay in Edo. Among them was Takahashi Kageyasu to whom Doeff had given the name Globius. Together with 50 others, he was arrested in 1828 for having passed on to Siebold forbidden materials, maps of Japan in particular. Some of these people were put to death, others received various punishments. Von Siebold himself was put under house arrest shortly before his departure, and was subsequently banned from Japan. His unbridled mania for collecting anything Japanese had aroused the suspicion of the authorities who believed that he was a spy. Hoping to be able to return to his beloved Japan, von Siebold tried to join Perry's expedition but was rebuffed by the Commodore. After the treaty of Kanagawa, Siebold was able to return to Japan where he stayed from 1859-1862. However, during this stay, von Siebold made no significant contribution to Western medicine. Ironically, the once-banned "spy" is revered today in Japan, and there is a museum dedicated to his work in Nagasaki.

Von Siebold, a vain and extremely ambitious man, was much disliked by his compatriots in Deshima, and he was known to appropriate as his own the works or endeavors of others. Among his many published books, *Fauna Japonica* and *Flora Japonica*, as well as his main oeuvre *Nippon* are still considered standard works. His collection of 5,000 pieces of Japanese ethnographica formed the basis of the present Museum of Ethnology in Leiden, which was founded in 1837 and is the world's oldest public museum. Recently, his house in Leiden has become a museum also.

Von Siebold's mistress Sonogi, from the Hiketaya teahouse, gave him a daughter, Oine, born in 1827, who became the first female Japanese doctor in Japan. She died in 1903.

Petition from Titia Cock Blomhoff to the governor of Nagasaki

To the Right Honorable Governor of Nangazacki

Your Honor

The undersigned, Titia Cock Blomhoff, nee Bergsma, housewife of Chief J. Cock Blomhoff, having recently learned of the order read to Chief Doeff and Chief Cock Blomhoff that she is to return this year to Batavia, feels extremely distressed, lost and frightened to have to part from her husband and to leave him in his infirm condition and to depart with her only child among strangers across the dangerous sea and to arrive helpless and forsaken in Batavia where she has neither friends nor acquaintances nor house. She is so utterly distressed and afraid over this that she cannot sleep at night and has no rest as she constantly weeps. As a result, she now too is ailing and in her great anguish respectfully beseeches Your Honor to have pity on her unfortunate situation and upon her innocent child of only 20 months of age who would have to miss his father and, as an orphan with her, would have to wander among strangers in strange hands.

If it would be possible to postpone this order and to grant her and her small child permission to remain here this year to look after and tend to her husband so that all grief, sadness and fear will cease, she would be eternally grateful to Your Honor and with her small child would pray for Your Honor's health.

Your Honor, please excuse the boldness of a distressed woman and do not become angry, because it is from fear and sorrow that she does not know what to do. Perhaps Your Honor has himself a wife and children and can feel himself how heart wrenching it is to leave them. Therefore, please take all this into consideration and take pity upon an unhappy woman. With all respectful esteem, Your Honor's sorrowful servant.

(signed) Titia Cock Blomhoff

Although Titia Cock Blomhoff was not the first Western woman to set foot on Japanese soil, she was the only Western woman known in Japan's pre-Meiji history to petition the Japanese government.

BIBLIOGRAPHY CONSULTED

Beasly, W.G. *The Rise of Modern Japan*. London: Weidesfeld and Nicolson, 1990.

Bowers, J.Z. *Western Medical Pioneers in Feudal Japan*. The John Hopkins Press, 1970.

Boxer, C.R. *Jan Compagnie in Japan* 1600-1817. The Hague Martinus Nijhof, 1950.

Boxer, C.R. *The Dutch Seaborn Empire* 1600-1800. New York: Alfred A. Knopf, 1965.

Catalogue Rotterdam Museum for Ethnology. *In het Spoor van de Liefde (In the Wake of the (ship) Charity)*. Amsterdam: The Bataafse Leeuw, 1986.

Dunn, C.J. *Traditional Japan*. Tokyo: Tuttle, 1972.

French, C.L. *Through Closed Doors: Western Influence on Japanese Art* 1639-1853. Meadow Brook Art Gallery, Oakland University Rochester, Michigan 48063, 1977.

Meadow Brook Art Gallery, *Shiba Kôkan: Artist, Innovator, and Pioneer in the Westernization of Japan*. Tokyo: Weatherhill, 1974.

Hesselink, R.H., *Twee Spiegels op Cambang. Een portret van de Japanners in de negentiende eeuw naar Nederlandse ooggetuigen verslagen. (Two mirrors on Cambang. A portrait of the Japanese in the nineteenth century through Dutch eyewitness reports)*. Utrecht. Hes Publishers

1984.

Keene, D. *The Japanese discovery of Europe* 1720-1830. Revised edition. Stanford University Press, 1969.

van der Kemp, P.H. *Decima, tijdens Nederlands Toevoeging aan Frankrijk. (Decima during the annexation of Holland by France.)* Nederlands-Indie Oud en Nieuw, derde jaargang. Afl 8, December 1918.

Meilink-Roelofsz, M.A.P., et al. *De VOC in Azie. (The VOC in Asia)*. Bussum: Unieboek b.v., 1976.

van Opstall, M.E., Vos, F., van Gulik, W. and de Vries, J. *Vier Eeuwen Nederland-Japan. Kunst, Wetenschap, Taal, Handel. (Four Centuries the Netherlands-Japan. Art, Science, Language, Trade)*. Lochem: De Tijdstroom 1983.

Parthesius, R., Schiermeier, K with a contribution by Yasumasa Oka. *Japanese Amazement: Shiba Kôkan, Artist under the spell of the West*. Amsterdam. Amsterdam Historical Museum 2000.

Paul, H. *De Nederlanders in Japan* 1600-1854. *De VOC op Desjima. (The Dutch in Japan 1600-1854. The VOC on Desjima.)* Weesp: Unieboek b.v., 1984.

Reischauer, E.O. *Japan. The Story of a Nation*. Third Edition, Charles E. Tuttle Company Inc. of Rutland, Vermont and Tokyo, 1981.

Sansom, G. *A History of Japan* (three volumes). London: Cresset 1958, 1961, 1964.

Sansom, G. *Japan: A short Cultural History* (revised edition). London: Cresset 1962.

Statler, O. *Japanese Inn*. New York: Random House, 1961.

Stellingwerff, J. *De Diepe Wateren van Nagasaki. Nederlands-Japanse betrekkingen sedert de Stichting van Deshima* (*The Deep Waters of Nagasaki. Dutch-Japanese relations since the foundation of Deshima.*) Franeker: T. Wever b.v. 1983.

Stellingwerff, J. *Roodharige Vreemdelingen op Deshima* (*Red Haired Strangers on Deshima*). Franeker: T. Wever b.v. 1983.

Storry, R.A. *History of Modern Japan.* Middlesex: Penguin, 1968.

Veenhoven, W.A. *De Strijd om Deshima, een onderzoek naar de aanslagen van Amerikaanse, Engelse en Russische zijde op het Nederlandse handels monopolie in Japan gedurende de periode* 1800-1817 (*Battle around Deshima, an investigation into the American, English, and Russian attacks on the Dutch trade monopoly in Japan during the period 1800-1817*). Drukkerij, J. B. Hemelsoet, Bloemendaal, 1950.

END NOTES

INTRODUCTION

[1]Personal communication of the original as yet unpublished research on Hendrik Doeff courtesy Dr. Johan Stellingwerff.

[2]In 1795, the French revolutionary forces had overrun Holland and the Republic of the United Netherlands had been renamed the Batavian Republic and by the treaty of The Hague in 1795 became closely allied to France if not its vassal. In a period of less than twenty years, Holland would subsequently undergo four name changes: the Batavian Republic from 1795-1805, the Batavian Commonwealth from 1805-1806, the Kingdom of Holland under Louis Napoleon from 1806-1810, and finally a department of the Empire of France from 1810-1813.

[3]*Haiku*, a traditional Japanese poem of 17 syllables.

[4]Veenhoven, W. A., *Battle around Deshima*, 1950.

[5]Two districts in Tokyo are also named after Adams and van Lodensteyn, the *Anjincho* and the *Yaesu*.

[6]Van Diemen sent Abel Tasman on an expedition which discovered Tasmania (van Diemen's land), New Zealand and the Tasman sea but missed Australia.

[7]*Het Groot Schilderboek*, Amsterdam, 1707.

[8]National Museum of Ethnology, Leiden, the Netherlands.

[9]Personal communication from Professor Tetsuo Najita of the University of Chicago.

[10]Sir Thomas Stamford Raffles, founder of Singapore.

[11]Translator's note (hereafter TN): See appendix.

RECOLLECTIONS OF JAPAN

[12]TN: From 1821 - 1829

[13]TN: King William I who reigned from 1815 to 1840.

CHAPTER 1

[1]TN: Doeff arrived on the American ship *Franklin*. As only Dutch and Chinese ships were allowed into the harbor, all hired American ships hoisted the Dutch flag upon entering the bay of Nagasaki.

[2]TN: The author uses the old term *Nederduitsch* or Low German.

[3]TN: Their number is variously reported as having been 11 or 20.

[4]It is written on Japanese paper (large format) which is known as *obosho*. I received this paper as a gift from the ruler of *Satsuma*, father-in-law of the present *shôgun*. This brand of paper is difficult to obtain, as it is mainly used at the court to write imperial orders, or occasionally given as a gift.

[5]TN: This copy is now in the Prefectural Library in Nagasaki.

[6]TN: This rule was obviously impossible to enforce. Although formal training was not available to them, most Dutch in Deshima learned some Japanese from their concubines *(yûjos)*, including Doeff. He truly mastered the Japanese language and its subtleties and even composed *haiku*, one of which is considered excellent. The Dutch called their concubines *taijos*, from the word *tayu* or highest ranked (and most expensive) courtesans, which they were indeed. Besides serving food and drink, they sang, played the shamisen and were considered more brazen than the other *yûjos*, *Oranda-yuki*, or those who went to the Dutch, wore bracelets and rings and learned to shake hands and kiss, which they called *umakuchi*, tasty mouths. They had their personal assistant (an apprentice) called *kabro*, from *kaburo*, someone with short hair.

[7]TN: It was called: *Dôfu Haruma* or *Doeff's Halma*.

[8]TN: Doeff indeed seems to have made many friends in Nagasaki as well as in Edo, including at the Court. On several occasions, he received substantial gifts from the Court in appreciation of his services.

[9]TN: *History and Description of Japan*, Amsterdam 1729. Kaempfer arrived on Deshima in 1690 and his posthumously published book gave the outside world a first image of this faraway and mysterious land. See appendix.

[10]TN: Johannes Camphuys, 1634-1695, chief in Deshima in 1671, 1673, and 1675, then from 1684 to 1691 the Dutch East India Company's Governor General of the Indies. See appendix on Kaempfer.

[11]TN: May 30, 1619. Batavia, now called Jakarta, is the capital of Indonesia. It was founded by Jan Pietersz Coen, 4th Governor General of the Dutch East Indies, on the ruins of the old city Jakarta, which he took and destroyed.

[12]TN: François Valentijn: *Oud en Nieuw Oost-Indien*, Dordrecht - Amsterdam, 1724-1726, vol. Iv., pp. 421-91.

[13]TN: Onno Zwier van Haren (1713-1779), *Proeve, op de leevensbeschijvingen der Nederlandse doorlugtige mannen: behelzende het leven van Joannes Camphuys*, haarlemmer, Tezwolle, 1772.

[14]TN: This *dairi* or emperor, is also known as *Jimmu*.

[15]TN: Abreviation of *Seiitaishôgun*, *shôgun* or supreme commander and sole ruler, literally means "barbarian killing general." The *shôguns* reigned from 1603 to 1868. This is called the Tokugawa era, also known as the Edo period.

[16]TN: Edo, door of the river in Japanese, became Tokyo, eastern capital, and Miyako became Kyoto under the Meiji in 1868. Under the Meiji, most place names were changed.

[17]TN: Minamoto Yoritomo: 1147-1199.

[18]In this manner, the *shôgun* or field marshall, just like the

imperator in Rome, acquired what was only a personal honor before, as a hereditary title which contained the highest authority. Similar examples of kings who by their own appointed generals or supposed protectors were removed from their office and destined to lead a vegetative life in their palaces, come to us from the history of the Orient, in *The Emirs El Omrah*, who totally controlled the Kalifs of Bagdad yet let them keep their titles and the trappings of their power (a few centuries earlier than Yorimoto). Examples from the West are the upper chamberlains or "maires du palais" of the good for nothing kings of the first Royal House of France in the 7th or 8th century. [The Merovingians] *Publisher*

[19]TN: This period is called *Sen Goku Jida*, age of the country at war. It was brought to an end in the first half of the sixteenth century by the successful efforts of three warlords, Oba Nobugana, Toyotomo Hideyoshi, and Tokugawa Ieyasu.

[20]TN: Toyotomi Hideyoshi: 1536-1598.

[21]One passes his former humble home on the way from Miyako to Edo which I did three times.

[22]Today the Hachijo islands, to the east of Japan, serve as the place of exile.

[23]TN: *Seppuku*, a ceremonial suicide accomplished by cutting the belly from left to right and then upwards with a very sharp short dagger called a *Tanto* or a larger dagger called a *wakizashi*. We are more familiar with the term *hara* (belly) *kiri* (cut), but it is of interest to note that this word is seldom used in Japan.

[24]TN: Tokugawa Ieyasu: 1542-1616. He established the Tokugawa dynasty which reigned from 1603 to 1868. Note that in Japanese, the last name comes first.

[25]TN: Tokugawa Ieyasu finally defeated his enemies at the battle of *Sekigahara* in 1600. Three years later, he had himself named *shôgun*.

[26]TN: Great King or Mikado.

[27]TN: Ceremonial suicide.

[28]The English acted in the same way in India with the great Mogul. *Publisher*

[29]Zimmerman, following the example of several old writers, calls him *Cubo Sama. Publisher.*

[30]The old Romans did likewise. *Publisher*

[31]We had given him this horse!

[32]TN: *Metsuke* are imperial spies independent from city government. They operated all over Japan.

[33]TN: *Dwarskijkers*, literally those that look diagonally across or snoops.

[34]TN: *Okobito metsuke* could be merchants, priests, travelers, beggars, and even blind men. One can make the case that in the Edo period, each Japanese spied on his neighbor. The reign of the *shôguns* rested almost exclusively on an apparatus of espionage and terror.

[35]TN: *Daimyô,* territorial ruler and lord over a number of samurai.

[36]TN: This system was called the *Sankin Kôtai* and was devised to control the princes, and more significantly, to deprive them of the means to take up arms against him, as they had to maintain two residences, in Edo and in their province, which necessitated large expenditures..

[37]TN: Arai is near Shimada on the river Ôigawa.

[38]TN: This was also the period, from 1639-1853, of *sakoku seisaku* or national isolation policy. During this period, it became a capital crime for a Japanese to attempt to leave the country or, having left, to return

[39]TN: Nagasaki, Long Cape in Japanese, was founded in 1570 especially for Portugese traders by Ômura Sumitada, Christian ruler of Omura. Nagasaki was a Jesuit city and a free city for Japanese Christians at that time. It boasted the first bishop

seat in Japan..

[40]TN: Like the accountants, chief banyos, repairmen, and government secretaries.

[41]TN: Shichigatsu.

[42]TN: Banjoosen in Dutch, a word derived from the Japanese word *banyoshu*, the Japanese police.

[43]TN: A Dutch word literally meaning masters of the secret or secrets sniffers.

[44]TN: *Oranda tsûji* in Japanese. The first Dutch translator's college was founded in 1640. Before, Portuguese had been the lingua franca. It wasn't until the end of the 17th century that the Japanese translators (whose services the Dutch had to pay for) seem to have gained a reasonable command of the Dutch language. Their difficulty, no doubt, was in part due tot he fact that the Dutch were not allowed to teach them. The college was organized like a guild and consisted of some 60 people; *dai-tsûji* or first class translators, *ko-tsûji* or second class translators, and then lower ranked or apprentice translators. In certain families, the profession of translator was hereditary.

[45]TN: The use of this French word refers to the fact that Holland was under French occupation. Perhaps the French were in need of spies as well at that time.

[46]Zimmerman talks about a strange case in his work, *The Earth and her Inhabitants*, chapter XI, page 65-66. Two noblemen met each other on the staircase of the imperial palace. Accidentally their swords touched. The nobleman who came from upstairs considered this an insult while the other, who was to carry a plate to the Emperor's table, wrote it off as an unintentional little accident. The latter nobleman however said in parting to the one who felt insulted: "anyhow, my sword is as good as yours." "I will show you right now what the difference between our sabers is," replied the other. He pulled his and cut open his belly. Without a word, the other left but returned after having fulfilled his duty to the Emperor, glad to find his adversary still

alive though mortally wounded. Apologizing for the fact that service to the Emperor had forced him to leave the scene, he instantly proved that his sword was every bit as valuable as the other's by cutting open *his* belly. He fell, dead, to the ground. Zimmerman compares this belly cutting with dueling in Europe. *Publisher*

[47]This was also the case in Rome under the first tyrannical emperors when someone was accused of lèse majesté. Hence, the many suicides of that period which Tacitus reports. In Japan, therefore, suicide is considered an honor, while in our laws it is considered a disgrace. *Publisher*

[48]TN: He was literally locked up in his own palace. All the doors and windows were nailed shut, and he was also not allowed to shave.

[49]New proof that the pure worship of God originates with man and that neither nature worship nor idolatry are the oldest forms of worship as so many modern writers claim. Publisher's note.

[50]TN: Shinto, literally way of the Gods, has no godhead as such. It encompasses a collection of rituals, traditions, pilgrimages and shrines which emphasize nature and ancestor worship. In Shinto, all living things are seen as an expression of the divine, but it has no systematic philosophy or well-defined moral code. Until the end of World War II, Shinto did also include the worship of the emperor as the direct descendant of the sun goddess Amaterasu who, according to legend, founded Japan.

[51]TN: Tabard, a loose jacket with wide sleeves, somewhat akin to a Greek toga.

[52]TN: Izumo, where an ancient God is said to have descended from heaven, is actually the oldest. The Ise shrine has been torn down and rebuilt, exactly as it had been built originally, every two decades since 1640.

[53]The *matsuri* is held to honor the Shinto God *Suwa*, patron

deity of Nagasaki. It was basically instituted to counteract the Christian deity.

[54]TN: Usually in the beginning of June, in order to arrive in July, the designated month for the arrival of Dutch ships. The distance from Batavia to Nagasaki is 3,300 miles and took from 4 to 6 weeks. Ships usually sailed by way of the Banka and Taiwan straits and the Nansei-Shôtô islands. They often stopped in Thailand or Taiwan to pick up deer pelts and shark skins which were much coveted by the Japanese. About 3.7% of these ships perished at sea.

[55]TN: Often, the Japanese guests at these banquets folded leftovers in paper and hid this "doggy bag" in their sleeves.

[56]TN: Buddhism originated in India and came to Japan via China. The Japanese date the official introduction of Buddhism into their country to the year 552, but it probably entered Japan even earlier. This date also marks the time when Japan started to learn from the Chinese, since Buddhism served as an important vehicle for the transmission of Chinese culture to Japan This "borrowed" Chinese civilization was eventually transformed into a native Japanese culture.

[57]Buddhists are spread throughout East Asia. They have many priests whose spirituality and ceremonies have a lot in common with Roman Catholic priests. They originate from Hindustan (India). Buddhism is the main religion of Ceylon, Indo China, and Tibet, and is the most numerous sect in China and Japan. Publisher.

[58]It really corresponds to the English "Lord," which is used both for an aristocrat as well as for God. *Publisher*

[59]TN: Literally representations of the Buddha.

[60]TN: It was not eradicated. The Roman Catholics of the village of Urakami, for instance, continued to practice their faith in secret during 200 years of persecution. They were called *Kakure Kirishitan* or crypto-Christians. In an ironic twist of fate, the atom bomb, falling short of its intended target, the Mitsubishi

shipyard and factory, fell instead on Urikami.

[61]TN: Around 1600, Catholics in Japan numbered already 1.75 million or about 1/10 of the population.

[62]TN: Toyotomi Hideyoshi.

[63]The Spaniard must have spoken here out of sheer arrogance or recklessness, as he could easily have predicted the consequences of such talk from a nation like Japan. On top of this, what he said was not even true. The innocent inhabitants of the West Indies, of Mexico, and Peru were conquered not by missionaries but solely by the sword, firearms, bloodhounds (in the real sense), and horses with their riders in the saddle which the Indians saw as superior creatures. The missionaries, especially the decent Las Casas, came only later to redress great evils. On the Philippine islands, they were surely successful in converting or forcing some inhabitants into that (so-called) Christendom, but usually after the country had been conquered. On the Muslim islands of the East Indies, their attempts at converting were inconsequential. It is possible that the Spaniard wanted to convey that his government operated more by management and reason than by force; but in any case, his silly and unsubstantiated loquaciousness did his country and the flourishing Christian community in Japan irreparable harm. Publisher.

[64]TN: The Portugueses were called *namban-jin* or southern barbarians.

[65]TN: In 1614, foreign priests were declared enemies of Buddha and the state and ordered to leave the country.

[66]TN: Twenty-six people were crucified in Nagasaki, 6 European friars and 20 Japanese Christians, among them a 12- and a 14-year-old boy. All 26 were canonized in 1862. Not only did many Japanese Christians suffer the agony of crucifiction, but other tortures as well: their genitals were branded; capes of straw, hung over their shoulders, were set on fire. Adult males had to rape their mothers, while others were boiled in the "hells" of

Unzen's sulphur springs in which they were thrown. Christian children were also tortured. In 1827, a *rangakusha* or Dutch scholar was crucified for owning forbidden Christian books.

[67]TN: The name of this ship was *"De Liefde,"* Charity, when *oranda-jin* as the Dutch were called, first set foot in Japan on April 19, 1600, in Sachibi in Bungo province. The Dutch, alone among the European nations, had the monopoly of trade with Japan from 1639 until the treaty of Kanagawa in 1853, whereby Japan opened two harbors to American ships and the Dutch-Japanese relation lost its unique character.

[68]TN: He received the Japanese name of *Miura Anjin*.

[69]This ship was badly outfitted by Jacques Mahu, Simon DeCordes and Sebalt de Weert. It sailed in 1598 but was, for the most part, shipwrecked. Publisher.

[70]TN: This was the Eighty years war of independence Holland waged against the mighty Spanish Empire. This war (1568 to 1648) ended in the Peace of Münster when the seven northern provinces of Holland, already united since 1579 (the Union of Utrecht) became independent.

[71]TN: The *Griffioen* (Griffin with 19 cannons) and the *Roode Leeuw* (Red Lion), a ship of at least 600 tons and 26 cannons. They arrived in Hirado on July 2, 1609.

[72]This Ongoshio is the same person who is frequently mentioned under the names of Zjejas, Daifu-Sama, and Gongen, the founder of the present reigning royal family in Japan, i.e. Ieyasu Tokugawa.

[73]TN: Hirado or wide gate in Japanese. The first European ship, a Portuguese one, came here in 1543. The Dutch started trading here in 1609 and the English in 1613, but the latter voluntarily retreated in 1623. During the Hirado period, the Dutch were free to travel, marry Japanese women, and take them and their offspring home. This all changed after the expulsion of the Portuguese. In this period, lots of ships arrived, 48 during the years of 1634 to 1638 alone. Trade flourished

and so did profits which in the year 1636 amounted to 1.2 million guilders. The first Dutch chief in Japan was Jacques Specx, one of the most important founders of the trade with Japan..

[74]TN: Deshima, variously spelled Decima, Dejima, or Desima, was an artificial, fan-shaped island built on high ground in the bay of Nagasaki in 1634-36. The name means "the isle that juts out," It was about the size of the Dam square in Amsterdam, or about 238 x 272 feet. Deshima, according to legend, was fan-shaped because, when the ruler was asked for his wishes as to its shape, he simply moved his wrist to open his ever-present fan. It was surrounded by a big rock stone wall, and along the main street were about 30 houses. A stone bridge connected the island to the city. The island had two gates, a land and a water gate, each with a guard post. On the land gate was written: no women are allowed except *yûjos* (public women who served the Dutch as concubines and housekeepers): no Dutchman can leave the island without a good reason or the permission of the governor of Nagasaki. This rule too became less strictly enforced over time. During the 17th century, this trading station was very profitable to the Dutch, but in the 18th century, profits steadily declined. However, Deshima became an extremely useful diplomatic contact point as well as a source of Western culture and technology for Japan. Only the knowledge thus acquired can explain Japan's rapid transformation from a feudal to a modern state in the second half of the 19th Century.

[75]TN: Spain and Portugal had formed a union in 1580, which lasted until 1640. The Dutch then made peace with the Portuguese.

[76]TN: Holland was called *Oranda* from the Portuguese Olanda. As the Japanese cannot say the letter L, Olanda became *Oranda*. According to the famous artist Hayashi Shihei, Holland lies in the northwest of the world and is a civilized European country. It is 13,000 miles from Japan, and, therefore, the Dutch, who visit us yearly, do not come directly from Holland but from

Java, south of Japan. The Dutch were called *Oranda-Jin*, and Japanese children called the Dutch *Oranda-ô-me* or Dutch big eyes.

[77]TN: Especially the English put Holland in a bad light as having aided a "heathen country" against fellow Christians.

[78]The Shimabara rebellion was led by Amakusa Shirô, a valiant Christian youth.

[79]TN: The Japanese knew very well that the Dutch ships had gunpowder, hence the invitation which was, at the same time, a test of loyalty. All Europeans were suspect in those days, and refusing to help might have led to the expulsion of the Dutch as well.

[80]TN: This ship was called the *Rijp*. In actuality, there had been four ships in Hirado, but two ships, the *Otter* and the *Oudewater*, had just left for Formosa. Koekebakker quickly sent the third, the *Petten* back to Batavia. That left only the *Rijp*, a relatively small ship.

[81]TN: They were directed at the fort of the insurgents but apparently without much success, which gave the *shôgun*, shamed by the insurgents' note, a good excuse to dismiss the Dutch.

[82]TN: The Shimabara rebellion began indeed for economic and political reasons. It became more of a Christian rebellion when flocks of Roman Catholics joined the insurgents.

[83]TN: F. Caron, former chief on Deshima, wrote a book titled *Description of the Powerful Kingdom of Japan*, Amsterdam, 1648. He also was one of the founders of Dutch trade in Japan.

[84]TN. The construction of a big fortified square building in Hirado bearing the inscription "Anno Christi 1640," almost caused the banishment of the Dutch. Caron, warned by his ally the daimyô of Hirado, that all the Dutch would be killed if he refused, immediately executed this order. Knowing the Dutch tendency to negotiate first, the Japanese government was pleased and mollified by this strict obedience, but nevertheless

remained wary. In May 1641, it ordered the Dutch trading station to be moved to Deshima. This heralded a new, restriction-laden period of Dutch trade in Japan.

[85]TN: This man settled as a merchant in Japan and sent letters to Holland requesting that the Dutch come to Japan. This finally materialized in 1609, and Santvoort went to Hirado to help the Dutch with all the formalities required to establish a trading post. He also accompanied the first two Dutch delegates, Mr. Puyck and Mr. van den Broek, who had a letter for the *shôgun* from Prince Maurits, on the first of what would become many treks to the Court in Edo.

[86]TN: They were on the ship the *de Liefde*, partially shipwrecked in 1600.

[87]TN: *De Verenigde Oost-Indische Compagnie* or the United East Indies Company was founded in 1602 by a charter from the States General with a dual purpose: to regulate and protect the already considerable trade carried on by the Dutch in the Indian Ocean and to help in prosecuting the long war of independence against Spain by opening up a second front in the Far East. The VOC had 17 directors called *de Heren XVII* or the Lords XVII. The VOC not only received the monopoly of the Asian trade, but a few sovereign rights as well, such as establishing trade pacts with foreign princes and potentates and enter into alliance with them against Spain.

[88]TN: This man later published the first eyewitness report of the persecution of the Roman Catholics in Japan in a sensational pamphlet called: *The Tyranny and Cruelties of the Japanese*, Amsterdam, 1637. After 1622, this persecution had become so extreme that the Dutch, pretty much inured by cruelty reports since the inquisition and their war with Spain, were appalled. Catholicism in Japan survived 200 years of persecution, however, by going underground.

[89]TN: In 1640, the inquisitor of the *shôgun* said this to the Dutch chief: His imperial majesty knows that you, like the Portuguese, are Christians. You keep the sabbath; you write the date of

Christ's birth on the facades of your houses in full view of our entire nation; you have the ten commandments, the Our Father, the faith, the baptism, the sharing of bread, bible, testament, Moses, the prophets and apostles... That you are Christians we knew, but we supposed that *you* had another Christ.

[90]TN: Fesodonne was an anti-Dutch governor of Nagasaki.

[91]TN: The 80-year war of independence.

[92]TN: The mainland above China and the island of Hokkaido. In 1690, it was not known whether it was connected to Tartary or America.

[93]*Jefumi*, from Je = idols and *Fumi* = trample, and *not* from the word *Jesumi*, or Jesus, as most writers claim. TN: called *fumi-e* by the Japanese.

[94]TN: *Tôjin* in Japanese, from *Tô*, their version of T'ang, the name of the Chinese dynasty. *Tôjin* thus means the People of T'ang

[95]TN: Gotô Rettô in Japanese.

[96]TN: Ambon, an island in the Ceram Sea, Indonesia, has an interesting history. In a 1619 pact, the VOC granted the English East India Company a lodge within its fort on this island. In 1623, ten Englishmen, ten Japanese mercenary soldiers, and one Portuguese were executed, as they had conspired to take over the Dutch fort. This incident heralded the end of Anglo-Dutch cooperation in the Far East and contributed to the beginning of the Anglo-Dutch wars, as the English called it "murder." "Revenge for Amboyna" remained for centuries a propaganda tool for rallying the English against the Dutch and was used as late as the Boer war, despite the fact that in 1654, at the Peace of Westminster, the VOC paid 43,000 guilders in reparation money to the heirs of some of the executed Englishmen.

[97]TN: This was the *Tôjin-yashiki*, or Chinese trading station and walled compound in the southeast corner of the City. The

Dutch trading station was called *Oranda-yashiki* and operated from 1641 to 1860.

[98]TN: J. A. Krusenstern, captain of the ship *Nadeida*, made the first Russian circumnavigation of the globe from 1802-1806. He related his experiences in a three-volume book with atlas, *Journey Around the World*, published in 1809-1813, and translated into German then English.

[99]TN: Ship's doctor of the Nadeida, Georg Heinrich Langsdorff wrote a book in two volumes published in 1812. *Reflections upon a Journey around the World*.

[100]TN: E. Kaempfer, a German physician, succeeded in seeing more of the country and collecting more information than any European before him. Kämpfer's book remained the standard work about Japan far into the 19th century. See appendix.

[101]Carl Peter Thunberg, a botanist and physician, had been a pupil of Linnaeus.

[102]*TN: Shôgatsu.*

[103]TN: This whole text is quoted in French.

CHAPTER II

[1]TN: Four copies of this trading pass were actually handed out, one of which survives and is in the General Archives in The Hague. The pass was handed over to Jacob Groenewegen on the 25th day of the 7th month of the 14th year of *Keichô*, i.e. on August 24, 1609. In a personal letter to Prince Maurits of Orange, Ieyasu granted the Dutch free access to all Japanese harbors, free trade all over Japan, as well as the same protection granted Japanese citizens. Some historians claim that this trading pass was not the reason that the Dutch were allowed to stay for 250 years after Japan became closed to the world. According

to them, the main reason was the fact that the Dutch strictly adhered to the ban on Christian missionaries.

[2]TN: The main exports from Japan were gold, silver, and copper. In 1668 silver could not longer be exported, while gold could only be exported in the form of coins, the gold kobans. As these coins had to be melted in India, the gold export became unprofitable, a 39% loss alone in 1720, and was therefore abandoned. Only the export of copper remained but was severely restricted through taxes and quotas.

[3]TN: A *pikol* is a Malay word. It connotes the weight a man can carry in two baskets which are suspended from a pole and carried over his shoulder, usually around 125 pounds.

[4]TN: Today we would call this a quota.

[5]TN: The VOC and its sister company, the VWC, formed a trading empire that stretched around the world. It was a global enterprise unrivaled to this day, as it made a profit in excess of 10% for almost 200 years. The VOC owed its success in large measure to the fact that it had its warehouses filled with specific goods at strategic points all over Asia. The VOC could fill orders more expeditiously than others could, as it knew exactly where to send its ships to pick up merchandise and deliver it. One might consider the VOC the FedEx of its time.

[6]TN: Hemmy died from a mysterious illness in 1789 on the return trip from Edo. Rumors had it that he was poisoned. He was buried in Kakegawa where his grave still exists. Recently, a commemorative stone slab was placed at the site.

[7]At his appointment, mister Wardenaar was able to accomplish that the government took over the cost and the risk involved in shipping the 700 *pikols* copper the chief receives as part of his salary to Batavia. Up till then, it was sent at his own risk and cost.

[8]TN: Actually the start of the fifth of the six wars the Dutch waged against the English.

[9]TN: A treaty between England and Holland, whereby England returned the colonies, was signed on August 13, 1814, but in reality the actual repossession didn't take place until a year or two later (variously reported as 1815, 1816 or, as here, 1817). Raffles left Java only in 1816.

[10]TN: The *Crown Prince*.

[11]TN: This ship brought the news that the Batavian republic was now the Kingdom of Holland under Louis Napoleon, brother of Napoleon.

[12]TN: This was the only American who gave Doeff real headaches. Apart from frequently not paying his crew, officers, or bills, Davidson was often roaring drunk and then became obnoxious, once even slapping the translators. Doeff received many complaints about him from the governor of Nagasaki, including that he once had received the translators without pants on and with his legs on the table. To top this off, he then proceeded to vomit. Davidson also kept the American flag on the stern which the governor, whose life literally was at stake here, noticed with great dismay. Doeff first asked, then ordered him to take the flag away which he did, but included the Dutch flag. At his departure, Davidson was so drunk he had to be carried on board, but Doeff, lest he pull one over on him, put two Dutchmen on board, including the experienced Dutch captain Voorman.

[13]TN: After the Arabic word hamman, bath house. Thick, densely woven cloth used as shawls during the cold season. Also bath towels.

[14]TN: *Ducaton*, an old Dutch silver coin worth three guilders and three stuivers. It is sometimes called a silver rider.

[15]TN: A word derived from the Chinese word tael is a weight as well as a monetary unit. One tael (37.8 grams of silver) was the basis of the monetary system in Japan. Until 1666, the worth of a tael was set at 57 *stuivers* (Dutch nickels), after that at 70, while in the French period it was set at 33 *stuivers*. It is

widely used in Asia as a standard to establish the price of luxury goods. Some claim that the word derives from the Malay word *tahil*, a weight unit for gold and opium.

[16]TN: A *stuiver* is the Dutch equivalent of a nickel, worth five cents.

[17]TN: *Maas* and *conderin* are smaller denominations of the *tael*.

[18]TN: Coromandel and Bengal contained two Dutch possessions.

[19]TN: Caesalpina sappan, or red dye wood. *Soboku* in Japanese.

[20]TN: An Indian root and ingredient for perfume and incense.

[21]TN: Gum.

[22]TN: Coins.

[23]TN: Coarse wool cloth.

[24]TN: *Ikje* is a Dutch bastardization of the Japanese word *ikken*. A *ken* is a measure of length consisting of six *shaku* (Japanese foot), i.e. about 1.81 meters or about six feet.

[25]TN: *Grijn*, a mixture of wool and goat or camel hair.

[26]TN: *Chitzen*, fine cotton material.

[27]TN: *Patnachen*, textile from the city of Patna, capital of the state of Bihar, India.

[28]TN: *Taffachelassen*, finely striped silk or cotton from the north west of India (the area around the city of Sinbri). Coast refers to either the coast of Bengal or Coromandel.

[29]TN: *Hassaku*, which refers to the first day of the eighth month according to the sun calendar. It was the day payments were made.

[30]TN: Doeff probably Japanized the word *ropijen* or *ropeys*, the Dutch plural version of *rupee* (India) or *rupiah* (Indonesia), a widely used currency in the Far East. A *ropey* at that time was worth one *rijksdaalder* (two and a half *guilders*).

³¹TN: This cemetery lies on the slope of Mount Inasa and dates from 1654 or even earlier.

³²TN: Old Spanish silver coin also called *piastre*.

³³TN: A guilder is divided into four *kwartjes* (quarters), or *ten dubbeltjes* (dimes), or twenty *stuivers* (nickels).

³⁴TN: The Dutch government had taken over the VOC in 1798, but the Japnese government was not informed of this change.

³⁵TN: The Japanese called this trade *Conpaniya* or the official trade.

³⁶TN: Kambang was the unofficial or private trade. The word is most likely derived from *kanban*, the signboard on which all the articles for sale were written.

³⁷TN: Areca palm or areca catachu. Betel nut.

³⁸TN: Aromatic resinous oils used for medicine and perfume.

³⁹TN: In Dutch *geld kamer* or *kaisho* in Japanese. Literally a money chamber, akin to a loan and exchange bank or chamber of commerce.

⁴⁰TN: Literally unicorns. These were in reality the pointed and curved single tusks of the narwahl, *monodon monoceros*, found in the Arctic seas. The Japanes believed that these horns had extraordinary life-prolonging, memory enhancing, and curative powers.

⁴¹TN: Most likely a contraction of (papaver) somniferum or opium.

⁴²TN: *Yûjos*, the prostitutes the Dutch kept as concubines, were also avid smugglers and made a lot of profit from this extracurricular activity. In addition, *yûjos* were useful *metsuke* (spies), as they informed Doeff of the intentions and plans of the translators.

⁴³TN: In 1828, Franz von Siebold was banished, when a map of Japan was found in his luggage among many other forbidden items. These were given to him by his pupils who were severely

punished, some by death, others by jail.

[44]TN: This word is probably derived from the Malay word kabaya — blouse. Here it connotes a long Persian coat fashioned after the flowered ones worn by the Mogul rulers. It eventually evolved into what we now call a kimono.

[45]TN: *Sake* sediment.

[46]TN: Big porcelain pots named after the city Martaban in India.

[47]TN: *Mieo-mame*.

[48]TN: It was through the *Kambang* trade that Japanese scholars ordered books, manuals, scientific instruments, and other articles from Holland.

[49]TN: This is a Portuguese word and basically means buyer. It certainly dates from the time when the Portuguese traded almost exclusively in Japan.

[50]TN: This word is a quaint expression meaning "narrow chestedness." Wardenaar was often short of breath as he was quite overweight. Some sources say he had asthma.

[51]TN: Chief Inspector.

[52]TN: This was a treaty, signed in 1802, between England, France, Spain, and Holland which made for a short pause in the Napoleonic War.

[53]TN: William Robert Stewart was an enigmatic figure, as it is not clear whether he was actually an American or an Englishman posturing as an American. Doeff firmly believed the latter.

[54]TN: The privilege of carrying swords was usually only accorded to nobles, samurai and priests. Samurai, the military aristocracy, regarded their blades as a symbol of their honor; treating their swords with disrespect could lead to dire consequences.

[55]TN: *Gobansho*.

[56]TN: From the Malay word *muson*, monsoon season, a period

of (usually) heavy rains in the Far East.

[57]TN: It had actually been a typhoon.

[58]TN: Stewart had named this brig *Emperor of Japan*.

[59]TN: Doeff by then knew very well that Stewart was a crook.

[60]TN: The name of this ship was the *Frederick*.

[61]TN: In 1803, the 6th and last war against England started, and all over Europe the Napoleonic Wars raged.

[62]TN: Start of the fifth war against England.

[63]TN: It has to be kept in mind also that Russia at that time was allied to England.

[64]TN: These demanded strict neutrality.

[65]TN: This was a small island, two kilometers from Deshima. The Japanese called it *Takaboko*, and it afforded the first full view of Nagasaki. After the Dutch sailed around the Papenberg, their ships had to be towed in by order of the Japanese.

[66]*Journey Around the World*, Dutch translation, H.D. page 48.

[67]See Langsdorff, page 50.

[68]TN: *Kugatsu*.

[69]The *tripang* is a sea cucumber (holothuria) abounding in East Indies waters. The Chinese and Japanese relish it. The latter are particularly fond of fish and shellfish; basically they are fond of all that the sea offers. Publisher

[70]This is a shellfish from which the Japanese extract the mother of pearl which they so artfully use in their lacquer work. TN: This Dutch word literally means reefsucker.

[71]TN: Pier is the space between windows.

[72]: From the French verb *chattouiller*, to tickle or please. Knick-knacks.

[73]TN: Palanquin, in India and other Eastern countries, is a

passenger carriage, usually for one person, consisting of a covered box-like litter carried by means of poles resting on the shoulders of several men. Random House Dictionary of the English Language.

[74]This is also the reason why the author preferred not to translate these papers into French, a language with which the Russian ambassador and his retinue were surely more familiar than Dutch. The Japanese did not know French, however, and this request could have fed their suspicion. Publisher

[75]TN: Matsumae.

[76]TN: *Bunka nengô* means Bunka period, Bunka 2 - 1805.

[77]TN: Nansei-shotô islands.

[78]TN: Red pepper.

[79]This became known in Europe through the travel writings of Langsdorff and Krusenstern.

[80]On the first mentioned page one read about a reminder given by the *Ginmiyakushi* (inspection commissioners) to Mr. Golownin; on the second page an address to Mr. Golownin by the governor of Matsmay (Matsumae).

[81]Who perhaps did so to save these people from inconvenience (sic!). Publisher's note.

[82]TN: In 1795 the French revolutionary forces overran the Netherlands, which then became the Batavian republic until 1805. Before 1795, it was the republic of the United Netherlands.

[83]TN: From 1633 to 1790, this trek to Edo took place every year but every four years thereafter. The Chinese did not have this honor, only the Dutch. The distance between Nagasaki and Edo was about 1,300 miles, and the arduous trek usually took from three to four months.

RECOLLECTIONS OF JAPAN

CHAPTER III

[1]TN: Original translation into Dutch by Professor Fritz Vos.

[2]TN: On one of his treks to Edo, Doeff glimpsed a beautiful young girl in Gion, Kyoto chopping tofu with lightning speed. This image was the inspiration for this *haiku*.

[3]TN: *Shôgatsu.*

[4]TN: *Nigatsu*

[5]TN: *Shukubamachi.*

[6]TN: The inland sea of Japan, *Seto Naikai.*

[7]TN: The famous *Tôkaidô* highway.

[8]TN: A colorful print of this barque hangs in the municipal museum of Shimoneseki.

[9]TN: The Dutch chief had the de facto rank of a *daimyô* and was the only Dutchman allowed to carry a sword.

[10]TN: *Norimono* in Japanese.

[11]It happens more often on the short than on the long country road that people crowd around us. On the main island of the realm (Nippon, now Honshû), the seat of the *shôgun*, the government, and the most important interior trade, the people are in general more polite and seemingly more civilized than on the more remote south western island. Proof of this is that the princes always have their troops accompany us on the short road, which they do not do on the long road as that would not be necessary.

[12]TN: *Honjin* were exclusively for *daimyô* and Court nobility. For a lesser grade of people, there was the *waki-honjin* which was also free to take ordinary people if not busy.

[13]TN: Now Honshû.

[14]TN: Now Murotsu.

[15]TN: Now Kobe. Fiogo is the Dutch version of Hyôgo.

[16]TN: Nishinomiya.

[17]According to Kaempfer, Osaka is one of the 5 big cities and agreeably situated in a fertile plain on the banks of a navigable river in the province of Set-Zu. A fortified castle protects it on the east side, and on the west side are two big gates that separate the city from its suburbs. The city is about 3 to 4,000 feet long and slightly less wide. The river Yodogawa brings countless treasures to this city, and to accommodate this traffic a big canal and several smaller ones were dug that criss-cross the city and over which more than a 100 bridges were built. Osaka is the best trading city in Japan as it is well situated for this. Many merchants, artists, and artisans live there, and the cost of living is low. The city is so densely populated that the Japanese pride themselves on being able to assemble an army of 80,000 men from this city alone!

[18]TN: Fine cotton materials from Patna (India) - chintz.

[19]Miyako, a long day's journey from Osaka, an area so densely populated that the road seems to be a continuation of a city street, is the second, or, as the seat of the *dairi*, really the first city of the realm. Situated in a big plain, the city is 3/4 of a German mile (almost 1½ hour on foot) in length and half of that in width. Green hills make the area very pleasant, and several rivers that originate in the area flow either through or past the town. The *dairi* lives on the North side in a separate part of the city that is encircled by walls and canals which cut it off from the city itself. To the west lies a big stone castle which serves as the *shôgun's* residence when he visits the *dairi*. Excluding the court of the *dairi*, Kaempfer estimates from real census data that 140 years ago, the city had a population of 477,557 lay people and 52,169 priests. Kaempfer, pgs. 342, 345-347

[20]TN: This is the famous *Tôkaidô* highway which runs from Kyoto to Tokyo. There were 53 stops on this road; the first was Otsu and the last Shinegawa.

[21]TN: Kuwana.

RECOLLECTIONS OF JAPAN 199

[22]TN: Miya.

[23]TN: An open gondola type canopied vessel, akin to a royal sloop.

[24]Mishima.

[25]According to Kaempfer, the Japanese call Mount Fuji an inactive volcano, its crater now filled with water. The Japanese climb this mountain for religious reasons to worship the God of the winds there. Poets cannot find words nor painters colors to do justice to this mountain. Kaempfer, page 363.

[26]TN: Shinagawa.

[27]TN: The Nagasaki-ya.

[28]TN: *Boontjes* literally means little beans in Dutch. As there are sufficient examples of coins in the form of a bean, it is likely that small coins came to be referred to as *boontjes* in the far East. Here they pertain to the small square Japanese coin called *ichibu* which was worth one fourth of a *koban*.

[29]TN: Baskets made out of rattan. Often used to transport sugar and tobacco. Canaster in old English.

[30]TN: *Nihonbashi*. Literally Nippon Bridge but the word nihon is used more often than nippon in Japan. It is the most famous bridge in Japan.

[31]According to Kaempfer, pg. 372, fires are multiplied here because Japanese houses are made of pine wood and their walls of clay. The insides are divided into rooms by paper sliding doors and windows, the floors are covered by mats and the roofs with woodchips. Publisher.

[32]TN: For over 200 years, the Dutch were the only Europeans the Japanese saw. They were fascinated by these *kômô-jin* or red-haired barbarians to whom they ascribed five characteristics: they were tall, had blue eyes, white skin, long noses, and red hair. They also thought the Dutch had no heels and therefore put them on their shoes, and they ascribed a phenomenal sexual prowess to them which could even be enhanced by mysterious

medicine. Still others held that because of their sexual excesses and drinking, the Dutch did not become old, 50 at most. Though many depictions of the Dutch were at first very unflattering (they were even supposed to lift their legs when urinating), with increased contact between Japanese scholars and the Dutch, these depictions became almost idealistic and therefore equally unreal. The Dutch, their ships, and the exotica they brought soon became the subject of numerous wood block prints.

[33]TN: Nagasaki had four governors called *bugyos*. Two stayed in Nagasaki and two were stationed in Edo.

[34]TN: *Sangatsu.*

[35]TN: Proof that the chief had the same status as a *daimyô*.

[36]TN: A Dutch bastardization of the Japanese word *bôzu*, singular as well as plural for monks.

[37]TN: Tatami mats.

[38]TN: *Oranda kapitan*, literally Holland Captain.

[39]Edo (Kaempfer says, page 372) lies in the province Musossi at 35° and 32 minutes N. latitude, in a big plain at the end of a bay which teems with fish, crabs, and shellfish. This bay is so shallow that no ships of any size can come to the city, but have to unload two hours distance below the city. Edo faces the sea in a half moon fashion. Like other cities, she is not surrounded by a wall or rampart but is bisected by many canals with high parapets on both sides on which rows of trees are planted; this was done not so much to defend the city as to prevent that fires which often rage here from causing too much damage. A big river, coming from the west side, crosses the city and finally disgorges in the harbor. This river has a big branch that runs around the castle to then empty into the harbor in five streams, each with a bridge spanning it. As far as the gaiety and bustle in the streets, Kaempfer is in agreement with Thunberg and this author, and ascribes it to the many officials and princely families. Edo, Kaempfer continues, is not built in as regular a

RECOLLECTIONS OF JAPAN

fashion as other cities in Japan, especially Miyako, because the city gradually was expanded to her present size. At certain points in the city, streets run in regular right angles which can be ascribed to the fires. Because many hundreds of houses can be destroyed all at once, new streets can be built wherever the builders want them. The houses in Edo are small and low, just like everywhere else in the country, but there are also many stately palaces. The castle is five miles in circumference and inside the palace square, a brilliantly white tower arises which is many stories high and provides a lovely view of the castle from afar, just as the other beautiful roofs adorned with dragons on top do. Behind the imperial palace are beautiful gardens, orchards, and woods. Edo is a hotbed of artists and artisans, merchants and shop keepers, but because of the great influx of people and the difficulty in supplying provisions, everything is sold at a higher price than anywhere else in the country. Publisher

[40]TN: Joseph Jerôme de LaLande, famous French astronomer who devoted himself to the improvement of the planetary theory and published a corrected edition of Halley's tables in 1759. He is best known for popularizing astronomy. Takehashi Yoshitoki and Hazama Shigetoki translated *Astronomia* in 1775.

[41]TN: Inhabitants of the *Nansei-Shotô* islands of which the main one is Okinawa.

[42]TN: Eager Japanese doctors received such names as Peter Healthy, William Recovery, or Philip Cured, names they carried like a badge of honor. The Japanese firmly believed that Dutch was a world language, and they had no idea how small Holland was in reality.

[43]TN: Possibly a pun as *pauw* means peacock.

[44]TN: In 1720, the *shôgun* Yoshimune lifted the ban on the import of non-religious books which heralded the penetration of western knowledge into Japan. Two years later, the first book, *Tafel Anatomia*, was translated from the Dutch and widely circulated. Japanese scholars eager to study Western medicine

and science, recognized the need to learn Dutch. To that effect, schools for learning Dutch were established in several parts of Japan. They were called *Rangaku*, a contraction of *oranda bangaku* or the science of the Dutch barbarians, and their students were called *rangakusha* or Hollandologists, Dutch scholars. They established the first school, the *Shirandô*, that taught Western medicine in Edo in 1789. They also painstakingly translated Dutch books and manuscripts into Japanese and ordered not only books but all kinds of scientific instruments as well. Over time, they became ever bolder in seeking contact with the Dutch, establishing *rangaku's* in other cities where, eventually, the Dutch were allowed to teach. In the last 75 years of the Dutch trading station, over 10,000 books on medicine, astronomy, geography, navigation, engineering, irrigation, horsemanship, and military sciences were imported via the kambang trade. *Rangakusha* still exist today, but they now learn Dutch to study that historical period of Dutch-Japanese relations. The Japanese microfilmed all the day registers of some 250 years and are in the process of translating them.

[45]TN: Franz von Siebold met this man, also known under the name Takahashi Kageyasu, as Globius in 1826. Undeniably the most brilliant scholar of his day, Takehashi met with a tragic end. In 1828, he was arrested and put in prison for having passed forbidden materials, maps in particular, to von Siebold. Before being sentenced, he died in prison on March 20, 1829. His body was subsequently pickled in brine, and once his sentence was passed, he was beheaded.

[46]It is under this nickname that this herbal specialist corresponded in our language with the famous professor Reinward when he was stationed in the Dutch East Indies, as I learned from this scholar himself.

[47]TN Kamiya Hiroyoshi.

[48]TN: Possibly after prince Frederik Hendrik of Orange.

[49]TN: Schuitje, literally a small boat. A block of silver poured into the form of a boat. It had a constant value in Japan of 4.3

RECOLLECTIONS OF JAPAN

tael. The little silver boat was the value basis of the Japanese monetary system as *tael* were converted into boat silver.

[50]TN: The Sanjûsangendo, a temple with a hall of 33 *ken* in length. It contains a principal statue of the Goddess of Mercy, Kannon Bosatsu, who is flanked by 1,000 smaller images, each in turn representing 33 images, hence Doeff's description of the temple with the 33,333 idols.

[51]This is really not surprising. The Dutch are the only foreigners the Japanese *ever* can see and, in the interior, they see them only once every four years. How different from theirs are the dress, customs, language, etc. of these foreigners.

[52]TN: Probably a Daibutsu temple, a temple with a big *(dai)* statue of Buddha *(Butsu).*

[53]TN: Nishinomiya and Kobe. Fiogo is the Dutch transliteration of Hyôgo as Kobe was called.

CHAPTER IV

[1]TN: They had to arrive in July.

[2]TN: The captain of the *Eclipse* was J. O'Cain. The ship was leased by the Russian-American Company to sail to Kamchatka, but some claim that its true aim was to open trade relations with Japan.

[3]TN: Louis Bonaparte, brother of Napoleon, became King of Holland in 1806. In 1810, Napoleon deposed his brother, and Holland was then incorporated into France and became a French department (until 1813).

[4]TN: Although America was neutral, its ships were nevertheless frequently attacked by the British, who were perhaps still smarting from the loss of their former colonies. This and other abuses led to the declaration of war in 1812.

[5]TN: Doeff was fluent in French as well as in English and

Japanese. In 1808, he started to teach French to six Japanese pupils.

⁶TN: Apart from exporting and importing goods, the VOC had another, unique mandate in Japan. It was expected to give other services such as translating foreign letters or requests and give a yearly report, the so-called Dutch newsletter or *Oranda Fusetsugaki*, of the political developments in Europe and elsewhere in the world. According to some, this mandate made the Dutch the foreign *metsuke* (spies) of the Japanese.

⁷TN: For the French word entêtement.

⁸TN: This was during the 6th war against England which lasted from 1803 to 1813.

⁹TN: A culture clash is in evidence here. For Doeff, the first and foremost priority was to save the lives of his two men and, if possible, prevent a carnage of innocent English sailors. For the Japanese, revenge for the insult meted out to them counted more than saving lives. Had the hostages been Japanese, their lives undoubtedly would have been sacrificed for the honor of revenge.

All through Doeff's writings, day registers included, his humanitarian instincts and respect for human life comes through. As many progressive Europeans of his time, he espoused the democratic ethos of the French and American revolutions, especially the rights of men. The slogan "Liberté, Egalité, Fraternité" resonated with the Francophile Doeff.

¹⁰One could call this the enthusiasm of slavery. Publisher's addition

¹¹TN: Doeff estimated that the *Phaëton* had 300 men aboard and was armed with at least 40 cannons. In fact, the *Phaëton* had 350 men on board, among whom was a Dutch sailor named Metzeler.

¹²What a despicable action, one among thousands showing the misuse of power of which the English have been guilty against

less powerful nations, especially against us! To enter a foreign neutral harbor and there lure two men by deceitfully flying their flag and using their language, until they can capture them by force, then *threaten them with death*, and, without any proof, accuse them of lying, something the English especially consider to be a mortal insult! What a baseness, like their actions in 1781, 1795, 1803, and 1832.

TN: The first of these three dates refer to the fourth, fifth, and sixth so called English Wars. Since 1652, the Dutch had fought the English in a total of six wars. The first four wars were purely trade wars. The last two were so-called coalition wars when Holland, allied to France, fought against England and its allies. Doeff made a slight (but understandable) mistake in the date of the fourth war which actually started in the last two or three weeks of 1780.

The date of 1832 refers to the London Conference, when England declared itself in favor of the partition of the Northern and Southern parts of Holland against the wishes of King William I who wanted to keep them together. England favored Prince Leopold of Saxen-Coburg as King of a future Belgium, since he was related to the English Royal Family through his first wife, Charlotte, daughter of a son of King George III. This partition issue had become a political process that lasted from 1800 to 1839, when Belgium became an independent nation under King Leopold I.

Clearly in Doeff's eyes, England had again acted against the interests of Holland.

[13]TN: It speaks for the esteem in which Doeff was held and the confidence in his judgment that he was twice able to dissuade the governor from a plan of action.

[14]TN: Fleetwood Pellew was the hot-headed and impulsive son of Rear-Admiral Sir Edward Pellew, later Lord Exmouth. In 1806, Sir Edward's fleet had approached the road stead of the city of Surabaya (Java) where his son Fleetwood, member of a delegation sent ashore, had been taken prisoner. After his raid

on Nagasaki, Fleetwood was involved in the opium war between China and England. When Perry came to Japan, Fleetwood was still signaled in the vicinity of Japan. As he continued to be hated in Japan, Fleetwood perhaps hoped for a chance to once more enter the harbor of Nagasaki, which he had never forgotten and about which he wrote lyrically, extolling its unsurpassed beauty.

[15]See the map of the harbor of Nagasaki in Kaempfer (p. 181). The Papenberg will not be found on that map, but instead the Japanese name of *Takaboko*. It is an island. I could not find the Cavallos on that map. Publisher.

[16]TN: On this last visit, Doeff noted that the governor wore his armor.

[17]TN: The biggest gold piece in general use, nominally with 1 *ryo* (18 grams) gold. In the 17th century, a *koban* was worth 21 Dutch guilders.

[18]TN: Kruithoff's ship was conquered by the English in Chinese waters, and he was sent back to Batavia.

[19]TN: Usually toward the end of October or the beginning of November when the typhoon season was over.

[20]TN: An example of Doeff's shrewdness. He played by the rules but knew how to manipulate them to his own advantage. Doeff was variously described as a man of principle, cautious and wily, a shrewd diplomat, politician and negotiator. The Japanese admired him as a scholar and ...as a womanizer. On one of several erotic wood block prints the Japanese made, which depicted the Dutch in compromising positions, the figure of Doeff is clearly identifiable.

[21]TN: Ilha Dos Cavallos, the Fukahori or Horses' Islands.

[22]TN: The flag consisted of three horizontal stripes, white-blue-white.

[23]TN: On this trip, Doeff was accompanied by the clerk Gozeman and the physician Jan Frederik Fijlke, who got sick

on the return trek and died six months later at the age of 35. A well known print shows Fijlke demonstrating the amputation of a left arm. The Japanese often paid more attention to the physician than the chief in their insatiable thirst for Western knowledge and tirelessly questioned him until late into the night.

[24]TN: This was a doubly difficult summer for Doeff. On August 11, 1810 he writes in the day register: "Death due to the red runs (hemorrhagic dysentery) is very high in Nagasaki, especially among children, with 50 of them being buried daily." On the 18th he writes: "This morning I lost my oldest daughter named Omon, 9 years of age and living in the city." Some 1,400 people died during that hot, dry summer.

[25]TN: On Cape Nombo or Nomosaki in Japanese.

[26]TN: Dutch gin made of Juniper berries.

[27]TN: Translated into Dutch from the original French *Dictionnaire Economique*, 1709, this was a sort of encyclopedia in seven volumes with lengthy articles about the natural sciences of the 18th century. In time, nine supplementary volumes were added with scientific data from such luminaries as Swammerdam and Leeuwenhoek, Linaeus and Camper. These volumes became the basis for the biggest translation enterprise of the Edo period.

[28]TN: A white beer with a distinctive taste, named after the Dutch town of Haarlem.

[29]TN: Among these women and children were Doeff's *taijo* Uryuno and their son Michitomi Yokichi born in 1807.

[30]TN: Some 377 houses burned down.

[31]TN: *Kura* in Japanese were not all that fireproof, as four of them burned down during this fire, two Chinese and two Japanese..

[32]TN: Literally "hailing letters." Basically these letters contained the information given when a new ship is hailed by a look-out boat.

[33]TN: Actually, Raffles had been appointed Vice Governor-General.

[34]TN: On August 4, 1811, the English attacked Java with some 2,000 men ferried over from Malacca on more than 100 ships. The leader of this expedition was Lord Minto, with general Auchmuty as head of the military operation. The engine behind it, however, was Thomas S. Raffles. On August 23, the Dutch troops under general Janssens suffered a decisive defeat but remnants of the army struggled on in mid-Java until their final defeat. On September 17, the capitulation of Tuntang was signed and Raffles was appointed Vice Governor-General. Previously, other Dutch possessions such as the Cape Colony, Guyana, St. Eustatius, Triconomale on Ceylon (Sri Lanka), and Negapatnam in India had already fallen into English hands. In a treaty signed in August 1814, the English reluctantly returned these Dutch colonies with the exception of the Cape Colony, Guyana and Ceylon. Holland received Banka in return for a few possessions in India.

[35]TN: The capitulation of Tuntang signed on September 17, 1811.

[36]TN: Basically, the Dutch were "guests" of the Japanese government which could expel them at any time.

[37]TN: Actually he was Dutch, but since Holland was annexed by France, he was technically speaking now a French citizen.

[38]TN: Wardenaar, basically a decent man, had succumbed to Raffles' bribe because he was in dire financial straits. At first, Raffles offered him 20 to 30,000 Spanish *piastres*, if he were willing to accept a commission to Japan. Wardenaar refused this offer but caved in when the ante was upped to 15% of the cargo *in natura* or about 50,000 *piastres*. However, he accepted on the condition that trade would proceed in the name of Holland. Wardenaar also vigorously opposed Raffles' imposition of Ainslie as a second commissioner, and the latter accompanied him as a ship's doctor instead.

[39]TN: Their names were Sukezaemon, Sakusaburô, Takichirô, Shôzaemon, and Tamehachirô.

[40]TN: Doeff shows a ruthless side here, as he lets Wardenaar slowly twist in the wind.

[41]TN: Doeff and the translators agreed on answers to give to certain questions, e.g. that the port of origin was Pondicherry, a French possession in Bengal. The Japanese had no idea that it had long since been taken over by the English.

[42]TN: Doeff was apparently not above a bit of blackmail.

[43]TN: Mainly because Doeff had made many friends, at the Court as well, during his long tenure. Many Japanese seemed to have liked and admired him.

[44]TN: This seems somewhat strange, as the Court coveted all kinds of exotic animals from afar. Already in 1646, the Dutch chief took with him on his trek to Edo two camels, a cassowary bird in a cage, two cockatoos, and a civet cat. In 1821, a camel and a dromedary accompanied the chief, while at other times, the menagerie of animals offered as gifts included an ostrich, Grevey zebras, several Persian horses, and assorted colorful tropical birds. The *daimyô* especially coveted dogs, big ones, and ones that could do tricks.

[45]TN: 87,500 guilders was a real fortune at that time.

[46]TN: Based on a conceptual plan as to how trade in Japan should continue. It basically said that it should continue as it had been, under the Dutch flag, since a transfer of the station was out of the question. The Japanese would never accept a political and commercial agreement with England.

[47]TN: A couple of weeks after Blomhoff left, Doeff, on Christmas eve 1813, wrote in the day register: "Last night, the little girl of Cock Blomhoff, living with her mother in town, died of diphtheria."

[48]On these ships, the steward Antoni Paschen, an able and in general a nice employee, who had given me excellent service

since 1804, also left. In a fit of rage, he had caused an eye injury to a Japanese worker whom he suspected of stealing, and for this he was expelled from Japan.

[49]TN: What sweet revenge for the anti-English Doeff!

[50]TN: Their gifts were refused!

[51]TN: An old Dutch ell was 69 cm. An English ell was 45 inches.

[52]TN: Raffles indeed did not have a high regard for the Dutch, just like Doeff had little regard for the English. Doeff, however, had a high regard and fondness for the Americans.

[53]Memoirs of the life and public service of Sir Th. Stamford Raffles by his widow, London, 1830, pages 68 and 183.

[54]TN: In fact, the station continued to exist until 1860, its importance not so much for the trade any longer, but for the unique foreign diplomatic outpost and link to the world it provided. The above-mentioned text, included in the memoirs, was sent from Malacca to Lord Minto on June 10, 1811.

[55]Memoirs, pp. 229-231.

[56]TN: Later George IV, 1762-1830, who was king from 1820 to 1830. When his father, George III, became insane as a result of intermittent porphyria in November 1810, his son became Prince-Regent in 1811 and King upon his father's death in 1820.

[57]TN: A hundred blocks of silver in the form of boats constituted a considerable amount of money.

[58]TN: The English occupied Java in August 1811.

[59]TN: In a surprise attack in July 1811, the Japanese captured the Russian frigate *Diana* off the coat of Kunashir, took captain Golownin, two of his officers, and four of his sailors prisoners and transported them to Matsumae, where they were kept for two years and three months.

[60]TN: Cassa was a far more dangerous opponent than Wardenaar. Although, like Wardenaar, Cassa had many debts, he had also far less scruples and would do anything to dislodge

Doeff.

61TN: Given the time it took for news to travel, this must refer to the battle of Leipzig (Oct. 1813) where Napoleon's Grande Armée was torn to shreds. This led to his eventual abdication in April 1814, after which he was banished to the Isle of Elba.

62TN: Actually King William I. Doeff must have been under the impression that he had succeeded his father, William the 5th, as stadholder, hence the title prince.

63TN: This is a euphemism for a *yûjo*, or prostitute, the only women allowed on Deshima. There were those who went to the Dutch, *oranda-yuki*; the Chinese, *kara-yuki*, and the Japanese, *nihon-yuki*. These *yûjo* came from two districts in Nagasaki, *Maruyama* and *Yoriai* and were high class prostitutes who also played the *shamisen* and sang. Of interest is that only the Dutch assigned prostitutes were allowed to bring children into the world, the others were not.

64TN: Their names were Namura Takechirô and Motoki Shôzaemon. From Doeff's daily register.

65TN: Their names were Sukezaemon, Sakusaburô, and Jinzaemon. From Doeff's daily register.

66TN: Once back in Holland, Doeff tried to get this money back from the British government. In a long official letter, detailing both the historical and present particulars of a Deshima chief's renumerations in order to legitimize his claim, Doeff requested he be reimbursed for the sum of 26,179.20 *ropeys*. At that time, a *ropey* was worth a *rijksdaalder*, so the request was for the not inconsiderable sum of almost 66,000 *guilders*. No evidence was found whether his request was granted.

67TN: Doeff was on thin ice here and knew it. In the worst case, nothing would have prevented these translators from revealing the "secret." Although normally the whole family shared in the disgrace of a member, it is of note here that Takichirô's son Mosaburô was allowed to stay on as vice sub-translator, and Shôzaemon's son Mokichirô as apprentice translator, each with a salary of 300 *tael* per year. (The fathers had earned 2,000 *tael* per year!) To ensure their father's silence, it is very possible that Doeff had been able to accomplish this.

[68]TN: As the first European women seen for over 150 years, Titia and her maid became the subjects of numerous wood block prints.

[69]TN: Taiwan. The Portuguese discovered this island in 1590, named it Formosa, but were unsuccessful at establishing more lasting settlements there. The Dutch and Spanish were more successful, the former settling at An-p'ing in southwestern Formosa. Until 1646, when the Dutch seized the Spanish settlement, northern Formosa was under Spanish domination, and the south under Dutch control. In 1661, the Dutch were expelled by Koxinga (Cheng Ch'eng-Kung) who was half Japanese, half Chinese.

[70]TN: The governor of Nagasaki returned the letter containing this request to Doeff, however, not daring to send it on, as he had already been reprimanded by the Court for having taken matters in his own hand and allowed two Dutch women to stay on Deshima. Blomhoff then sent a request to the governor as well.

[71]TN: Prince William, oldest son of prince William the 5th, had become King William I of the United Kingdom of the Netherlands in 1814.

[72]TN: This order was given to "those who had shown evidence of tested love of country, of particular diligence and faithfulness in the execution of civil duties, or of extraordinary aptitude in science and art."

[73]TN: And indeed it was, as this Knighthood was rarely bestowed on colonial officials. In fact, they received one of the first decorations the king of the Netherlands could bestow after the congress of Vienna. See appendix.

[74]TN: Titia Cock Blomhoff herself wrote a heart-wrenching letter to the governor in a desperate attempt to avoid a

separation from her husband. Titia's lack of knowledge of Japanese customs might have caused serious problems, as the governor could well have seen her action as one inspired by Doeff and Blomhoff. Fortunately, the governor overlooked her actions "as being of no consequence as it was written by a woman." See appendix.

[75]TN: Caspar Georg Reinward, physician and botanist, was sent to Java in 1815 as director of agriculture, arts, and science. He returned to Holland in 1822 and became professor of chemistry, botany, and natural sciences at the university of Leiden.

[76]TN: This separation was a final one. Titia Blomhoff died in 1821 before her husband's return to Holland.

[77]TN: As chief, Mr. Blomhoff later celebrated his wife's birthday, unaware of the fact that she had died some 10 months earlier.

[78]TN: This was approximately 150 kilograms of silver, quite a fortune.

[79]TN: To his great regret and anguish, Doeff also had to leave behind his nine-year-old son Yokichi, who had the legal right to carry the name *Dôfu* and was raised in Deshima. Despite Doeff's not inconsiderable influence, the Japanese stuck to the rule that Japanese-Dutch children were not permitted to leave the country. Doeff, who was close to his son, provided well for him and his mother. He kept up a correspondence with his son until Yokichi died, at age 17, of tuberculosis and melancholy. Michitomi Yokichi Dôfu was buried in the Japanese cemetery which lies behind the Kôtaiji temple. His well maintained grave, high up a slope of the Hikosan mountain, bears the encircled initials HD on a small separate column, the only Latin script to be found in this cemetery. The sphere on which the temple head rests bears the Chinese symbol for love. A father's moving tribute to a beloved son.

[80]TN: In 1814, Elout, van der Capellen and Buyskes were appointed commissioners-general to take back the Dutch East Indies colonies from the English. At that time, it was also

decided that van der Capellen would become the governor-general. Due to Napoleon's return from Elba, the commissioners did not arrive in Java until 1816. The English, reluctant to give up the colonies, created all sorts of difficulties with the result that van der Capellen was only officially installed as the governor-general in 1819. Mr. Elout later became minister of colonial affairs.

[81]TN: After his arrival in Batavia, Doeff married Elisabeth Rebecca Steenboom on June 18, 1818.

[82]TN: In those days, a frigate was a fast sailing, three-masted ship.

[83]TN: Due to the Napoleonic wars and the English occupation of Java, the Dutch fleet was in terrible disrepair.

[84]TN: Today Ile de la Réunion.

[85]TN: Half way between Mauritius and Ceylon (Sri Lanka).

[86]TN: She died on board the *Pickering* on April 26, 1819.

ADDENDUM, EPILOGUE & APPENDIX

[1]TN: This dictionary was first published in 1710. Dutch was rendered at that time as *Nederduitsch* or Low German.

[2]TN: Once back in Holland, Doeff became the advisor of Japanese affairs to the minister of colonial affairs, Mr. Elout. This man also persuaded Doeff to write down his recollections to "uphold the name of Holland vis-à-vis Raffles." In a review of Doeff's book in the *British Quarterly Review*, vol. 56, 1836, there is an admonition "not to simply believe Raffles only!"

[3]TN: Mr. von Siebold, a bright but vain and ambitious man, was known for the fact that he often appropriated other people's work without giving them credit. See appendix.

[4]TN: Mr. Siebold never really mastered the Japanese language.

[5]*Dictionarium, Sive Thesauri Linguae Japonicae* Compendium a D. Collado Roma Prop. Fid. 1632 4 to. Additiones ad Dictionarium Japonicum auctore D.C (sine anno).

[6]TN: This dictionary was extremely important, as Dutch was the only foreign language (apart from Chinese) used in Japan. It remained the foreign language for science and correspondence with foreigners until 1870. The first two American ambassadors to Japan employed Dutch translators.

[7]TN: The adjacent and identical property is now the van Loon museum.

ISBN 155395849-7